Seized with the Temper of the Times

A Journal of the American Revolution Book, Don N. Hagist, Series Editor

Seized with the Temper of the Times

Identity and Rebellion in Pre-Revolutionary America

ABBY CHANDLER

WESTHOLME
Yardley

© 2023 Abby Chandler

All rights reserved under International and Pan-American Copyright Conventions. No part of this book may be reproduced in any form or by any electronic or mechanical means, including information storage and retrieval systems, without permission in writing from the publisher, except by a reviewer who may quote brief passages in a review.

Westholme Publishing, LLC
904 Edgewood Road
Yardley, Pennsylvania 19067
Visit our Web site at www.westholmepublishing.com

ISBN: 978-1-59416-410-1
Also available as an eBook.

Printed in the United States of America.

For Jim, with all my love.

Contents

List of Illustrations — *viii*
Preface — *ix*
Introduction — *xiii*

1. Founding Rhode Island and North Carolina — 1
2. Before the Stamp Act — 21
3. The Stamp Act in Rhode Island — 39
4. The Stamp Act Riots — 55
5. The Regulator Rebellion Begins — 74
6. The Regulator Rebellion and the Imperial Crisis — 93
7. Imperial Crisis to Revolutionary Era — 110
8. Rhode Island and North Carolina: New Battles — 127

Notes — *145*
Bibliography — *193*
Index — *211*

List of Illustrations

The Wanton-Lyman-Hazard House	xi
Martin Howard's statement in the *Newport Mercury*	xv
Letter to *Newport Mercury* editor Solomon Southwick	xxx
"A Plan of the Town of Newport in Rhode Island"	3
"A Compleat map of North-Carolina from an actual Survey"	7
The Colony House, Newport, Rhode Island	23
The Redwood Library, Newport, Rhode Island	27
The Franklin press	35
A Letter from a Gentleman at Halifax, to his Friend	43
Advertisement for "A Vindication of the British Colonies"	47
Engraving of the Boston Stamp Act Riots	59
Marker at the site where William Houston was forced to resign	71
Tryon's Palace	79
"The Humble Petition of Us the Inhabitants of Orange County Bordering on Cumberland"	87
The Edmund Fanning marker in Hillsborough	103
"North Carolina Hillsborough District Court Record"	105
The Alamance battlefield	119
The Regulator monument	121
"A Chart of the Harbour of Rhode Island and Narragansett Bay"	131
"Plann of the County of Mecklenburg"	141

Preface

This book began at the Newport Historical Society in 2005. As part of a summer internship, I was asked to create a first-person interpretive program about a Loyalist named Martin Howard who lived in the historical society's Wanton-Lyman-Hazard house in the mid-eighteenth century. As I scoured the historical society archive for clues to his life, I came across a transcription of a letter Howard sent to his friend James Iredell in 1777. "My little family would have been glad to see you, and you would have seen, I think, the best piece of meadow in Carolina," wrote Howard. "When I leave this country, you might [observe] that I had made two blades of grass grow where only one grew before—a circumstance among some nations of no small honor and renown."[1] I am a gardener, and I found Howard's blend of horticulture and grace of language completely irresistible. They lingered at the back of my mind until spring 2015, when I was finally able to expand my initial research on Howard. In his own words to Iredell, he was an "unimportant character." Nevertheless, Howard's life and career encompassed the major political activity of the 1760s—the Stamp Act crisis, the Regulator Rebellion, and the transition toward the Revolutionary era. This period is deeply understudied, but it has much to offer modern scholars, and my hope is that more of Howard's contemporaries will see the light of day in the coming years. For me, an unexpected pleasure while writing this book has been making the acquaintance of Howard's second wife, Abigail Greenleaf Howard, and I look forward to learning more about her years in Boston following the American Revolution.

As I finally bring this research to a close, I am grateful to all the librarians and archivists who located the hundreds of documents that brought the Stamp Act crisis and the Regulator Rebellion to life for me. I would especially like to thank Kaela Bleho, Bert Lippincott, Bridget Newton, and Ingrid Peters at the Newport Historical Society; Erin Bradford, Josh Hager, and Sarah Koonts at the State Archives of North Carolina; and Rebecca Valentine and Rick Ring at the Rhode Island Historical Society. In addition, I would like to thank the American Antiquarian Society, the Library of Congress, the New York Public Library, and the Yale University Library for their digital archives. I am also grateful to the North Caroliniana Society for the Archie K. Davis Fellowship, which allowed me to begin my research in the State Archives of North Carolina in spring 2015.

I am equally grateful for feedback received while presenting my research at the British Group in Early American History, the War College of the Seven Years' War, the Consortium on the Revolutionary Era, History Camp-Boston, the Massachusetts Historical Society, and the World History Association. I would like to thank Helena Yoo Roth for inviting me to talk about my research at the City University of New York Early American Republic Seminar, and Geralyn Ducady for inviting me to give a talk at the Revolutionary Ideals Summer Teacher Institute. I am also grateful to Benjamin Carp for his feedback and support as the book made its way along the final path toward publication.

Portions of this book and its arguments were originally published as articles. These include "'Unawed by the Laws of their Country': Finding Local and Imperial Legitimacy in North Carolina's Regulator Rebellion" in the *North Carolina Historical Review*; "Reexamining the Remarkable Career of Martin Howard" in *Newport History*; "'Let us unanimously lay aside foreign Superfluities': Textile Production and British Colonial Identity in the 1760s" in *Early American Studies: An Interdisciplinary Journal*; "'The Basis of Alienation will never be healed': The Historicity of Protest in Ezra Stiles' Stamp Act Notebook" in *Protest in the Long Eighteenth Century*; and "'But by the Law of this Colony': The *Gaspee* Affair in American History" in *The Bridge: The Gaspee Affair in Context*. I am grateful to the editors of all those publications for their feedback during the writing process and for their permission to present this work as part of a longer book project. I also wish to thank Don N. Hagist and Bruce H. Franklin for their interest in publishing my book as part of the Journal of the American Revolution book series.

The History Department at the University of Massachusetts Lowell comprises the world's best students, colleagues, and historians. Grants from

The Wanton-Lyman-Hazard House is the oldest surviving house in Newport, Rhode Island. Built c. 1697, it was purchased by Martin Howard in 1757. (*Newport Historical Soci-*

the department helped fund my archival trips to North California and Rhode Island and made my research possible. I particularly wish to thank Christoph Strobel, Shehong Chen, Michael Pierson, and Chris Carlsmith for their support as I transitioned from first book project to second book project and from assistant professor to associate professor. I also wish to thank Betsy Herbin-Triant, Elizabeth Williams, and Jane Sancinito for many walks, cups of tea, and conversations about history as we write our way through a past that never seems very far away.

I am equally grateful to the family members and friends who also have lived with political revolts in the 1760s during the past several years. Along with my parents and sisters, I wish to thank Brookie McCulloch for providing me with a place to stay in the next town over from the Newport Historical Society. The community of garden volunteers at Steven-Coolidge Place has distracted me with plants when needed, as has my own garden. Bree and Io Beal are, as always, champions of good history from Oregon. I am also grateful to Lilly Chandler, without whom this book would not exist. Finally, in honor of our twentieth wedding anniversary, this book is dedicated to Jim Riordan, my dear and loving husband.

Introduction

The streets of Newport, Rhode Island, had begun to still and the day's heat was ebbing when Martin Howard settled at his desk in the house on Broadway Street he had purchased ten years earlier. He and his wife, Ann Brenton Conklin Howard, had flung themselves into renovations, adding paneling to the rooms on the lower floor, choosing paint colors, selecting porcelain dishes to be displayed on the newly installed shelves.[1] Ann had died of a fever the year before, and now Howard shared the house with their ten-year-old daughter, Annie.[2] A few days earlier, he had read an article in the *Newport Mercury* reporting that an effigy of "Mr. O____" had been found hanging on a tree in Boston's South End on August 14.[3] Like many New England colonists in the 1760s, Howard would have known the effigy represented Andrew Oliver, the man responsible for enforcing the Stamp Act in Boston.[4] The article further detailed an attack on the Oliver family home by a group of men who "beat in all the Windows ... abused his furniture very much; and gather[ed] all the Fruit in the Garden." Howard read the article through one last time. Then he picked up a quill to compose a statement expressing his concerns about the unrest roiling the British North American colonies in summer 1765.

The words spread slowly across the page. "The Author of the *Halifax Letter* gives out to the Public, That he is a Native of the Colonies, and has a heart as warmly attached to their true Interest as any man whatever."[5] Just as Martin Howard had known that "Mr. O____" referred to Andrew Oliver, Howard's neighbors knew he was the author of the *A Letter from a*

Gentleman at Halifax to his Friend in Rhode Island pamphlet published seven months earlier.[6] They also knew that Howard was one of the cofounders of the Newport Junto, a local political organization that championed Parliament's right to tax the British North American colonies. The act of accepting the position of Stamp Tax distributor had made Oliver vulnerable to attack in Boston. Now, Howard's long-standing support for Parliament's policies for its North American colonies had placed him, Annie, and the other members of the Newport Junto in similar danger.

Still, he wrote on. He had published his beliefs "with that freedom, which is the privilege & ought to be the Boast of every Englishman," and he could not "repress his Astonishment, at the mistaken Notions of those, who, under a pretense of serving the Course of Liberty, would take away the Right of Private Judgement, and stop the Avenues to Truth." Furthermore, he feared that some Newport colonists, like their Boston counterparts, were preparing to "invest the populace, and endeavor to point their Fury against the Person and Interest of a Man, merely because he happens to differ in Opinion from his Countrymen."

Howard dipped his quill in the ink one last time before penning his final sentences. He would not "retract any Position contained in the Halifax letter" and if "his Person and Interest bec[a]me the Objects of popular Revenge for these Sentiments, he [would] never lament the Cause, whatever may be the Consequences." With his statement complete, Howard held the paper in the still August air for a moment to dry, then crawled into bed for a few hours' sleep. Later, he would deliver it to newspaper editor Samuel Hall and wait as the type was set and the paper distributed to the Newport community.

Martin Howard's statement appeared on the front page of the *Newport Mercury* on August 26, 1765.[7] By dawn the following day, gallows were being prepared on the Newport Parade, and crowds of men were gathering in the streets. Howard and his fellow Newport Junto members, Thomas Moffat and Augustus Johnston, took refuge on HMS *Cygnet* in Newport Harbor while mobs hung them in effigy before attacking their houses.[8] A few days later, Howard, Annie, and Moffat fled to London, where Howard and Moffat testified before Parliament about the Stamp Act crisis in Rhode Island.[9] Howard was made chief justice for North Carolina in 1767.[10] This new position brought him back into the spotlight during the Regulator Rebellion, as he oversaw many of the trials for the men who sought to regulate, or reform, North Carolina's political and legal systems. The Howard family's time in North Carolina came to an abrupt end when the American Revolution caught up with them in 1777.[11] Howard's trajectory from

Introduction

> THE Author of the Halifax Letter gives out to the Public, That he is a Native of the Colonies, and has a Heart as warmly attached to their true Interest as any Man whatever: That the Sentiments he has adopted, in Print, have since appeared to be the Judgment of the Parliament of Great-Britain; and the Opinion of Nine-Tenths of the British Nation; and he has published them with that Freedom, which is the Priviledge, & ought to be the Boast of every Englishman. He therefore cannot repress his Astonishment at the mistaken Notions of those, who, under a Pretence of serving the Cause of Liberty, would take away the Right of private Judgment, and stop the Avenues to Truth, by instigating the Populace, and endeavouring to point their Fury against the Person and Interest of a Man, meerly because he happens to differ in Opinion from his Countrymen: And in that Instance, only exercises the same Priviledge which they claim and enjoy.
>
> The Writer does not retract any Position contained in the Halifax Letter; and therefore does not meanly sollicit any Favour or Exemption from the Abuse intended him, because if his Person and Interest become the Objects of popular Revenge for these Sentiments, he thinks he shall never lament the Cause, whatever may be the Consequences.
>
> CUSTOM-HOUSE, NEWPORT, RHODE-ISLAND.
> INWARD ENTRIES.

Martin Howard's statement published on August 26, 1765, in the *Newport Mercury*. (*Newport Historical Society*)

Rhode Island to North Carolina to permanent exile in London spanned the late eighteenth-century Atlantic world. It also encompassed the Stamp Act crisis and the Regulator Rebellion, two understudied movements with new insights for historians of this period.[12]

If the Stamp Act crisis is traditionally portrayed as a starting point for the American Revolution, the Regulator Rebellion is considered a local issue with little or no relevance outside the immediate contexts of North Carolina. Instead, the documentary record demonstrates that the Regulator Rebellion and the Stamp Act crisis were equally driven by the imperial crisis, the collective term used to describe the transatlantic tensions created by Britain's rapid geographic and political expansion in the years following the end of the Seven Years' War.[13] These two paradoxes—a local crisis cast as imperial affair and an imperial affair cast as local crisis—require a reconsideration of the motives and outcomes for both movements. Without preexisting local tensions, the fury of the Stamp Act crisis may not have spilled over in summer 1765, and without the added strains posed by colonial challenges to the British Empire, the Regulator Rebellion may have ended as swiftly as North Carolina's earlier rebellions.

The Stamp Act crisis was fueled by the chain of colonial responses to the Duties in American Colonies Act passed by Parliament on March 22, 1765.[14] Thus, the Stamp Act crisis would appear to have been the starting point for the political movement that became the American Revolution.

Historian Edmund Morgan noted in 1995 "that what the colonists had to say about Parliamentary power and about their own rights deserved to be taken seriously."[15] Historians Joshua Fogarty Beatty and Zachary McLeod Hutchins examined the Stamp Act crisis through the lenses of individual communities in the early twenty-first century.[16] More recently, scholar Ken Shumate stated in 2021 that "the year 1764 marked the beginning of a long and unhappy argument between America and Great Britain; it was the first year of the American Revolution."[17] Like Beatty and Hutchins, I believe the Stamp Act crisis needs to be examined in context with the communities that responded to its challenges. Incorporating preexisting community tensions provides a more nuanced examination of the Stamp Act crisis and a greater understanding of the diverging paths taken by the colonies to independence in 1776 and political union in 1787. The goal of the Stamp Act response was not revolution, and so it is necessary to examine these events in their immediate moment.

Scholars have also offered a range of explanations for why and how the Regulator Rebellion unfolded in late-eighteenth-century North Carolina. Historian A. Roger Ekirch examined recurring tensions between eastern and western settlements in North Carolina, while acknowledging the colony's economic challenges, in *"Poor Carolina": Politics and Society in Colonial North Carolina, 1729–1776*. Historian Wayne E. Lee placed the Regulator Rebellion in context with North Carolina's history of internal rebellions dating back to the seventeenth century in *Crowds and Soldiers in Revolutionary North Carolina: The Culture of Violence in Riot and War*. Historian Marjoleine Kars considered the populist influences of the First Great Awakening on the Regulators' writings and actions in *Breaking Loose Together: The Regulator Rebellion in Pre-Revolutionary America*. Finally, historian Carole Watterson Troxler offers a demographic approach to the earlier research from Ekirch, Lee, and Kars in *Farming Dissenters: The Regulator Movement in Piedmont North Carolina*.[18] I argue, however, that while local issues informed the Regulator movement, it was ultimately shaped by political interests and consequences reaching far beyond New Bern, Hillsborough, and the forests and creeks of North Carolina.

A comparative history of the Stamp Act crisis and the Regulator Rebellion must begin with a recognition of its own contradictions. One of these movements took form in most, if not all, of the British North American colonies; the other was confined to a single colony. The many commonalities between Rhode Island and North Carolina do, however, lend themselves to such a study. Both were founded in the second wave of colonization in their respective regions, as many Rhode Island colonists traveled overland from Massachusetts or Connecticut, while many North Carolina colonists came from Virginia or South Carolina. Rhode Island's and North Carolina's economies were economically distinct from their immediate neighbors. Rhode Island was a northern colony whose economy was fueled by every aspect of the transatlantic slave trade; North Carolina was a southern colony where slavery was initially less intrinsic to the overall economy. Both colonies experienced prolonged periods of internal unrest, ranging from North Carolina's Culpeper Rebellion in the 1670s to Rhode Island's Dorr Rebellion in the 1840s.[19] In addition, whether in the colonial period or in contemporary scholarship, Rhode Island and North Carolina have long been overshadowed by their immediate neighbors. Political fervor on both sides of the imperial crisis led to early action in both Rhode Island and North Carolina, and yet most accounts of these activities focus on Massachusetts and Virginia. These experiences laid the groundwork for Rhode Island and North Carolina's shared concerns about the balance between local and imperial/federal control and identity, an issue that remains equally unresolved in the present-day United States.

Rhode Island and North Carolina's interlocking experiences also support a deeper study of the political and ideological shifts that underscored the turn from imperial crisis in the 1760s to Revolutionary era in the 1770s.[20] The Revolutionary era was rooted in the broader imperial crisis created by the expansion of the British Empire in the 1760s, but it was by no means an inevitable conclusion to debates over imperial and local political control within the British Empire. Instead, there were multiple paths forward from the imperial crisis, some ending in revolution for the thirteen colonies that became the United States and others ending in a renewed bond between Britain and the colonies in Canada and the Caribbean.[21] Still, these bonds would continue to be tested in the coming years. Both Canada and the Caribbean colonies would seek independence from Britain in the nineteenth and twentieth centuries. If the colonies of Rhode Island and North Carolina embraced the coming war before many of their counterparts, they would later be reluctant participants in the rising union envisioned by the US Constitution.

A multiplicity of voices fueled the Stamp Act crisis and the Regulator Rebellion. Overall, they can be divided into four primary groups: the Newport colonists who supported the Stamp Act, the Newport colonists who opposed it, the North Carolina colonists who supported the Regulator Rebellion, and the ones who opposed it. With the exception of Governor William Tryon, most of the North Carolina colonists who opposed the Stamp Act were also opposed to the Regulator Rebellion, while many Regulators would eventually support the British Empire through the American Revolution. Teasing out their individual voices provides a better understanding of the many divisions, paradoxes, and commonalities informing and shaping these movements. The Newport Junto is the only identifiable group involved with either the Stamp Act crisis or the Regulator Rebellion whose members did not turn to violence. It is also nearly impossible to distinguish between the ideas and actions of the individual Newport Junto members. By contrast, the Sons of Liberty, a larger and more fluid organization, struggled to craft a unified response to the Stamp Act. Historian Pauline Maier writes that "almost immediately after the outbreak of mob activity . . . colonists consciously retreated from mere ad hoc violence to an ordered opposition."[22]

The work of Maier and other scholars has done much to isolate the motives and actions of individual Sons of Liberty members, but scholarship on the Regulators has paid less attention to such divisions.[23] Nevertheless, my research demonstrates the existence of two Regulator movements; one, a legal center that tried to work within the North Carolina political system, the other, an extralegal center that turned to violence as frustrations grew. Once reports of the Regulator Rebellion's sudden end on the banks of the Alamance Creek were reported in other colonies in fall 1771, another division emerged. Colonists outside North Carolina eagerly claimed the defeat of the Regulator Rebellion as further evidence of parliamentary overreach, while the North Carolina General Assembly worked to downplay the Regulators' struggles.

In turn, paying attention to individual voices reminds us of the rhetorical links, however unrealized at the time, between the Stamp Act crisis and the Regulator Rebellion. Both the Newport Junto and many of the Regulators advocated for an older agricultural economy, while both the Sons of Liberty and the North Carolina elite sought the mercantile world of the rising Industrial Revolution, and these connections will be examined in greater depth in later chapters.[24] These same issues would be revived in 1787 at the Constitutional Convention, where delegates struggled to balance the interests of rural Americans with their urban counterparts.[25] The late eighteenth century also saw the emergence of rebellions whose instigators, like the Regulators, were protesting against political systems seemingly designed to support the interests of urban residents.[26]

A full examination of the individual voices of the Stamp Act crisis and the Regulator Rebellion also needs to acknowledge their offscreen participants. Martin Howard's statement of August 26, 1765, celebrated his right to publish his views "with that freedom, which is the privilege & ought to be the Boast of every Englishman."²⁷ A shared faith in this freedom infuses the documentary record from the Stamp Act crisis and the Regulator Rebellion. Some participants in these movements questioned whether British colonists had the right to object to parliamentary taxation. Others asked whether the right to criticize Parliament could be equally applied to backcountry colonists' desire to critique their own colonial government. These were questions designed to highlight restrictions on speech stemming from geography and economic standing rather than gender or race. This did not mean, however, that they were questions asked in a space empty of female or nonwhite participants.

Debates on women's roles in a period of crisis appear throughout the political rhetoric of the 1760s and 1770s. In both Rhode Island and North Carolina, enslaved labor was a crucial part of the colonial economy. Martin Howard and other British officials repeatedly questioned the motives of Patriots who called for political freedom while keeping others enslaved.[28] The Regulator Rebellion was also a battle about the economic interests of slave-holding and nonslave-holding colonists. Consequently, these stories can, and should, be read as warp threads running through both the Stamp Act crisis and the Regulator Rebellion.

Surviving sources for the Stamp Act crisis and the Regulator Rebellion consist of published and unpublished writings composed between 1764 and 1772; political and legal documents from North America and the United Kingdom; and such papers as correspondence and tax and probate records. All three are essential for better understanding the motivations and interests of the participants in these movements.

The invention of movable type and the printing press by Johannes Gutenberg in the early fifteenth century provided literate Europeans with a plethora of newspapers, pamphlets, and other reading materials throughout the early modern period. Increased access to political cartoons and pictorial engravings made it easier to reach illiterate Europeans on the streets of Paris, Amsterdam, London, and other major urban areas. Anna Pavord notes that "information [began] as a personal asset or property, passed at its owner's discretion from hand to hand, by word of mouth or by letter. Each person in possession of information could add or subtract from it before passing it on." By contrast, "the printed book changed the way information was received. It sent the same message to all. It was not necessarily the right one, but it set an agenda; it was a fixed point from which the fight for elucidation could continue."[29] Most political and military leaders had become accustomed to the ready ability to disseminate these "fixed points" by the late eighteenth century.

Printing presses were, however, relatively new technology in Rhode Island and North Carolina during the imperial crisis and the Revolutionary era. The documentary record demonstrates that participants in both the Stamp Act crisis and the Regulator Rebellion were expert shifters between printed texts and handwritten missives as opportunity and necessity warranted. A decade and a half later, the lack of easy access to printing presses in North Carolina would stymie the Continental army. Frustrated with his efforts to stir up support for the American cause, cavalry officer Henry Lee suggested to Major General Nathanael Greene in 1781 that a "public press as the communicator of events would tend very much to stir up the patriotism of the people."[30] Greene agreed, noting that "Nothing will contribute more to the recovery of these Southern States than a proper channel to convey intelligence to the people."[31] Printing presses, however, remained confined to the coastal communities in the south rather than in the backcountry where most military campaigns were conducted. Such struggles may also have contributed to the later resistance to the Constitution found across the rural United States in the late 1780s. By that time, most political leaders were unaccustomed to using purely verbal channels to convey messages to their constituents.

The first printing press in Massachusetts arrived in Cambridge in 1638, but neither Rhode Island nor North Carolina had presses until well into the eighteenth century.[32] The first challenge facing a new press owner was generating enough funds to support his or her press. Ink could be concocted from ingredients readily available in North America, such as walnut shells or soot, but paper had to be imported from Britain throughout the colonial period.[33] Most colonial printers relied on government contracts to print warrants, announcements, and the other documents necessary for a functioning political society for their primary income, while trying to gain enough subscribers to run newspapers.[34] Pamphlets were a growing source of income for press owners in the 1760s and 1770s, as they provided an efficient, relatively affordable method for disseminating ideas to a wider audience, though they often left printers open to sedition charges from colonial leaders with different viewpoints.[35]

Towns like Newport and Wilmington struggled to support weekly papers while larger cities like Boston and New York were able to sustain two or more.[36] Print runs in Rhode Island were more regular than in North Carolina, but all of these enterprises struggled with changing editors, dwindling finances, and, occasionally, intervention from local colonial governments. Nevertheless, the output from these presses remain a crucial source for tracing the evolution of political movements since they provided dated commentary on rapidly shifting events. Benjamin Carp writes that "eighteenth-century urban political culture flowed through multiple avenues of communication, association, and social interaction [moving] from the press to the streets, taverns, and churches."[37] These channels allowed news to travel through all levels of society while providing space for public comment at multiple levels. They also helped to sustain the reciprocal contract between political leaders and their constituents, which allowed the latter to express their responses as laws were created, a system apparent throughout the Stamp Act crisis and the Regulator Rebellion.[38]

Essays from members of the Newport Junto and the Sons of Liberty published in the *Newport Mercury* and the *Providence Gazette* provided the backbone for my research on the Stamp Act crisis in Rhode Island, as they offered weekly updates on the shifting tensions between the two groups. Other key sources were the two Rhode Island pamphlets on the Sugar and Stamp Acts. Stephen Hopkins's *The Rights of the Colonies, Examined* was published in Providence on November 30, 1764, while Martin Howard's *Letter from a Gentleman at Halifax to his Friend in Rhode Island* was published in Newport on January 20, 1765.[39]

The first printing press reached Rhode Island in the late 1720s or early 1730s when James Franklin, Benjamin Franklin's brother, moved to Newport.[40] Franklin's widow, Ann Franklin, took over the business after his death and founded the *Newport Mercury* in 1758.[41] In 1762, she was joined by business partner Samuel Hall, who continued publishing the paper after Franklin's death in 1763. Most eighteenth-century newspaper editors only published on topics aligned with their political views. By contrast, Hall took a broader approach by publishing essays from multiple political perspectives in the early 1760s.[42] He was questioned by the Rhode Island Superior Court later that winter, an ordeal described by the Newport Junto as being "without any kind of warrant or legal process . . . in contemplating this matter, Judge Jeffries, the Star Chamber, the Spanish Inquisition rush into our minds." Despite Hall's best efforts to portray himself as a staunch supporter of anti-imperialism after the Stamp Act crisis, he continued to be regarded with suspicion by the Sons of Liberty in Newport.[43] Hall was eventually replaced in 1769 by Solomon Southwick whose pro-Patriot views eventually led him to bury his press to protect it during the British occupation of Newport in the 1770s.[44]

Perhaps reflecting its location in highly literate New England, Rhode Island was able to support two printing presses by the mid-eighteenth century. The second press was in Providence, where Sarah Updike Goddard and her children, Mary Katherine and William, jointly founded the *Prov-*

idence Gazette in 1762.[45] Once William Goddard had left Providence in 1767, his mother continued publishing the *Providence Gazette* with her business partner, John Carter.[46] Unlike Samuel Hall, both the Goddard family and Carter managed the *Providence Gazette* on a strictly partisan basis. Their press provided a reliable outlet for pro-Patriot voices in the decade preceding the American Revolution.

Printed documents were less essential for my research on North Carolina during the imperial crisis. Maurice Moore published the pamphlet *The Justice and Policy of Taxing The American Colonies, in Great Britain, considered* in North Carolina that, like Stephen Hopkins's *The Rights of the Colonies*, advocated against parliamentary taxation.[47] Herman Husband published two pamphlets discussing the Regulators' concerns in 1770 and 1771, but neither appears to have been printed in North Carolina. Their primary purpose was, instead, to alert British colonists in other regions to the Regulators' plight.[48]

The North Carolina Assembly agreed on October 17, 1749, to advance Williamsburg, Virginia, printer James Davis the "sum of Eighty Pounds, Proclamation Money being half a years Salary" in order to "enable him to print the said Laws, and such others as have passed since the said Revisal."[49] Persuading him to move to North Carolina was the most cost-effective means of bringing a printer and his press to North Carolina since he was located in an adjoining colony. A few years after moving his press to New Bern, Davis began publishing the *North-Carolina Gazette* on November 15, 1751. Unlike the weekly print runs of the *Newport Mercury* and the *Providence Gazette*, this paper was printed only when he had enough information to fill a complete issue.[50] Davis eventually ended the *North-Carolina Gazette* around 1761 and founded another journal, *North-Carolina Magazine; or, Universal Intelligencer*, in 1764.

A second printer, Andrew Steuart, arrived in North Carolina in June 1764 and settled in Wilmington, which served as the de facto capital for the colony at that time. It appears likely that Governor Arthur Dobbs persuaded Steuart to leave the press he had previously established in Philadelphia to replace James Davis as the official colonial printer.[51] Unfortunately for Steuart, Dobbs's invitation placed him at the center of the feud between the North Carolina government officials who received their appointments from the British Crown and the ones who received their positions via local elections. The North Carolina General Assembly reappointed Davis as the official printer for North Carolina on November 26, 1764, and required Dobbs to pay Steuart's salary out of his own funds. Steuart reestablished the *North-Carolina Gazette and Weekly Post-Boy* in October 1764 but again found himself caught between the colonial government and the royal governor during the Stamp Act crisis in 1765. Following Steuart's death by drowning in the Cape Fear River in 1769, Wilmington resident Adam Boyd purchased Steuart's press and began publishing the *Cape Fear Mercury*, which remained in circulation until 1775.

Other print sources include Ezra Stiles's "Stamp Act Notebook" and William Smith's writings about North Carolina during the imperial crisis. Both accounts raise the question of whether they should be considered as the work of a journalist/participant or a historian. They are contemporary accounts composed by men with firsthand information. Their primary intent, however, was to contextualize and analyze the causes and events of the imperial crisis for future audiences. Stiles and Smith were working at a time when the crafting of history was increasingly seen as a deliberate enterprise. Thomas Hutchinson published the first volume of his *History of Massachusetts Bay* in the 1760s.[52] Benjamin West's 1770 portrait *The Death of James Wolfe* initially shocked viewers for its efforts to realistically portray General Wolfe's death at the Battle of Quebec, but it led to the emergence of a new, and more realistic, style of painting.[53] Consequently, this intent to shape the narrative for future audiences must also be considered when assessing the writings of Stile and Smith.

Ezra Stiles was the Congregationalist minister in Newport between 1766 and 1769. Edmund Morgan writes, "I first became acquainted with Stiles through the notebook he kept on the Stamp Act crisis, in which I discovered information on the subject that I had found nowhere else."[54] Despite this endorsement from Morgan, Stiles's work remains one of the most underutilized sources from British North America in the 1760s, which is unfortunate, as it offers such a comprehensive perspective on the Stamp Act crisis.[55] This particular source was never published, and it is unclear why, because it reads like a document written for a public audience. Perhaps by the time Stiles was winding down his chronicle of the Stamp Act crisis in 1769, it felt like old news compared to the new tensions over the Townshend Acts.

The "Stamp Act Notebook" consists of five individual sections, each with its own particular goal or purpose.[56] The first section contains a seventeen-page poem documenting the evolution of British colonization in North America, while the second section chronicles the long wait for news of the parliamentary debate and notes the arrival dates of the ships that brought news of the repeal to the British colonies. The third section provides information on the Stamp Act protests in all the British colonies, including Canada, Florida, and the Caribbean. The fourth section lists the names of the Parliament members who voted for and against repealing the Stamp Act, and the fifth section documents the annual commemorations of the repeal of the Stamp Act between 1766 and 1769 in multiple colonial communities.

The nonchronological layout of the "Stamp Act Notebook" and the presence of several blank pages between the end of the second section and the beginning of the third are the elements that led me to classify the "Stamp Act Notebook" as a protohistory of the imperial crisis. They suggest that Ezra Stiles wrote his history of the colonies, recorded the first news of the parliamentary debates and, while he was waiting for further updates, flipped ahead to begin writing about the passing of the Stamp Act and the protests in summer 1765. Newspapers are intended to inform contemporary audiences about current events. Consequently, their accounts contain little in the way of contextual information since their readers are assumed to be familiar with such details, which was the case in the *Newport Mercury*, the *Providence Gazette*, and other eighteenth-century newspapers.[57] Histories are usually recorded after the fact by authors whose lack of firsthand knowledge of the events in question is balanced by their access to a wider array of perspectives and viewpoints than is often available in the moment.

The "Stamp Act Notebook" was composed in 1765 and 1766, the years the Stamp Act crisis occurred. Nevertheless, it reads as a supportive and definitive history that blends Stiles's firsthand experiences in Newport with supplementary information. It also was clearly crafted for a wide range of audiences. Readers who might question the validity of the protestors' cause are provided with arguments and explanations dating back to the founding of the British North American colonies in the early seventeenth century. Readers searching for evidence to support the protestors' cause are provided with documentation from all the British colonies of the period arrayed alongside multiple character witnesses for the participants. Stiles's records on Newport were the most complete, but he also went to great effort to broadly document the British North American colonies in the 1760s.

Like Stiles, New York Chief Justice William Smith Jr. was interested in documenting British North American history, and his *History of the Province of New-York* had been published in 1757.[58] After William Tryon was appointed as what turned out to be the last royal governor of New York in summer 1771, Smith appointed himself as Tryon's champion in the colony.[59] Smith's first move in this direction was his "Notes and Extracts from papers of Governor William Tryon," which detailed Tryon's family connections as evidence of his qualifications.[60] Later efforts drew from Tryon's letter book to document his time as North Carolina's governor between 1764 and 1768 and 1769 and 1771.[61] Years later, Smith noted that the reading of Governor Tryon's commission in Manhattan was greeted by a crowd that was "neither great nor joyful."[62] In an effort to win New York residents over to their new governor, Smith set out to document Tryon's thoughtful approach to governing North Carolina. Rumors of Tryon's intractability and disdain for his colonial subjects were countered with tales of negotiations between Tryon and the North Carolina Assembly. Both Stiles and Smith are invaluable chroniclers of the 1760s and 1770s, but their particular blends of history, journalism, and propaganda need to be carefully assessed when using them as documentary sources.

Documents from political and judicial systems in North America and the United Kingdom made up my second category of source materials. Rhode Island's unique position as a chartered colony whose governor and legislature both opposed the Stamp Act meant the colony generated less formal discussion on the act than colonies where it was supported by the royal governor but opposed by the legislature. The Rhode Island General Assembly issued its resolves on the Stamp Act in September 1765, but these were a more generalized statement condemning the Stamp Act than the resolves targeted at royally appointed governors in other colonies.[63] Unlike Rhode Island and many other colonies, North Carolina did not issue a statement condemning the Stamp Act, as Governor Tryon had prorogued the colonial government. Instead, this portion of my research came from reports on colonial unrest in the Cape Fear region published by Andrew Steuart in the *North-Carolina Gazette*.[64]

The surviving documentary record from the Regulator Rebellion comes from the Regulators, Governor Tryon, members of the North Carolina General Assembly, and the judiciary. David Zaret writes that while "rulers had ceremonies, priests, printers, assize judges, and more for sending political messages ... highly ritualized forms of collective behavior afforded a limited opportunity for crowds to send messages to local and national rulers."[65] Governor Tryon and the assembly relied heavily on proclamations, which had long provided medieval and early modern governments with a highly ritualized means of public communication. First, they were read aloud, whether on the street, in the courtroom, or in church, to illiterate members of society. Afterward, they were posted in public spaces so literate citizens could refer to them at will and, if the technology was available, published. This two-part conveyance of information served to legitimize the proclamations by embedding them in their respective audiences' daily political structures, whether as repeated vocal pronouncements or in print in newspapers or pamphlets.

Ordinary subjects like the Regulators were allowed to submit petitions that "conveyed complaints, decried miscarriage of justice, or requested relief from taxes, forest laws, and other regulations."[66] Like the proclamations, petitions were highly ritualized, and petitioners were expected to demonstrate their deference to authority alongside their concerns. It is not surprising that Tryon was familiar with the use of public proclamations to support governmental actions, but the Regulators' use of carefully worded petitions to express their grievances reveals that they were equally knowledgeable about the English political process. This same emphasis on legitimacy is equally apparent in the legal records, as the Regulator Rebellion's participants continually battled each other in the courtroom as well as on the printed page.

My third category of source materials was the surviving personal papers from the participants in the Stamp Act crisis and the Regulator Rebellion. Papers from the Rhode Island families who opposed the Stamp Act and from Governor Tryon and the North Carolina families who made up the assembly and other government positions are easily found in state and local archives. By contrast, the Newport colonists who supported the Stamp Act and the North Carolina colonists who supported the Regulator Rebellion left behind few records, albeit for different reasons. As pressures increased on British colonists who supported the Stamp Act and, in time, the British Empire after the Declaration of Independence in 1776, many fled the United States for other parts of the empire. Surviving letters written by Martin Howard number fewer than a dozen despite his prominent positions in Rhode Island and North Carolina. Likewise, few records survive from the men who supported the Regulator Rebellion. Paper was scarce in the rural parts of North Carolina where they lived, and, like Martin Howard and the Newport Junto, the later decision made by many Regulators to remain loyal to the British Empire disrupted the preservation of any surviving personal papers.

Given these gaps in the documentary record and the fact that familial connections can often animate and inform the actions of the involved players, I turned to the long-standing sources used by social historians to understand the past: probates, tax lists, vital records, and town histories. Genealogies were another invaluable source for this research, though they can come with blind spots of their own. Usually written by family members, most genealogies were created in the midst of the colonial revival of the late nineteenth and early twentieth centuries. In the effort to glorify their families, some authors offered coy hints while others chose sweeping deletions of unpleasant facts. Nevertheless, genealogies and political and judicial records remain closely linked, with one often informing the other. Delving into these records helped me to better understand how and why these men came to their positions in the newspaper essays and pamphlets and in the petitions, resolves, and proclamations, while also helping me to draw links between the individual players. In turn, these sources helped me to better understand these movements and their particular moment in time.[67]

Chapter 1 discusses the commonalities of experience shared by Rhode Island and North Carolina. Both colonies were early advocates for religious toleration in British North America and so had more diverse populations than their neighbors in Massachusetts and Virginia. While there were few similarities between Rhode Island and North Carolina's economies, both diverged from the broader mercantile systems used, respectively, in their home regions of New England and the Low Country colonies. If Rhode Island and North Carolina were home to some of the earliest proponents of independence, they also were home to some of the first vocal defenders of the British Empire. These shared histories of religious toleration, economic divergence, and internal political tensions created similar climates in Rhode Island and North Carolina. Both colonies had reason to suspect their larger and more powerful neighbors, which in turn made the question of local control even more pressing than in other British North American colonies.

Chapters 2 and 3 discuss the political currents churning through Rhode Island prior to Newport's Stamp Act riots in August 1765. Chapter 2 introduces the individual members of the Newport Junto, while chapter 3 introduces Newport's various Sons of Liberty. The Newport Junto supported multiple causes in 1764 and 1765. These included arguments in favor of parliamentary taxation in the colonies, a bid for Rhode Island to become a royal colony, and plans to expand home textile production in Rhode Island, all of which were intended to restore order in a turbulent society. These ideas were contested by the members of Newport's Sons of Liberty chapter, who were increasingly working with other Rhode Island colonists to oppose the Newport Junto. Martin Howard and Providence resident Stephen Hopkins emerged as the primary voices in the colony during this period. Howard's *Letter from a Gentleman at Halifax* and Hopkins's *The Rights of the Colonies, Examined* and their respective newspaper editorials transmitted the rapid evolution of political thought in Rhode Island to the wider Atlantic world. By documenting preexisting political tensions in Rhode Island, these two chapters lay the groundwork for my argument that the Stamp Act crisis was fueled equally by local issues in the British colonies and concerns about parliamentary overreach.

Chapter 4 examines the Stamp Act riots in Massachusetts, Rhode Island, and North Carolina. It also considers how these colonies' particular experiences of the Stamp Act crisis were shaped by their individual statuses within the British Empire. Massachusetts and North Carolina were royal colonies whose governors were appointed by the British Crown. By contrast, Rhode Island was a chartered colony whose governor was elected locally. The chapter focuses on the use of violence during the riots in Boston and Newport and the demonstrations against the Stamp Act in North Carolina. It also introduces Maurice Moore's *The Justice and Policy of taxing the American Colonies*, the most vocal opposition to the Stamp Act in North Carolina when it was published in 1765.

Chapters 5 and 6 discuss the early stages of the Regulator Rebellion prior to its conclusion at the Battle of Alamance in 1771. Chapter 5 introduce the North Carolina colonists who referred to themselves as Regulators, while chapter 6 introduces the broad cadre of political and legal officials who responded to the Regulator Rebellion, including newly arrived Chief Justice Martin Howard. North Carolina was a relatively poor colony that provided minimal salaries for government employees. Instead, sheriffs could collect commissions based on a percentage of the tax money collected, while attorneys, registrars, and clerks could collect a percentage-based fee for services such as notarizing a land sale. Responses to these challenges varied widely, and two centers of the Regulator movement emerged by the end of 1768. The legal center worked to have its concerns addressed via petitions to Governor William Tryon and the General Assembly and the court system. The extralegal center increasingly turned to violent protests, including attacks on courtrooms in 1770 and 1771. These chapters also examine the impact that contemporaneous colonial responses to the Townshend Acts and the Boston Massacre had on these actions in North Carolina. By contextualizing the Regulator Rebellion with these events, these two chapters lay the groundwork for my argument that the Regulator Rebellion was fueled equally by concerns about the rising imperial crisis and by long-standing tensions within North Carolina.

Chapter 7 discusses the time preceding and following the end of the Regulator Rebellion at the Battle of Alamance. The passing of the Johnston Riot Act by the General Assembly in 1771 led directly to Governor Tyron's decision to turn to the colonial militia to quell the Regulator Rebellion by the use of force. Fallout from the Regulator Rebellion would shape North Carolina's progression toward the American Revolution in the years following the Battle of Alamance. Newly appointed Governor Josiah Martin's efforts to investigate the Regulators' concerns about North Carolina's colonial government was portrayed as further evidence of parliamentary overreach by the General Assembly. In turn, these concerns contributed to the passing of the Mecklenburg Resolves, which ended the royalist government in North Carolina in 1775.

Chapter 8 examines the legacy of North Carolina's and Rhode Island's colonial experiences in the 1770s and 1780s and the role these experiences played during the founding years of the United States. Tensions continued to grow in Rhode Island, where a group of colonists burned HMS *Gaspee* in spring 1771. The American Revolution and the years immediately following the war only deepened the lingering divides that had fueled the Stamp Act crisis and the Regulator Rebellion. Both Newport and parts of North Carolina were occupied by the British army in the later years of the war. The war effort also largely silenced Loyalists in Rhode Island and North Carolina. The war years also saw ruptures within the Regulator community, as some remained loyal to the British Empire while others joined the Revolutionary cause. After the American Revolution, North Carolina and Rhode Island were the final states to ratify the Constitution, in 1789 and 1790 respectively. Their inhabitants' questions about the intersecting roles played by local and imperial interests and identities in the 1760s had become questions about the roles played by local and federal interests and identities in the 1780s.

One of the many documents in the archives of the Newport Historical Society is an undated letter to *Newport Mercury* editor Solomon Southwick.[68] It depicts a dialogue between Lucius, the author of the piece, and an "elderly gentleman" on the "state of [our] menaced, invaded and abused Country." The elderly gentleman assures Lucius that "a few regiments trained, as are some in Virginia, to join Indians and Europeans together, would puzzle the best troops in England," a remark implying service in the Rogers's Rangers regiment during the French and Indian War.[69] He further reassured Lucius that these regiments would be joined by others for "every man seems to be siezed with the Temper of the Times, and this Great Britain knows or will know." This letter was never published in the *Newport Mercury*, but the phrase "temper of the times" echoes throughout the writings of this period.[70]

An early sentence in Lucius's dialogue expressing a desire for "a repeal of the most intolerable of the Coer. Acts" suggests a composition date no earlier than spring 1774, when the first news of Parliament's Coercive Acts, known as the Intolerable Acts in the colonies, reached North America.[71] Likewise, the reference to regiments trained "as are some in Virginia" appears to be a nod to the rifle company organized by Virginia colonist Daniel Morgan in summer 1775.[72] While this letter was written a few years after most of this book's events had come to their respective ends, the phrase

An undated letter to *Newport Mercury* editor Solomon Southwick depicting a dialogue between "Lucius" and an "elderly gentleman," who claims that "every man seems to be siezed with the Temper of the Times, and this Great Britain knows or will know." (*"Lucius to Solomon Southwick," date unknown, Box 121, Folder 13, collection of the Newport Historical Society*)

"siezed with the Temper of the Times" is equally emblematic of the concerns that drove the Stamp Act crisis and the Regulator Rebellion. When defined as a verb, the word "temper" describes the process of bringing a substance "to a proper or suitable condition, state, or quality, by mingling with something else; to qualify, alloy, or dilute by such mixture or combination."[73] Whether they supported or condemned the Stamp Act or the Regulator Rebellion, participants in both of these events were fiercely committed to tempering their worlds by any available means. They were also products of a world in which British North American colonists were still testing the bonds and divisions among themselves in equal measure. This book tells their stories, while placing the Stamp Act and Regulator Rebellion in the broader context of the turn from imperial crisis to Revolutionary era.

Chapter One

Founding Rhode Island and North Carolina

THE COLONIES OF RHODE ISLAND AND NORTH CAROLINA emerged in very different regions of British North America, one in New England, the other some seven hundred miles to the south. Despite these geographic differences, their many political and cultural similarities lend themselves to a comparative study. Rhode Island was often overshadowed by the Massachusetts and Connecticut colonies, while North Carolina was equally overshadowed by Virginia and South Carolina.[1] Both were largely settled by colonists who traveled overland from neighboring British colonies and so were already familiar with the North American landscape. Many of these colonists were, as Patrick Conley notes, "outcasts" known for their "individualism and separatist tendencies."[2] Both colonies also welcomed a multiplicity of religions, and later efforts to increase the role of the Anglican Church in North Carolina were met with resistance from non-Anglican colonists.

While Rhode Island and North Carolina had little in common with one another economically, both colonies developed economies that were distinctive from their immediate neighbors. Rhode Island was a northern colony whose economy was fueled by all aspects of the transatlantic slave trade. North Carolina was a southern colony where enslaved labor was less intrinsic to the overall economy than in neighboring Virginia and South

Carolina, though this would change in the period following the American Revolution. Both experienced prolonged periods of internal unrest, ranging from North Carolina's Culpeper Rebellion in the 1670s to Rhode Island's Dorr Rebellion in the 1840s. Rhode Island and North Carolina were also home to some of the earliest proponents for independence as well as some of the first vocal defenders of the British Empire. These elements made Rhode Island and North Carolina early testing grounds for the debates over political legitimacy and the intersecting roles played by local and imperial governments that encompassed British North American in the late eighteenth century. Understanding the respective histories of these colonies is essential for contextualizing their political activities in the 1760s.

Rhode Island's founding period began in fall 1635, when Roger Williams was expelled from Massachusetts for his sermons questioning Puritan religion, political rule, and the treatment of Native Americans.[3] Williams then spent the winter with a Wampanoag community on the eastern side of Narragansett Bay. In the spring, he purchased from the Narragansett tribe land for a settlement he called Providence, which was soon populated by his wife, children, and some of his followers.[4] Anne Hutchinson, William Coddington, and John Clarke, all later religious dissidents from Massachusetts Bay, founded Portsmouth on the north end of Aquidneck Island in 1638. Coddington, Clarke, and their followers then broke away from Portsmouth to found Newport in 1639. Following several years of wrangling with authorities in the Massachusetts and Plymouth colonies, Samuel Gorton added a fourth settlement called Warwick in 1643. These four settlements—Providence, Portsmouth, Newport, and Warwick—lacked a common political identity, which left them vulnerable to imperial ambitions from Massachusetts Bay and Connecticut, which wanted Rhode Island's deep harbors and rich farmland.

Roger Williams drew on his vision of a "livelie experiment" that allowed for (relative) democracy and religious toleration to persuade the largely unwilling Rhode Island towns to join together as a single colony in the early 1640s.[5] Unlike the Puritan colonies of Massachusetts Bay and Connecticut, suffrage in Rhode Island did not require church membership. After moving to the colony and acquiring enough land, white male heads of household could apply for voting rights from their towns, a process that took anywhere from three to ten years.[6] Once accepted, these men voted for political leaders who then created laws for the colony; but women, non-Protestants, Native Americans, African Americans, and servants of all races remained barred from voting. Rhode Island's commitment to religious toleration attracted groups of Baptists and Anglicans who were later joined by a com-

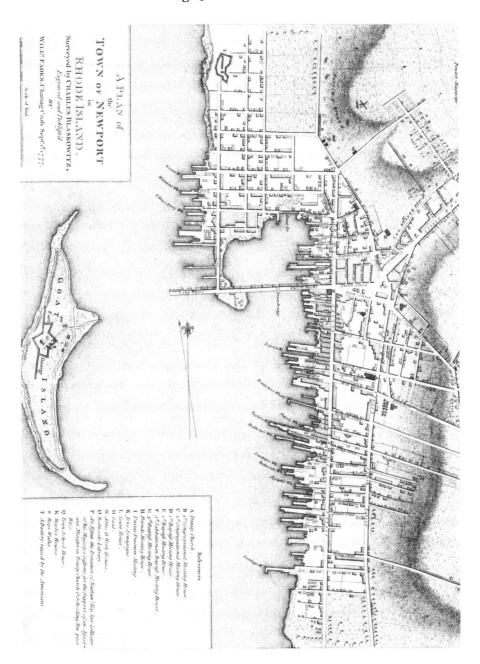

"A Plan of the Town of Newport in Rhode Island," Charles Blaskowitz, 1777. (*Object Number 01.952, collection of the Newport Historical Society*)

munity of Sephardic Jews in Newport in 1656 and a community of Quakers in 1657.[7]

The newly unified settlements were recognized with a patent in 1644 for the "Colony of Rhode Island and Providence Plantations," a name carefully chosen to reflect the Rhode Island towns of Portsmouth and Newport on Aquidneck Island and the mainland towns of Providence and Warwick. The patent may have created a political union among the four settlements, but each town still maintained its own legal system for addressing criminal acts, which created a "crazy quilt of mutually antithetical political and religious views."[8] This changed in 1647, when the first colony-wide legal code was created, though court sessions continued to rotate between Providence, Portsmouth, Newport, and Warwick until the court was moved in 1663 to Newport, the largest and most financially stable town in the colony.[9]

The restoration of Charles II to the English throne in 1660 posed new challenges for the colony of Rhode Island and Providence Plantations. Minister John Clarke traveled to England to negotiate for the best terms obtainable at the time.[10] Charles II agreed to provide Rhode Island with an official charter in 1663, which further established that the colony would be ruled by an annually elected governor, deputy governor, and General Assembly.[11] The General Assembly consisted of ten assistants and ten deputies, with representatives from all Rhode Island towns. These men also served as justices in the colony's court system for much of the seventeenth century, though they were eventually replaced by a separate judiciary.[12]

The early years of British settlement in North America led to the creation of three types of colonies: chartered, proprietary, and royal.[13] Chartered colonies allowed white male property-owning colonists to elect all political positions and to create legal codes for their colonies; proprietary colonies placed all political and legal power in the hands of one or more of the families who founded the colony; and royal colonies were under the direct supervision of the British monarch and Parliament, who appointed most political positions in these colonies. Most chartered and proprietary colonies had been transformed into royal colonies by the early eighteenth century, including the previously chartered colony of Massachusetts and the proprietary colonies of Maine and New Hampshire in New England. Rhode Island was one of the final chartered British North American colonies where some colonists still elected their own colonial governments, though this status was increasingly straining relations within Rhode Island in the 1760s.

Carolina Colony, established near modern-day Charleston, South Carolina, in 1663, was the first successful English colony south of Virginia.

Unlike Rhode Island, whose political identity rested on its inhabitants' obtaining first a patent and later a charter from the British monarch, Carolina began as a proprietary colony. This system was popular in the early colonial period since most funding for establishing the new colony came from the families who were granted the proprietorships rather than having to be raised by the joint-stock companies that funded the other British colonies. Unlike the other proprietary colonies that went to individual families, Charles II created eight separate proprietorships for Carolina that were expected to pool their resources and create a jointly run colony, though each proprietor was responsible for the residents in his section of the colony.[14]

The eight lords proprietor, as they were known, received their lands on March 4, 1663. Their first challenge was attracting British settlers to a colony in close proximity to Spanish-held Florida.[15] Colonists who took up land in proprietary colonies were required to pay a land tax to the proprietors known as a quitrent, which "was levied by the acre without regard to the location, productivity, or value of the land," though the Carolina proprietors agreed to waive this tax in the early years in the hope of enticing further settlers.[16] Some colonists had already begun traveling overland from Virginia to settle in the region around the Albemarle Sound.[17] Other Carolina settlers came from British colonies in the Caribbean and so arrived with a long-standing familiarity with plantation systems and enslaved labor. The English philosopher and political theorist John Locke created The Fundamental Constitutions of Carolina in 1669, which outlined the government and laws for the new colony. It noted that since "the natives of that place . . . are utterly strangers to Christianity . . . and those who remove from other parts to plant there will unavoidably be of different opinions concerning matters of religion," it would not be "reasonable for us, on this account, to keep them out."[18] Furthermore, "any seven or more persons agreeing in any religion, shall constitute a church or profession, to which they shall give some name, to distinguish it from others," a statement that not only protected "Jews, heathens, and other dissenters" in Carolina Colony but allowed them to form their own houses of worship. These provisions attracted multiple religious denominations, including English Baptists, Quakers and Methodists, Scots-Irish Presbyterians, German Lutherans and Moravians, and Sephardic Jews, many of whom were fleeing regions under Spanish control.

Over time, Carolina Colony faced increasing political challenges. Many Carolina colonists found that having eight individual families invested with proprietorships worked better in theory than in practice. By the early eighteenth century, Parliament and the Crown preferred the greater control provided by royal colonies rather than proprietorships or chartered colonies of the early settlement period.[19] Tensions with the Yamasee, Chickasaw, Creek, Catawba, and Cherokee tribes led to the outbreak of the Yamasee War near Charleston in 1715, which nearly destroyed Carolina Colony altogether.[20] Following the war, the area around Charleston became the royal colony of South Carolina in 1719. Descendants of seven of the original eight lords proprietor transferred their lands to the Crown on July 25, 1729, in exchange for payments of £2,500, along with an additional £5,000 to cover any outstanding quitrents, and these lands were then converted into the royal colony of North Carolina.[21] John Carteret, the Earl of Granville and a descendent of Sir George Carteret, one of the original lords proprietor, was allowed to keep his lands in exchange for relinquishing his political role in the colony. The Carteret family continued to maintain control over the massive tract of land known as the Granville District until the American Revolution, when it was confiscated by the newly formed state of North Carolina.

Similar to other royal colonies in the eighteenth century, most political power in North Carolina rested in the hands of the governor and his council, who received their appointments from the Crown, although the governor was allowed to recommend members for his council. This body served as the upper house for the General Assembly, while the lower house was elected by property-owning white men and comprised members of the same group. North Carolina's chief justice was appointed in England, but the colony's two associate justices were appointed by the governor. They presided over the colony's superior court, and the inferior courts were maintained by the individual counties, each with its own justices and clerks of court. All lower positions were elected offices, but they generally went to families who lived in eastern North Carolina rather than the rapidly expanding western parts of the colony, which, in turn, contributed to tensions between the geographic regions.

Rhode Island's early economy was rooted in the same blend of farming and fishing that supported the five New England colonies with access to the Atlantic Ocean.[22] The rich farmlands found on the shores of Narragansett Bay and on Aquidneck Island in the center of the bay had long sustained the Narragansett tribe.[23] Roger Williams's initial agreement with the Narragansett in 1635 allowed him and his followers to establish their settlement in the area around modern-day Providence, which was followed by the settlements on Acquidneck Island in the late 1630s. Cotton Mather's *Magnalia Christi Americana or the Ecclesiastical History of New England* would later rail in 1702 about the "lewd things which have been done or

"A Compleat Map of North-Carolina from an actual Survey," by John Collett, published in London, 1770. (*Louis Round Wilson Special Collections Library, University of North Carolina, Chapel Hill*)

said by the giddy sectaries of this Island" who now possessed "the paradise of all New England."[24] Like their neighbors in Massachusetts, Plymouth, and Connecticut, early Rhode Island farmers raised cattle and sheep, which were sold directly to surrounding colonies along with the cheese, butter, wool, and leather produced by some families, while early fishermen dried their cod and haddock to sell up and down the Eastern Seaboard.[25]

In time, it became apparent that Rhode Island's small size and relatively late start would limit any efforts to expand its agricultural efforts. Consequently, many colonists turned to trade on a much broader scale by "assemble[ing] cargoes from other colonies to supplement Rhode Island cattle, horses, and cheese" to ship throughout the Atlantic world. These efforts drew Rhode Island into the expanding triangular trade, which moved goods and enslaved people between ports in Europe, Africa, and the Americas.[26] Coastal Rhode Island communities drew on New England's ready supply of timber and labor to build the ships and provide the captains and crews needed for slaving voyages across the Atlantic. Wealthy families expanded their agricultural interests to include Rhode Island farms and sugar plantations in the Caribbean. These enterprises were locked together by the food raised by enslaved peoples on the rich soils of Acquidneck Island to feed the enslaved people who labored in the sugar fields and mills on Barbados and Jamaica.[27] If some of the resulting profits were plowed back into this forced agricultural system with the purchase of more and more enslaved people, others were spent on imported calicoes and silks from the Far East, which were then sold and purchased in Newport's shops. This led to an uneasy dynamic between agricultural and mercantile interests in Rhode Island, which later helped to fuel tensions during the Stamp Act crisis.

Economic distinctions also emerged between North Carolina and its neighbors in Virginia and South Carolina. The early establishment of tobacco plantations stabilized Virginia's economy by the mid-seventeenth century and led to massive agricultural expansion as hundreds of thousands of acres of land were turned into tobacco fields. The portions of Carolina Colony near Charleston, South Carolina, turned first to rice in the 1670s and later to indigo in the 1740s.[28] Most of the labor for these endeavors was done by enslaved peoples after the 1660s, though relatively few colonists in Virginia and South Carolina became involved with the slave trade, preferring instead to rely on transport provided by Rhode Island ship captains and others. By the mid-eighteenth century, Virginia and South Carolina were thriving colonies whose annual economic outputs deepened the pockets of planters and mercantile coffers alike, albeit at a staggering human cost.[29]

The waterways and marshes in southeastern North Carolina allowed for some rice production but never on the same scale as the rice plantations of South Carolina. The region around the Albemarle Sound was too cool to grow much rice, and the colonies of Virginia and Maryland were too deeply embedded in the tobacco trades for another colony to enter the already crowded tobacco marketplace. The sandy shorelines along the North Carolina coast also made commercial crops difficult since the colony had almost none of the deep-water ports needed to send goods into the wider world. Eighteenth-century historian William Smith noted that planters along the Chowan, Roanoke, Neuse, and Cape Fear Rivers relied on a mixed economy of "Tar Pitch, Turpentine, Lumber, Ship Shares, Deerskins ... Rice, Peas, Beeswax and Tobacco."[30] The first three of these items made up approximately 80 percent of all exports from North Carolina from 1768–1772 and were the only trade goods whose North Carolina production outstripped all the other British North American colonies.[31] Some of these planters also turned to land speculation in the mid-eighteenth century, which helped set the events of the Regulator Rebellion into motion in the late 1760s.

South Carolina was a relatively small colony, claiming less than two hundred miles along the Eastern Seaboard. The rice plantations along the coast were productive enough to deter most colonists from moving inland. By contrast, the North Carolina coastline spanned more than three hundred miles. The Algonquian, Iroquoian, and Siouan tribal groups who had inhabited North Carolina for centuries before the arrival of European colonists had long used the region's many rivers as trading paths reaching far into the North American interior.[32] The first documented journey by English colonists into inland North Carolina took place in 1673, when Virginia merchant Abraham Wood sent James Needham and Gabriel Arthur overland from Fort Henry, Virginia, through North Carolina and on to Kentucky, Georgia, and Alabama.[33] These travels brought them into contact with dozens of Native American tribes, including the Siouan-speaking Occaneechi tribe, whom they found on an island in the Roanoke River near Clarksville, Virginia. Eight years later, English explorer John Lawson organized a second expedition into the North Carolina interior, where he encountered the Occaneechi tribe living on the banks of the Eno River in a community called Achonechy. This would later become the town of Hillsborough, North Carolina.[34]

John Lawson's tales of swamplands and alligators living under his floorboards intrigued armchair travelers in Britain, who eagerly perused the pages of *A New Voyage to Carolina*.[35] Colonists living in coastal North Carolina were more interested in Lawson's descriptions of grasslands, forests, and shallow, swift-moving rivers in the interior. Grasslands, in their eyes, could become farmlands, forests could become timber for houses and ships, and the rivers could power the mills needed to grind their grains and saw their lumber. The first European settlers reached the Piedmont region in the 1730s and 1740s, following the long-established Great Indian Trading Path, which began in Petersburg, Virginia, and traveled southwest into the Carolinas. Later settlers would use the Great Wagon Road, which was established in the 1750s and ran from Pennsylvania through the Shenandoah Valley and into North Carolina. These colonists included groups of English Quakers, Methodists, and Baptists, Scots-Irish Presbyterians, and German Moravians, who gradually established a rough polyglot of languages in order to communicate with one another as they established their far-flung farms across the North Carolina interior.[36]

The early influx of European settlers into the Piedmont immediately led to rising tensions with the Cherokee, Catawba, and Creek tribal groups who lived in this region, though many of them were recent arrivals who had been pushed west by the first waves of English settlers in North Carolina.[37] Relations between European colonists and Native Americans worsened during the French and Indian War and led to the 1756 construction of Fort Dobbs in what is now Iredell County. Fort Dobbs was garrisoned with a North Carolina militia contingent under the command of Hugh Waddell who would later lead forces against the Regulators at the Battle of Alamance.[38] In the end, the spread of smallpox would have a far greater impact on the Catawba and the other tribes than military attacks, as hundreds of tribal members died during this period.[39] Following the close of the French and Indian War, four governors of Southern colonies, the British Indian agent for the Southern Department, and "twenty-five chiefs and seven hundred warriors, including many from the Catawba and Cherokee nations" gathered in Augusta, Georgia, to compose a treaty designed to resolve issues between English colonists and Native American tribes, establish trade relations and "the punishment, by each party, of offenders of its own race for crimes against the member of the other race," and create a reservation of about fifteen square miles for the Catawba tribe.[40]

Following the signing of this treaty, a wave of new European settlers arrived in the Piedmont. The early colonists in the region had largely been small farmers, with the exception of the German Moravians, whose urban community of Salem offered adjoining neighbors access to its tavern, pottery, gristmill, and sawmill.[41] The new arrivals, by contrast, were land speculators, merchants, and lawyers who planned to expand on their earlier financial successes in London and along the coast.[42] They advocated for the creation of towns and counties, courthouses and shops, and the necessary infrastructure for supporting them via the local tax base. Unsurprisingly, these contrasting visions for the Piedmont led to growing tensions in the early 1760s, particularly since they were fully supported by the North Carolina General Assembly and the royally appointed governors.[43]

These tensions between eastern/urban colonists and western/rural colonists were typical of many of the internal rebellions in North America before and after the American Revolution. Historian A. Roger Ekirch writes that "regional disputes disrupted politics in several provinces during the eighteenth century . . . in Connecticut conflict occurred between religious and economic factions drawn along east-west lines. Similarly, east-west divisions polarized New Jersey."[44] Daniel Shay and Job Shattuck would organize central Massachusetts farmers in Shays's Rebellion in 1786 to express concerns about the plight of small farmers who were unable to vote owing to property restrictions but who were still required to pay their rising taxes following the American Revolution.[45] Shays's Rebellion was followed by the Whiskey and Fries Rebellions in western Pennsylvania in the 1790s, which again saw small farmers struggling to pay rising federal taxes.[46] Ekirch adds that "Rhode Island experienced a struggle during the 1750s and 1760s between the trading centers of Providence and Newport. Certainly regional conflict was not unique to North Carolina."[47] North Carolina did, however, have multiple internal conflicts, including the Culpeper Rebellion in 1677, Cary's Rebellion in 1711, and the Enfield Riots and the Sugar Creek War in the years immediately before the Regulator Rebellion.

Rhode Island's beginnings as four separate communities in the 1630s set the stage for decades of internal turmoil in the colony. Roger Williams, John Clarke, and others had successfully fused the towns of Providence, Portsmouth, Newport, and Warwick into a single colony. Nevertheless, colonists in the Providence Plantations towns of Providence and Warwick continued to distrust the colonists in the Rhode Island towns of Newport and Portsmouth, and vice versa. Allowing all white male landowners in Rhode Island to vote regardless of church membership had seemed generous in the mid-seventeenth century. Once Massachusetts was no longer allowed to restrict suffrage to church membership under the terms of the second charter issued by William III in 1691, there were no differences in voting rights between Massachusetts and Rhode Island.[48] Furthermore, by the 1820s, many politicians were in favor of ending property restrictions on suffrage for male voters. After Virginia extended suffrage to all male voters in 1830, Rhode Island became the only state to link voting rights with property ownership. It was also the only state still using its colonial charter to craft its political systems in the nineteenth century.

Rhode Island's minimum freehold for voting rights was set at $134 in the 1820s and early 1830s. Patrick Conley estimates that "close to sixty percent of Rhode Island's free adult males were relegated to the status of second-class citizens by the freehold qualification" in 1829.[49] As the numbers of factories and landless factory workers continued to expand, the percentage of Rhode Island residents with voting rights was likely to diminish even further. Older landed families in Rhode Island argued in favor of continuing to use the 1663 charter with its property restrictions on suffrage, while rising numbers of factory workers argued in favor of expanding white male suffrage. Not surprisingly, this division closely resembles the older tensions between landed Rhode Island families and the newer mercantile families in the eighteenth century. This same period also saw the emergence of the abolition movement, which advocated for the ending of African American slavery and, in time, led to the women's suffrage movement. Similar to the rest of the United States in this period, advocates for universal white male suffrage and advocates for the abolition of slavery and the expansion of suffrage for African Americans and women did not always agree with one another, though these groups did, occasionally, find common ground in the 1830s and 1840s.

Thomas Dorr was an early supporter of the abolition movement whose actions led to the short-lived Dorr Rebellion in Rhode Island in the early 1840s.[50] His efforts eventually led to universal white male suffrage in Rhode Island, but they came at a high cost for Dorr himself. Most Rhode Island residents agreed in the 1830s that the 1663 colonial charter needed to be replaced with a state constitution. They did not, however, agree on the governments and political systems to be created by that constitution. This resulted in two separate constitutional conventions in 1841, one officially sponsored by the state legislature and one sponsored by Dorr and his supporters. The first of these conventions created a document known as the Landholder's Constitution, which "gave the franchise to those white, male native-born citizens who met age residency requirements, but retained the real estate requirement for naturalized citizens," a provision intended to target the many immigrants working in Rhode Island's textile factories.[51] The second convention created a document known as the People's Constitution, which advocated in favor of removing all property restrictions for voting in Rhode Island. Disputes also emerged between delegates at the convention for the People's Constitution. Forty-six delegates wanted their constitution to specify that voters had to be white, while eighteen delegates, including Dorr, felt that race should not be a barrier to suffrage.[52]

The People's Constitution was submitted to all male citizens of Rhode Island on December 27, 1841, and they voted overwhelmingly to ratify it. The Rhode Island legislature refused to recognize this election and submitted the Landholder's Constitution "to a vote on March 23, 1842 in which all who would be granted the franchise under the new document were permitted to vote"; it was narrowly defeated.[53] Both groups then called for elections to select new governments. The existing state legislature, which opposed the People's Constitution, issued a law stating it was the only entity in Rhode Island that could organize elections. Anyone who took part in unsanctioned elections faced fines and imprisonment, and anyone who assumed office under the People's Constitution would be tried on treason charges. Governor Samuel King then asked President John Tyler to provide federal assistance, but Tyler refused to do this on the grounds that there was no evidence of insurrection in Rhode Island.

The supporters of the People's Constitution and the Landholder's Constitution held elections in mid-April; King and Dorr were elected governor by their respective constituents. The federal government responded by moving artillery companies to Fort Adams in Newport, Rhode Island, in early May as observers. King and Dorr were then, respectively, inaugurated as governor of Rhode Island in Newport and Providence. Dorr's supporters unsuccessfully attacked the Providence Marine Corps of Artillery armory on May 17.[54] Dorr fled to New York and returned in June with about 250 armed supporters who gathered on Acote's Hill in Chepachet, Rhode Island. Governor King ordered the state militia to attack Dorr's men, and Dorr asked his men to stand down. The legislature placed the state under martial law, and multiple Dorrites, as they were commonly called, were arrested. Dorr surrendered to King in 1843 and was convicted on treason charges in 1844. He was imprisoned for a year and then pardoned by the state legislature, which eventually also restored his civil and political rights. Rhode Island approved a new state constitution in November 1842 that expanded suffrage to white men who could pay a one dollar poll tax. Despite the grounding provided by the new constitution, unease about sources of political legitimacy and the intersecting roles played by local and imperial governments continued to linger in Rhode Island.

North Carolina experienced multiple internal rebellions in the century before the American Revolution, including the Culpeper Rebellion in 1677, Cary's Rebellion in 1711, and the Enfield Riots and the Sugar Creek War in the years immediately before the Regulator Rebellion. All four had echoes of the divisions between rural and urban settlers found in most of the North American rebellions. They were also products of North Carolina's geography and unique political structures, which easily lent themselves to concerns about political legitimacy and the intersecting roles played by local and imperial governments.

The lords proprietor had divided Carolina Colony into two provinces in the late seventeenth century, Albemarle in the north and Clarendon in the south, though each of the proprietors also maintained a level of control over the lands allotted to his family. Britain passed the first laws known as the Navigation Acts in 1651, which limited British subjects to trading within the British Empire and only on British ships. Any goods coming from countries outside the British Empire were required to enter in London, where parliamentary taxes were paid before they were shipped to the rest of Britain and its colonies in the Americas. The Navigation Acts were reinforced by the Plantation Duty Act of 1673, which required that certain goods, including tobacco, be shipped directly to Britain for taxing rather than be traded within the British North American colonies.[55] English colonists living in Albemarle province had established a thriving tobacco trade with the colonies of Massachusetts and Rhode Island whose small trading vessels were shallow enough to navigate the region's narrow, sandy rivers. Not only would the Navigation Acts disrupt this trade, but it stood to make it nearly impossible for North Carolina to trade anything since the colony lacked the deep water ports necessary for loading vessels capable of making the long voyage across the Atlantic to London.

John Jenkins, the governor for Albemarle province in 1673, responded to the Plantation Duty Act by refusing to assign men who would enforce the new law as tax collectors. Thomas Eastchurch, the speaker of the Albemarle assembly, promptly informed authorities in Britain about Jenkins's refusal to support the new tax law. When Jenkins tried to dissolve the Albemarle assembly, its members refused to disband and voted instead to have the governor removed from office and imprisoned in 1676. At this time, Eastchurch and his supporter, Thomas Miller, traveled to Britain, where Eastchurch was made governor of Albemarle province. He promised to enforce the new tax on his return to North Carolina. But this return was delayed by his marriage to a wealthy widow in Nevis, so he sent Miller ahead to serve as acting governor for Albemarle. Miller's eager efforts to seize hundreds of pounds of tobacco, interfere with local elections, and fine and imprison various colonists triggered outright rebellion from John Culpeper, George Durant, and Valentine Bird in December 1677 in an event known as Culpeper's Rebellion.[56] After taking over Albemarle province, the rebelling colonists tried and imprisoned Miller and other high ranking officials. Culpeper was made customs collector and traveled to London to explain their actions to Parliament, who ordered a full investigation. Anthony Ashley Cooper, one of the lords proprietor, defended Culpeper in court and successfully argued that he and his associates were guilty only of rioting since there had been no settled government in Albemarle at the time of their actions.

The lords proprietor had agreed to defend Culpeper's actions, but they remained concerned that further unrest in Albemarle would lead to the loss of their charter and chose a man named Seth Sothel to serve as the province's next governor, a decision undoubtedly precipitated by the fact that Sothel had just purchased Edward Hyde's proprietorship and so would have both a financial and personal interest in the colony's stability. Sothel was captured by Turkish pirates on his way to North America and imprisoned in Algiers for the next two years. While Sothel was detained, John Jenkins served as governor for Albemarle province. He was assisted by George Durant, whom William Powell describes as the "ablest leader in the province" for his ability to restore order, collect customs duties without issue, and arrange for pardons for all the rebelling colonists. Sothel was eventually released from prison in Algiers and arrived in Albemarle in 1683. His time as governor proved disastrous, and Sothel was tried in 1688 by the Albemarle General Assembly on charges of "oppression, tyranny, extortion, and bribery."[57] Sothel finished his time in Carolina Colony by forcing out the governor of Clarendon province in South Carolina, which eventually led to his being removed from office there as well.

The next major unrest in Albemarle province was Cary's Rebellion, which began in 1711.[58] The Fundamental Constitutions of Carolina created by John Locke in 1669 had included protections for "Jews, heathens, and other dissenters," and hundreds of non-Anglicans had flocked to the colony in the late seventeenth century.[59] John Archdale, a recent convert to the Quaker faith, served as governor for Albemarle province in the 1690s, which further led to members of the Quaker church holding a majority of the seats in the General Assembly. The proprietors replaced Archdale with his Anglican son-in-law, Henderson Walker, in 1699. Governor Walker created a law in 1701 that ordered the use of tax money to support the Anglican Church.[60] Members of other churches could still attend their own religious services, but all colonists were required to financially support the Anglican Church. A 1703 law required members of the General Assembly to take an oath of allegiance to the newly crowned Queen Anne. The Quaker faith prevented its members from swearing oaths, and British law had long since granted them the right to make affirmations for political leaders instead, something Walker refused to allow Quakers in Albemarle to do.[61]

The proprietors then made Thomas Cary governor. He forced all Quakers from their positions in the General Assembly and requied its members to swear an oath of allegiance to Queen Anne. The Quakers sent John Porter to London to plead their case in person to the proprietors, who ordered that Cary be removed from office and that all laws requiring oath swearing be suspended. The Albemarle governorship was then assumed by William Glover, who promptly began reinforcing the oath swearing. This led to an election in 1708 in which Glover ran against Cary, who had agreed to work with the Quaker Church. By this time, the lords proprietor had decided they needed greater control in Albemarle province and sent Edward Hyde, a cousin of the lord proprietor of the same name, to serve as governor of North Carolina, the first time the colony was identified in this manner.

Governor Hyde arrived in North Carolina in spring 1711. His first course of action was creating laws punishing seditious actions against the colony's government, followed by nullifying all laws passed during Cary's tenure. Cary and his followers gathered a store of arms and attacked the house on the Albemarle Sound where Hyde and his advisers were meeting. Cary was eventually captured and sent to Britain for trial on sedition charges. He was later released due to lack of evidence, though this may have been because nobody was sent to Britain to testify against him. This period of feuding between Anglican and Quaker colonists in North Carolina greatly weakened the colony, as did repeated crop failures owing to a drought. These tensions were further heightened by growing Native American attacks on North and South Carolina, which culminated in the Tuscarora War in 1711 and the Yamasee War in 1717.

The next major political unrest in North Carolina was the Enfield Riots in 1759 and the Sugar Creek War in 1765, the final protests before the start of the Regulator Rebellion in 1768.[62] North Carolina continued to struggle economically in the mid-eighteenth century, and the arrival of new wealthy colonists hoping to expand their fortunes had added further tensions to an already unstable colony. This was also the same period in which Parliament had required the proprietors to sell their tracts of land to the Crown to transform North Carolina into a royal colony. Seven of the eight proprietors agreed to this process, but John Carteret, the great grandson of one of the original proprietors and the second Earl of Granville, refused to sell his lands and was eventually allowed to keep them and the right to collect quitrents from his colonists.[63]

Carteret was faced with two new challenges in the 1740s. His agents were struggling to collect quitrents from the far-flung colonists on his lands. Wealthy London merchant Henry McCulloh had just arrived in North

Carolina and was taking up as many land grants in central North Carolina as he could obtain from the Crown, which Carteret saw as a direct challenge to his authority. Fortunately for Carteret, in 1742 he became the secretary of state for the Northern Department.[64] While this position was not directly connected to the management of the British North American colonies, it expanded his influence in Parliament, and he was able to persuade the Privy Council to add to his previously existing lands in North Carolina. The resulting Granville District contained more than twenty-six thousand square miles of land that bordered on Virginia to the north and, at the time, had only about thirty thousand people in residence. Eager to entice new settlers to his lands, Carteret "chose to grant lands in fee simple, subject to an annual quitrent of 3s. sterling or 4s. proclamation money per hundred acres [while the initial purchase price] was £4 19s. Virginia currency [per tract of land], plus an additional 5 s. for every 50 acres included in the patent." Colonists were required to return half the profits for any gold or silver found on their lands to the Crown, but Carteret placed no restrictions on the sale of timber, North Carolina's primary export, or the right to fish or hunt on lands in the Granville District. New colonists flocked to the district, some establishing farms of their own, others amassing tracts of land of their own, which they then resold.[65]

Problems first emerged in the Granville District in the late 1740s. Because John Carteret remained in Britain during this period, he appointed two agents, Edward Moseley and Robert Halton, to manage his lands for him in 1746. This continued until the two men died within three months of one another in 1749. Carteret's first replacement agent, Thomas Child, returned to Britain within the year. The second, Francis Corbin, took advantage of Carteret's absence to expand and consolidate his own power in North Carolina by cheating and extorting numerous would-be landowners.[66] These activities brought Corbin in direct conflict with Henry McCulloh, the other major landowner in North Carolina, as the two men frequently claimed and then sold the same tracts of land.

Francis Corbin's land dealings eventually attracted the attention of North Carolina's colonial officials. Attorney General Robert Jones was encouraged by multiple colonists to prosecute Corbin late in 1758, but the investigation only led to near total exoneration for Corbin and the surveyors who assisted him in his work. Finally, men from Edgecombe, Halifax, and Granville Counties kidnapped Corbin from his home in Edenton on January 25, 1759, and held him hostage until he agreed to "open all land records for public inspection and to dismiss corrupt deputies." The later Regulator Rebellion was also fueled by concerns about illicit land sales and extortionate fees, but A. Roger Ekirch notes that the Enfield Riots should be seen as a "dispute between rival land magnates as much as an expression of settler disaffection."[67] The leader of the men who kidnapped Corbin was almost certainly Alexander McCulloh, Henry McCulloh's nephew, who was more than happy to exploit wider frustrations with Corbin's land dealings. The end result was a divided North Carolina General Assembly, which almost led to the unseating of Governor Arthur Dobbs.

The central figures in the Sugar Creek War of 1765 were the McCulloh family, John Carteret's primary competitors for control of land of North Carolina.[68] Henry McCulloh had received a massive tract of land in 1755 to the west of the Granville District consisting of most of present-day Rowan, Anson, and Mecklenburg Counties. He then sold portions of this land to George Selwyn and Governor Dobbs, while keeping the rest of it for his own land-speculation activities. By that time, floods of settlers from Pennsylvania and Virginia were pouring into North Carolina on the newly created Great Wagon Road. They saw the lands on which they had established their farms as theirs by right of possession, and few were willing to purchase these lands from men they viewed as absentee landlords. Surveyors were increasingly attacked by settlers, and these attacks grew particularly violent in the area around the Sugar and Reedy Creeks, land previously purchased by Dobbs from McCulloh. After he was captured by a group of men in this region in 1752, Dobbs eventually agreed to rent his land to the men farming on it for a reduced price, and the disruptions on his lands ceased in 1763.

Henry McCulloh purchased his lands back from George Selwyn in 1764 and arranged to lead a surveying expedition on them in March 1765. He also was confronted by farmers living on his lands who offered reduced rent prices, but, unlike Governor Dobbs, McCulloh refused to accept their offer and ordered additional surveying work, which led to new attacks on surveyors in May 1765. During this time, Dobbs died and was replaced by North Carolina's lieutenant governor, William Tryon. John Polk submitted a petition to Tryon asking him to investigate McCulloh's actions. Tryon initially ordered McCulloh to stop surveying his lands but later agreed to order investigations into the rioters who had attacked the surveyors on McCulloh's lands, though this investigation was eventually dropped. The Sugar Creek War was resolved in 1767 when McCulloh agreed to return disputed tracts of land to North Carolina, which then began the redistribution process all over again as other colonists flooded into central North Carolina.

Martin Howard, a resident of Newport, Rhode Island, became chief justice of North Carolina in 1767 because he was a qualified and, in the eyes of Parliament, deserving candidate at a time when the colony needed one. But Howard was not the only point of connection between Rhode Island and North Carolina in the colonial period. Colonists in Massachusetts and Connecticut were focused on agricultural production. By contrast, settlers in Rhode Island turned their economic attentions to the coastal trades. In the south, Virginia and South Carolina had the deep harbors and rich farmlands needed for the transatlantic trade. North Carolina's narrow ports and sandy creeks needed the shallow-keeled vessels used by ship captains from Rhode Island along the Eastern Seaboard. As these trade relationships between Rhode Island and North Carolina developed throughout the late seventeenth century, so did their cultural and political relationships.

Ship captain Roger Jones first traveled to North America in 1680, where he became a merchant and coastal trader in Virginia.[69] His son, Frederick, settled near Edenton, North Carolina, in the early 1700s. Like his father, Frederick Jones also became a merchant, as well as serving as the colony's chief justice from 1718 to 1722. He married Jane Harding and had six children, including a son named Frederick who married Mary Vail and had two sons, Harding and Frederick. In the early 1750s, the Jones family sent Harding to Yale University, where he was tutored in theology by Newport, Rhode Island, minister Ezra Stiles. Stiles introduced Harding Jones to Newport resident Mary Whiting, the daughter of John and Phebe Greenman Whiting. Shortly after Harding's graduation, Stiles conducted their wedding ceremony in Newport on October 17, 1756. Harding's cousin Frederick wrote to his mother from New Bern, North Carolina, on December 10, 1756, that "my cousin Harding has just returned from New England where he has been for education for several years past, with a very agreeable young woman to his wife."[70] The young family appears to have returned to Newport soon afterward as Harding died of tuberculosis in Newport in 1759. Mary Whiting Jones then returned to New Bern with their daughter, Mary Jones, who would marry Abner Nash in 1772. Nash became the second governor of the state of North Carolina in 1780.[71]

Mary Whiting Jones gave her father power of attorney to address her business affairs in North Carolina following the death of her husband. John Whiting transferred power of attorney to New Bern attorney John Fonville soon afterward, but Jones appears to have returned to North Carolina in the mid-1760s, as she married New Bern merchant Richard Ellis in 1764. Whiting visited his daughter and her new husband in New Bern in spring 1767 and sent Ezra Stiles a letter, noting, "I have had the honour of dining & drinking tea, with my lord chief justice [Martin] Howard, sundry times;

he is very alert, in high spirits, and extremely complaisant." Stiles undoubtedly shared this news with other Newport residents and so continued the ongoing chain of communication between Rhode Island and North Carolina.[72]

These shared histories of religious toleration, internal political tensions, and economic connections created similar climates in Rhode Island and North Carolina by the mid-eighteenth century. Both colonies had reason to suspect their larger and more powerful neighbors, which, in turn, made the question of local control even more pressing than in many of the other British North American colonies. Likewise, the rhythms of crafted dissent forged by decades of internal dissent gave colonists in both Rhode Island and North Carolina a playbook for expressing their concerns about the worlds around them. Wayne E. Lee writes that "the rioters began as petitioners. When their petition apparently failed, they carefully constructed their ensuing actions. They limited their targets and they restrained their violence while using symbols and figures of legitimacy."[73] Elements of these actions would appear and reappear in both the Stamp Act crisis and the Regulator Rebellion, though it is increasingly apparent that the men who launched the civil dissents were not the same ones who took part in the increasingly violent riots in the later stages of both movements. These conversations would reappear in Rhode Island and North Carolina in the decades following the American Revolution. Both states would question whether to take part in the forging of a central American government and, later, would be reluctant participants in the ratification of the Constitution in 1789 and 1790.

Chapter Two

Before the Stamp Act

The town of Newport, Rhode Island, stretches down a hill to Newport Harbor, where dozens of wharves reached into the harbor in the eighteenth century.[1] Thames Street runs parallel to the waterfront, with most warehouses and shops on the northern end of the street while the ever-growing number of homes of Newport's merchants and sea captains filled the southern end before spilling into neighboring Water Street. A short walk up Queen Street from Thames Street took passersby along the open land known as the Parade to Newport's Colony House, a large brick building constructed in the 1730s for political and legal gatherings. Around the corner from the Colony House was the printing press established by James and Ann Franklin in the late 1720s. The Parade became an enclosed space in the 1760s, with the Colony House on the eastern end and the newly constructed Brick Market Building on the western end, with houses lining the southern and northern edges of the Parade. Churches dotted the Newport streets, with the spire of the Anglican Trinity Church gazing serenely down at the harbor from Spring Street while two Congregationalist churches, four Baptist meetinghouses, a synagogue, and a Quaker meetinghouse formed a half circle around the Colony House.[2]

Readers of the *Newport Mercury* perused their weekly copies of the local periodical in taverns and coffee shops, at home and along the stretches of the Parade. Like most eighteenth-century newspapers, the *Newport Mercury* offered readers coverage of local events, editorials from members of the Newport community, advertisements, and news copied from other papers in the British Empire. The opening essay in the April 23, 1764, issue set off a wave of comment by declaring that Rhode Island's long-cherished charter had become "the source of all our evils, by giving too much to the people, and reserving too little in the crown."[3] This pronouncement from a pseudonymous Z.Y. was the opening salvo in a struggle that would explode during the Newport Stamp Act riots in summer 1765. Its roots, however, lay deep in Rhode Island's past. Competing visions for Rhode Island's identity had been part of the colony since it was founded in the 1630s. Where once the four original towns had jousted for prominence, now many Rhode Islanders were questioning whether the colony's economy should maintain its agricultural roots or join the rising ranks of the mercantile classes, whose interests had expanded alongside the British Empire following the Seven Years' War. This issue tore through political races, inspired endless newspaper columns, and, in time, merged with the debates over parliamentary taxation.

Z.Y. was a pseudonym used by the group of men known as the Newport Junto, or, in some circles, the Tory Junto. Their goal was to use the presence of their organization in Newport as a conduit for their many political and economic interests.[4] Months before the Stamp Act was passed early in 1765, the Newport Junto had already taken public stances on two seemingly disparate causes: Rhode Island's status as one of the last chartered British colonies and promoting domestic textile production in Rhode Island. The men in Newport and Providence who would later form Rhode Island's Sons of Liberty chapters became the Newport Junto's primary opposition as the two sides laid the groundwork for the fury that would unfold during the Newport Stamp Act riots in August 1765. Despite these tensions, the two sides occasionally shared common viewpoints, as they both questioned whether female colonists could also be held responsible for addressing Rhode Island's economic and political challenges. The campaigns launched by the Newport Junto and the Sons of Liberty were also influenced by Newport's dire economy in the period immediately following the French and Indian War, and the last vestiges of Stephen Hopkins's and Samuel Ward's efforts to dominate the governor's office and the Rhode Island socioeconomic identity in the mid-eighteenth century.[5]

Joshua Fogarty Beatty describes the Stamp Act crisis as a "multilayered struggle in which actors used many different culturally-defined forms of communication, including print, oratory, rituals of celebration and justice,

The Colony House, Newport, Rhode Island. (*Author's Photograph*)

and face-to-face speech, to advance their own goals."[6] Like their opponents across British North America, the Newport Junto began in the public arena of Newport's many civic and cultural institutions, moved onto utilizing every inch of available space in the pages of the *Newport Mercury*, and transitioned to pamphlet writing in spring 1765.[7] Massachusetts colonist James Otis infamously referred to the Newport Junto as a "little, dirty, drinking, drabbing, contaminated knot of beggars and transports . . . made up of Turks, Jews, and other infidels, with a few renegado Catholics and Christians."[8] Surviving records demonstrate, however, that these allegations were little more than hyperbolic slander from Otis.

The Newport Junto's three central figures, Martin Howard, Augustus Johnston, and Thomas Moffat, had all lived in Rhode Island for decades by the time of the Stamp Act crisis. Howard came from an Anabaptist family in Newport and described himself as a "Native of the colonies" in 1765.[9] Howard's marriage to his first wife, Ann Brenton Conklin Howard, in 1754 linked him with one of Rhode Island's oldest families.[10] By the time the Z.Y. letter was published in 1764, Howard had represented Rhode Island at the Albany Congress in 1754 and Newport in the Rhode Island General Assembly.[11] His work as an attorney was buttressed with further civic activities, including serving as moderator for the Newport Town Council, an overseer of the poor, and clerk for the Queen Street market.[12] Johnston was another "native of the colonies" who moved to Rhode Island from New Jersey with his family in the late 1740s.[13] Like Howard, Johnston was an attorney, and he served as Rhode Island's attorney general between 1757 and 1766. Moffat was a Scottish physician who trained at the University of Edinburgh and moved to Rhode Island in the late 1730s, while his brother John Moffat took up residence in Boston.[14] Moffat appears to have been a member of one of Newport's Baptist churches, as he wrote the epitaph for Baptist minister John Callendar in 1748.[15]

Other identifiable members of the Newport Junto included Peter Harrison, William Hunter, and George Rome. Harrison moved to Newport in 1739 with his older brother, Joseph Harrison, and the two initially worked as merchants and sea captains. The Harrison brothers came from a Quaker family from Yorkshire, England. Both men eventually converted to the Anglican faith, but their religious roots lay at the more radical end of the Protestant scale, which would not have appeared out of place in Newport. Peter Harrison's wife, Elizabeth Pelham Harrison, inherited a large estate known as Leamington Farm from her father in 1748, and the couple settled there while Harrison developed his career as an architect. Like Thomas Moffat, William Hunter completed his medical training at the University of Edinburgh. Historian Carl Bridenbaugh notes that Moffat and Hunter added "a decidedly 'philosophical' tone to the group as a whole." George Rome was the agent for the London firm of Hopkins and Haley and was tasked with persuading Newport's merchants to pay their export bills, which may have contributed to his unpopularity with many of his neighbors in town.[16]

Martin Howard, Augustus Johnston, Thomas Moffat, Peter Harrison, William Hunter, and George Rome were the core authors of the Newport Junto's public rhetoric. These writings were probably informed by the voices of fellow travelers who shared familial and economic connections with the group's more active members. Harrison's brother, Joseph, had moved to New Haven, Connecticut, by the early 1760s but delivered petitions and letters to London for the Newport Junto.[17] John Robinson was the customs collector for Rhode Island in 1764 and 1765, and his efforts to collect customs dues from Newport's merchants probably brought him in contact with George Rome.[18] James Honeyman Sr., the minister at Trinity Church, Newport's Anglican church, conducted the marriage ceremony for Martin Howard and Ann Brenton Conklin Howard in 1749 and christened their daughter, Annie Howard Spooner, in 1754.[19] Howard studied law with Honeyman's son, James Honeyman Jr., who was Rhode Island's attorney general between 1732 and 1740.[20] The estate adjoining Peter Harrison and Elizabeth Pelham Harrison's Leamington Farm belonged to Jahleel Brenton, a cousin-in-law of Martin Howard's who, like the Harrisons, was investing heavily in agriculture in the 1750s and 1760s.[21] Ann Howard's cousins, Mary and Margaret Sanford, were married to, respectively, Andrew Oliver and Thomas Hutchinson.[22] Like the more active members of the Newport Junto, the Honeyman, Brenton, and Hutchinson families largely remained loyal to the British Empire during the American Revolution. They also suffered financial losses in the 1770s as their lands were attacked and, later, confiscated by the newly formed state of Rhode Island and Providence Plantations.[23]

Martin and Ann Howard purchased a home on Broad Street around the corner from the Colony House in 1757, which placed them near the center of all political and legal activity in Newport. Fellow Newport Junto members Augustus Johnston and Thomas Moffat both lived close to the Howards, and it is likely William Hunter did as well. For his part, George Rome divided his time between a home near the Newport waterfront and his farm outside the town, while the Harrisons also lived on their estate during this period. By this time, Peter Harrison's architectural career was flourishing, and he designed Newport's Redwood Library in 1747, the Touro Synagogue in 1759, and the Brick Market Place in 1762, as well as providing plans for King's Chapel in Boston in the early 1750s.[24]

Thursday afternoons often found Martin Howard walking from his home on Broad Street, angling to the right on Bull Street, and continuing up Griffin Street to reach the Redwood Library, which was very nearly in the countryside in the mid-eighteenth century.[25] This institution had been designed by Peter Harrison and was modeled on a Roman Doric temple with portico and wings.[26] The building itself was constructed from wood that had been carefully shaped to resemble stone so it could be made from materials readily available in Rhode Island while also resembling the English Palladian style of the period. Merchant Abraham Redwood donated £500 to the town of Newport for, as he phrased it, "a collection of useful Books suitable for a Publick Library . . . having nothing in view but the good of mankind," which led to the initial purchase of 751 titles in London in 1747.[27] Harrison arranged for fellow Yorkshire merchant John Thomlinson to buy the books in London, and they were conveyed to Newport by Harrison's friend Stephen Greenleaf.[28]

The Redwood Library provided its readers with books on subjects ranging from theology and medicine to history and law to mathematics and architecture.[29] A small section offered poetry, the plays of Shakespeare, and a single novel, Henry Fielding's *Joseph Andrews*. The founders also agreed to appoint a librarian who would catalogue the library's collection and monitor the distribution of books into the community. Early records further note that this position required its holder to be present on Thursday afternoons when the library was open to all its members and their guests.[30] Thomas Moffat served as librarian for the Redwood in 1750; in 1752 he was replaced by Howard, who held the position until 1755.[31] Sundays sent most Newport residents scattering to their individual churches, while the Jewish community made its way to the synagogue on Saturday. Church and state were undoubtedly separate in Rhode Island, but political differences in Newport were often informed by religious differences, and the reverse was often true as well.[32] Yet the Redwood's patrons came from multiple congregations and held a multiplicity of political opinions. Like public libraries today, the goal was to provide common ground for Newport residents, or at least those residents whose purses could afford the cost of a library subscription.

Another venue providing common ground for Newport residents in the mid-eighteenth century was Samuel Hall's *Newport Mercury*. Unlike most eighteenth-century newspaper editors who only published on topics aligning with their personal views, Hall welcomed writings on a wide range of political topics in 1764 and 1765. The Z.Y. letter published by the Newport Junto on April 23, 1764, described Rhode Island colonists as "an ignorant and giddy multitude, always led to their own destruction by the flimsy eloquence, and pretended patriotism of knaves, fools, and enthusiastic madmen." Having dismissed their Rhode Island neighbors, the Newport Junto turned to the topic of Rhode Island's charter.[33] While "no friend to a popular or republican government," Z.Y. was willing to concede that "in the beginning or infancy of a state, when its members are few and virtuous," it is appropriate that "the whole power may be lodged with the people, and the government be purely democratical." This status was possible in the early stages of a political entity because its inhabitants could be trusted to rely on "simplicity and integrity of heart and manners" when designing their laws and government. However, as societies mature, this ceased to be the case. In the eyes of the members of the Newport Junto, developed societies inevitably turned to "licentiousness of manners, and universal distrust," a view not unlike the portrayals of the transition from innocent childhood to amoral adulthood that were increasingly prevalent in the eighteenth century.[34] At that time, it became necessary for "a coercive power" to "regulate and keep it within bounds." The use of the word "regulate" is particularly interesting in light of the coming Regulator Rebellion, and these parallels will be discussed in chapter 5. Consequently, the Newport Junto believed their colony was in need of the guidance provided to the British North American colonies, whose governors and councils were appointed by the British Parliament and Crown.

The Redwood Library, Newport, Rhode Island. (*Author's Photograph*)

The Z.Y. letter concluded by noting that its author(s) had "reason to think" that their hoped-for reforms in the British North American colonies were "now under the consideration of our rulers at home." This statement appears to refer to a petition sent to King George III by the Newport Junto asking him to consider making Rhode Island a royal colony. British subjects were allowed to submit petitions to their governments, whether local or imperial, that "conveyed complaints, decried miscarriage of justice, or requested relief from taxes, forest laws, and other regulations."[35] While there were no guarantees that petitions would lead to results, they were seen as a legitimate form of exchange utilized by many British colonists during this period, including the Regulators a few years later. They were also generally considered to be more effective if they were submitted in person, and it appears that the Newport Junto had tasked Joseph Harrison, Peter Harrison's brother, with this job.

Rhode Island and Connecticut were the last remaining chartered colonies in 1764. At that time, there was also one remaining proprietary colony, Pennsylvania. Martin Howard had met Pennsylvania resident Benjamin Franklin at the Albany Congress in 1754. Like Howard and the other members of the Newport Junto, Franklin was concerned that Pennsylvania was being mismanaged by its colonial government. It seems likely that Howard and Franklin had discussed their mutual concerns for their respective colonies at the Albany Congress. Franklin's correspondence includes a letter sent on May 1, 1764, to London barrister Richard Jackson that noted,

"The Rhode island People, too, are tired of their Charter Government, as you will see by one of their late Papers, which I send you."[36] The enclosed paper has not survived, but the timing of Franklin's letter suggests it was an early draft of the Z.Y. letter sent to Franklin by either Howard or Thomas Moffat. Six months later, Howard sent Franklin, who by that time was in London, a letter asking for additional assistance with the presentation of their petition.[37] Nothing came of Howard and Franklin's discussions of their concerns about Rhode Island and Pennsylvania's political structures, but it was not the last time the two men would correspond on a topic of mutual interest in the 1760s.

There is no evidence that the petition was ever submitted to George III, and its primary impact was to worsen relations between the Newport Junto and their neighbors in Rhode Island. The records for the Rhode Island General Assembly in late October 1764 noted that Governor Stephen Hopkins had sent a message to Joseph Sherwood, Rhode Island's colonial agent in London, imploring him to "use his utmost endeavors to prevent the evil intended by the said petitioners." Hopkins also asked Sherwood to send a copy of the petition and the names of the men who had signed it home to Rhode Island. He also spoke before the Rhode Island General Assembly on November 4 to express his concerns about parliamentary taxes and the Newport Junto's petition. The assembly then voted to submit to King George III a petition of its own that stated "apprehensions of a different treatment from the mother country, suffer us to go no further; we must be silent, or we must complain; we have a good cause, we have a gracious King."[38] This statement reminds us that the 1760s were a very different decade than the 1770s. Hopkins and the Rhode Island legislature were eager to maintain their position as a chartered colony, with the right to conduct their own elections, but they also saw themselves as part of the British Empire who answered to George III and Parliament.

On the surface, the Newport Junto's efforts to have Rhode Island transformed into a royal colony would seem little more than an extension of their support for the British Parliament. They were, however, also motivated by Rhode Island's internal turmoil in the mid-eighteenth century. Political campaigns had pitted neighbor against neighbor and town against town for the last decade. Dating back to the creation of Rhode Island as a united colony in the 1640s, Providence and Newport had always represented Rhode Island's two halves. Newport was located on Acquidneck or Rhode Island, while Providence was the mainland half of the colony, described in its full name of Rhode Island and Providence Plantations. The older landed families supported gubernatorial candidates who advocated for maintaining an agricultural lifestyle, while the newer families sought candidates who supported the transition toward trade and commerce. Mack Thompson writes that as Newport "extend[ed] its economic and political influence into the southern agricultural communities," another commercial center was emerging in the north so that "by the mid-1750s Providence was a thriving port with a young and enterprising group of merchants."[39] Potential Rhode Island leaders from Acquidneck Island championed rural interests, while potential leaders from the area around Providence argued in favor of a mercantile economy.

The political candidates identified most closely with these opposing sides were Providence resident Stephen Hopkins, and Samuel Ward, who had grown up in Newport. Hopkins's family was among the first colonists to join Roger Williams in the Providence area in 1636.[40] By the time Hopkins was born in 1707, his family had a long history of serving in the Rhode Island legislature. Hopkins turned to the law as his first occupation and became Rhode Island's chief justice in 1751; he turned to politics in 1755 with his first gubernatorial run. Ward's mother's great-grandfather was Roger Williams, which gave him an even more immediate connection to Rhode Island.[41] His father, Richard Ward, was Rhode Island's governor in the early 1740s, and the Ward family first moved to the Newport area in the 1660s. Ward moved to Westerly, a growing agricultural community on the Connecticut border, in the 1730s and later was Westerly's representative to the Rhode Island House of Deputies.[42] The competing visions for the colony's future offered by Hopkins and Ward nearly tore Rhode Island in two in the mid-eighteenth century.[43] In addition, Hopkins favored increasing the use of paper money, while Ward championed keeping Rhode Island's currency tied to hard money or specie. Both men campaigned for the creation of a University of Rhode Island, but Ward wanted it in Newport and Hopkins wanted it in Providence.

Hopkins won his first gubernatorial election in 1755, though he was defeated by his predecessor, William Greene, in 1757. Both Greene and Samuel Ward accused Hopkins of using his governorship during the French and Indian War to financially benefit his family. Greene died in office in 1758, and Hopkins was relected in a special election. Despite his success in this latest election, Hopkins sued Ward for libel and £20,000 in damages shortly afterward. Ward petitioned the Rhode Island General Assembly to have the case settled outside of Providence County since he doubted he would receive a fair trial in Hopkins's home county. The resulting trial in 1759 was held in Worcester, Massachusetts. James Otis was tasked with representing Hopkins, while Ward was represented by Edmund Trowbridge. The court ruled in Ward's favor, and Hopkins is reputed to have threatened that he "would blow Ward's brains out if he did not get satisfaction at law," though there is no evidence of any attempts on Ward's life.[44] Hopkins held the governorship until 1763, when he was defeated by Ward, who was replaced by Hopkins in 1764, who was replaced again by Ward in 1765, who was replaced by Hopkins for the second time in 1767.[45]

The members of the Newport Junto nearly universally supported Ward in the 1750s and early 1760s. Martin Howard ran for attorney general on the Ward ticket in 1761, though he was defeated by future fellow Newport Junto member Augustus Johnston, who would hold the position until 1766.[46] The Newport Junto's support for Ward stemmed from their shared bonds to the community of the Newport and Rhode Island landed families. Martin Howard's first marriage to Ann Brenton Conklin in 1754 connected him with the Brenton and Hutchinson families, who owned massive tracts of land alongside Narragansett Bay and who may have been silent members of the Newport Junto. Peter Harrison's marriage had provided him with similar connections, while Newport Junto member George Rome had acquired an estate of his own by this period.[47] By the time Ward was elected governor in 1765, relations between him and the Newport Junto appear to have cooled, and there is no evidence to suggest he supported their efforts to have Rhode Island's charter revoked.

On the surface, the Newport Junto's next campaign suggested a complete transformation in their interests and political affiliations. Beginning in August 1764, the organization spent months persuading neighbors to invest more heavily in domestic textile production.[48] Earlier scholars portray these writings as possessing little meaning beyond riling their neighbors. David Lovejoy describes them as having been "ostensibly written to encourage the cultivation of hemp, flax, and the raising of sheep within the colony" in order to "thrust upon the people their own loyal and unpopular ideas about dependence and necessary submission of the colonies to Parliament."[49] Edmund and Helen Morgan add that "they were not interested in bringing pressure to bear on Parliament but rather in diverting their countrymen's energies away from disloyal protests against its enactments," while Bernard Bailyn writes that "with vigorous pamphlets on the rights and wrongs of Anglo-American relations on all sides, essays on the joys and techniques of hemp production were losing whatever appeal they might once have had."[50] Joshua Fogarty Beatty recognized the possibility of connections between the Newport Junto's political interests and their advocacy for textile production but did not delve more deeply into these connections.[51]

Depicting the Newport Junto's textile essays as little more than a distraction for their opponents is problematic on two levels. First, the Newport Junto's advocacy for home textile production in Rhode Island was deeply rooted in their desire to promote agriculture in the colony. Second, it does not address the seeming irony posed by would-be Loyalist colonists advocating for home textile reform, a cause that T. H. Breen has trained scholars of early American history to associate with colonists who opposed parliamentary taxation on imported goods.[52] A close reading of the twenty essays promoting textile production published in the *Newport Mercury* in 1764 and 1765, and the twenty-three essays published between 1766 and 1770, helps to unravel this quandary while providing further insight into the tensions dividing Newport colonists on the eve of the Stamp Act crisis in 1765.

The Newport Junto's twenty essays in 1764 and 1765 can be divided into three categories that highlight their authors' specific motivations and interests. Fourteen essays took the form of signed letters to editor Samuel Hall that were published between August 20, 1764, and March 18, 1765, and used the pseudonym O.Z.[53] An unsigned letter from September 3, 1764, on a similar topic appeared between the first O.Z. letter, on August 20, and the second O.Z. letter, on September 10, and two more unsigned letters on similar topics appeared on October 1 and 15 between the O.Z. letters published on September 24 and October 22. It is also likely that the Newport Junto submitted the two essays on textile production in Pennsylvania and one on the history of cloth production in Great Britain published in the *Newport Mercury* in summer 1764 and spring 1765.[54] These essays also covered a wide range of topics, including fourteen treatises on the skills and materials needed to produce hemp, wool, and flax; five arguments for industry and self-denial in the colonies; and six discussions of politics in Rhode Island and the British Empire. This last topic is particularly helpful for scholars since it provides the concrete evidence necessary for linking the Newport Junto with these twenty essays from the *Newport Mercury*.

The fourth O.Z. letter, from September 17, 1764, stated "we gave early Hints of our profound Submission and Reverence to the Mother Country, and we cannot repress our filial Gratitude, when we consider that . . . Molasses is reduced to Three Pence per Gallon Duty."[55] The law known as the Sugar Act of 1764 replaced the Molasses Act of 1733 with a new tax that reduced the tax on molasses from six pence to three pence per gallon in the British North American colonies, and added new taxes on white sugar, coffee, "all callicoes, painted, dyed, printed or stained," "wrought silks, Bengalls and stuffs mixed with silks," and "all foreign linen cloth, called cambric."[56] Since most other Newport colonists were fiercely opposed to the Sugar

Act, this statement can only have come from the members of the Newport Junto. Likewise, the penultimate O.Z. letter on March 11, 1765, opened by informing readers that "these moral tablatures [are] far more useful and beneficial to the inhabitants of Rhode-Island, than *the rights of the colonies examined*" and that "they will afford more pleasure and satisfaction than the fruitless and unnecessary enquiries about the writer of *a letter from Halifax*."[57] Stephen Hopkins had published the pamphlet *The Rights of the Colonies Examined* on November 30, 1764, objecting to the Sugar Act, to which Howard had responded with the pamphlet *A Letter from a Gentleman at Halifax to his Friend in Rhode Island*.[58] The explicit references to the Hopkins and Howard pamphlets in this letter can leave no doubts as to the identity of the author(s) of the O.Z. letters, and these pamphlets will be discussed in greater length in chapter 3.

The first topic covered by the O.Z. letters was a campaign encouraging Rhode Island colonists to raise and process hemp, which could then be used for a wide range of purposes. The Newport Junto's decision to start with hemp was prompted by the announcement in the *Newport Mercury* on July 14, 1764, that Parliament had promised £100 to whoever could "produce the greatest quantity, not less than 20 tons, of good merchantable hemp, fit for cordage ... in any part of the provinces of Nova-Scotia, New Hampshire, Massachusetts Bay, Connecticut, and Rhode Island," with the remaining British North American colonies divided into three further districts, each with its own financial reward.[59] Farmers raising smaller amounts were encouraged to compete for smaller cash bonuses. Eager to improve the status of their colony, the Newport Junto hoped that providing their neighbors with practical information would enable the farmers of Rhode Island to raise enough "good merchantable hemp" to win the full parliamentary premium. Their first essays detailed for readers the process of preparing fields, planting seeds, and harvesting the resulting crop. Another noted that when "carefully attended to, and passed through a series of Heckles, [hemp] would make excellent Thread, and beautiful Stockings, superior far to any Thing made from Flax and Cotton," a description intended to appeal to female readers.[60]

The Newport Junto's essays on hemp production attracted swift attention from Rhode Island's other newspaper, the *Providence Gazette*. A letter "inserted in this Paper at the Request of a constant Reader" appeared on September 15, 1764, a little over three weeks after the publication of the first O.Z. letter.[61] It noted that "SEVERAL dull and unentertaining Pieces have lately appeared in the *Newport Mercury* about raising Flax and Hemp—making Cloth ... *Newport* Bucks reeling Yarn, —and I know not what Stuff." The author of this letter briefly acknowledged the need for "spirited Recommendations of Industry, Frugality, and Manufactures . . . at this time" before questioning the intentions of the authors of the O.Z. letters. Readers were reminded that "some, if not all, of the Members of this wonderful Club, are at this Time actually conspiring against the Liberties of this Colony." This letter's hyperbolic tone suggests it was written by Stephen Hopkins, whose public ire was turning toward Martin Howard by that time and would later culminate with the Stamp Act crisis.[62]

A week after the September 15 letter in the *Providence Gazette*, the Newport Junto announced that as "we find many of the opinion that enough has been said of Hemp," they would now turn their attention to "Wool and the enormous Abuses of it within the Colony of Rhode Island." Their next O.Z. letter reminded readers that Rhode Islanders generally sold their wool unprocessed, but if it was "spun, knit or woven all up within the colony of Rhode-Island; it will require few figures to shew the difference of value between a pack of raw wool, and the same weight or quantity of stockings, flannel, or broad cloth."[63] This was followed with further essays on keeping sheep, spinning, knitting, and weaving wool, which were then followed with the last two O.Z. letters in March 1765, which discussed best practices for raising flax to then be made into linen yarn for knitting or weaving.

At first glance, articles encouraging wool production would appear apolitical to the modern eye. The first O.Z. letter, published on August 20, 1764, pointed out that "a compleat Habit of Apparel, from the Wool and Fabric of this Colony, should entitle the Person to an upper Seat at a Town-meeting or Meeting on Sunday."[64] What could be more self-sufficient and practical than raising sheep whose wool could be made into the layers of warm clothing needed to survive a New England winter and so demonstrate their moral superiority to their neighbors? Raising sheep was, however, increasingly associated with colonists who supported parliamentary policies and a return to the landed estates, which had made up the English economy for most of the medieval period. The Brenton family owned massive tracts of farmland alongside Narragansett Bay, and Ebenezer Brenton Jr. had left his son-in-law, Martin Howard, a "farm in South Kingstown . . . with all [its] stock of creatures" in 1765.[65] A farm belonging to Jahleel Brenton, Howard's Loyalist cousin-in-law, which lay next to the estate owned by Newport Junto member Peter Harrison, would be raided in 1775 by a mob who carried off Brenton's one thousand sheep, an attack as symbolic as it was economically destructive.[66]

The Newport Stamp Act riots in August 1765 marked a turning point in the publication of the *Newport Mercury*. Martin Howard and the other members of the Newport Junto had either left the colony or been effectively silenced. Samuel Hall no longer dared to publish their opinions, and his successor, Solomon Southwick, had no interest in doing so.

Spring 1766 saw a return to the promotion of domestic textile production in Rhode Island as twenty-three more essays on this subject would be published by 1770. However, while the Newport Junto's essays in 1764 and 1765 began with raising hemp, wool, and flax; continued on to spinning; and finished by explaining how these products could be made into hemp ropes, woolen stockings, or linen cloth, the new essays published from 1766 to 1770 almost never moved past the stage of spinning raw wool or flax into yarn. This may seem a small distinction at first, but it holds the key to understanding the differences between the arguments in favor of home textile production made in Newport before and after the Stamp Act crisis. The Newport Junto wanted Rhode Island to resemble Britain before the Industrial Revolution, and so its members encouraged home textile production. By contrast, future Sons of Liberty members Samuel and William Vernon placed an advertisement for "an assortment of Checks, Broad Cloths [and] Calamancoe" on the same page of the August 20, 1764, edition of the *Newport Mercury* as the first O.Z. letter.[67] If the Newport Junto succeeded in creating a commercially viable home textile production in Rhode Island, the business practices of the Vernon brothers and other merchant families, which were increasingly built around providing their customers with imported goods, would be disrupted.[68] Since their primary goal was to draw parliamentary attention to the economic dangers posed by colonial-wide boycotts on imported fabrics in North America, and they had no intention of actually transforming Rhode Island's domestic economy, the Sons of Liberty could focus their attention on spectacle rather than action.

Uneven labor ratios between spinners and weavers led to a long history of putting poor women to work as spinners in both the medieval and early modern periods. Unfortunately, these efforts met with continual failures, as this work "rarely provided enough income for the necessities of life outside the workhouse."[69] But since spinning, whether done on walking wheels or the smaller upright or Saxony wheels, was highly visual labor, it quickly became the preferred vehicle for making political statements in the late 1760s. Laurel Thatcher Ulrich has identified some forty-six New England events involving spinning between 1768 and 1770, over half of which took place in 1769.[70] Some of these occasions were spinning matches; others were educational events in which women gathered to either gain new skills or perfect existing ones. An essay in the *Newport Mercury* announced on

The press on display at the Newport Historical Society Museum used by Benjamin Franklin's nephew, James Franklin, Jr., to print the *Newport Mercury* and other broadsides. (*Franklin press, Object Number L 93.54.1, collection of the Newport Historical Society*)

March 10, 1766, that "20 young Ladies of the best families in Providence, had a Spinning Match at a Gentleman's House last Tuesday."[71] Moreover, the "[Ladies had] made a brilliant appearance, and had a Dance in the Evening." The essay finished by observing that this was a "laudable Example for all Ladies in Newport, and elsewhere, who purpose to promote Industry." The Providence spinning match was the first of nine such events described in the *Newport Mercury* between March 10, 1766, and May 22, 1769, with three taking place in 1766, one in 1768, and five in 1769, and many of these descriptions detailed the amounts of yarn spun at each gathering, though none of them ever said just what the spun yarn would be used for.[72]

Only one of the *Newport Mercury* textile essays published between 1766 and 1770 mentioned weaving. Published on February 1, 1768, it boasted about a "Gentleman [of South-Kingstown] who married a Lady . . . remarkable for Frugality and Industry who has for some years entirely cloathed eleven of his family" and who now planned to employ the "Industrious poor around him" in producing cloth.[73] Unlike the earlier textile essays from the Newport Junto, this essay offered no further information on how other colonists might emulate the family from South-Kingstown. The "industrious poor," rather like the impoverished women of earlier decades, were to be put to work weaving, but what of their more prosperous neighbors? And, in any event, the *Newport Mercury* provided no coverage on whether the worthy gentleman had carried out his plans. The Newport Junto hoped to transform Rhode Island's economy while their counterparts hoped instead to maintain the status quo prior to the Townshend Act's implementation of rising taxes on imported goods.[74] Economic interests throughout the British Empire were closely intertwined with political interests, and Rhode Island colonists were deeply opposed to each other's economic and cultural visions for their colony, which, in turn, fueled their growing anger during this period.

Rhode Island's older agricultural families believed that land-based economic systems, including the raising and processing of wool and flax, were the best choice for supporting stability in the Anglo-American world. Like hundreds of manor owners in Britain, their own economic positions were supported by this approach. John Dwyer and Alexander Murdoch have detected "a defense of the landed interest and a corresponding distrust of monied men and the *nouveaux* riches" in the Scottish journals the *Mirror*, the *Lounger*, and the *Caledonian Mercury*.[75] The Newport Junto, three of whom had been educated in Scotland, made similar arguments throughout the O.Z. letters.[76]

By contrast, the members of Rhode Island's rising mercantile families had more difficult needles to thread with their arguments in favor of home textile production. They tapped into the centuries-old "luxury debate" as they constructed their arguments.[77] At its heart, this discourse questions whether material goods used to fulfill needs beyond basic survival have the potential to destroy human society. Ancient Greek and Roman philosophers focused their discussions on the dangers luxury goods posed to political societies, while early Christian writers linked individual human behavior and morality with the dangers posed by luxury. Consequently, Newport's mercantile elite warned their neighbors that their lack of discipline "would eventually lapse into the pursuit of unnecessary and useless desires [and] from there it is but a short step to the pursuit of unlawful or unnatural desires which characterize the tyrant."[78] Public displays of their commitment to shunning goods imported from India would, they believed, help shield them from a slippery slope toward tyranny. There was also another basis for their arguments: the less vocal hope that the economic pressures created by boycotting these temptations would provide them with a more equal trading partnership within the British Empire.

The philosophers who pondered the luxury debate throughout European history may have disagreed on the individual dangers posed by luxury goods, but they largely agreed that they were equally harmful to men and women. By the eighteenth century, however, these writings were increasingly driven by male concerns about female consumption. The first O.Z. letter, on August 20, 1764, asked "some of the youngest and most beautiful of the lovely Sex [to consider taking] Vows not to marry, until they had spun a great part of the Linen necessary for that solemn happy Occasion."[79] Five years later, an essay published May 8, 1769, from *American Watchman* praised unmarried women for their patriotic efforts but cautioned them "not to wet your thread with your sweet lovely Lips (which ought to be far *otherwise* employ'd) but use a Spunge, &c. which will be a great Advantage to your Healths and Complexions."[80] An advertisement in the same issue announced that "since I am unmarried, and determined to take the swiftest SPINNER, provided her other Accomplishments be agreeable (provided likewise, *she will have me*) I have been very inquisitive with regard to Spinning Matches," though the paper did not report on whether this proposal received a response from one of the female spinners.[81]

An essay published by "A Farmer" in the pages of the Philadelphia journal *American Museum* in 1787 helps to highlight the underlying concerns in these essays.[82] The "Farmer" explained that when his oldest daughter married, he had equipped her with the wool and flax needed to construct her own clothing and allowed her to purchase the cotton that could be spun and woven for bed sheets, much as his wife's father had done for her some thirty years earlier. But then his wife encouraged their second daughter to request purchased goods for her dowry, including a calico gown, stoneware cups, and pewter spoons. Even worse was the further request that both their third daughter and their own household be equipped with imported silk and china, which had brought them nearly to the brink of financial ruin. Consequently, he was now requiring his family to eat and wear only those goods that could be produced in their immediate vicinity and to remember how happy they had been decades earlier when this was their customary way of life.

Historian Carole Shammas argues, however, that this tale of American frugality was apocryphal because British North American colonists had always fed and clothed their families with a blend of home-produced and imported goods, and, if anything, "the costs of self-sufficiency would have exceeded the resources available to many households."[83] Following the timeline presented by the "Farmer" suggests that his wife and oldest daughter had willingly produced all necessary household goods in the 1750s and late 1760s. The *Newport Mercury* textile essays, however, demonstrate that colonial households were as dominated by imported textiles in those decades as the household described in the 1780s. If, writes Shammas, the Farmer's story appealed to conservatives for its ability to "highlight the self-reliance and frugality of the good old days . . . to the Left, [it] illustrated the purity and simplicity of life before capitalists and industrialists botched things up."[84]

These recurring themes speak to societal concerns shared by many European men at a time of expanding global trade and the early stages of the Industrial Revolution. If women became consumers rather than producers, what wider impacts might this have on society?[85] Would the household order celebrated by all of the essays on textiles in the *Newport Mercury* break down altogether? Producers were now portrayed as hard working and industrious, the sort of people who could be trusted as subjects and citizens, while consumers were described as frivolous, wasteful, and untrustworthy. These essays are also a reminder of the importance of reading documents in their own historical context. Colonists who would later face each other on opposing sides of a bloody civil war were still eager to demonstrate their entitlement to the privileges and protections of British subjecthood through their identities as textile-producing Britons. Home textile production was an issue that concerned British subjects across the empire, regardless of political affiliation or revolutionary interests. In the 1760s, revolution was still a long way off.

Chapter Three

The Stamp Act in Rhode Island

THE EARLY 1760S WERE A TURNING POINT for the British Empire. A decisive victory in the global Seven Years' War led to the Treaty of Paris in 1763, which doubled British land holdings in North America and extended British power in Africa and Asia.[1] During the war, Britain had sold government bonds and borrowed money from European banks, particularly in the Netherlands.[2] With the war finally over, that same triumphant victory now needed to be paid for. The British Parliament created a wide array of taxes on various goods and services in the mid-1760s, which led to rising anger in Britain and North America. American popular culture has largely forgotten the taxes levied in Britain in this period, but the writings of British North American colonists demonstrate that they were equally aware of the pressures faced by their counterparts on the other side of the Atlantic Ocean.

The two men most connected with these taxes were John Stuart, the third Earl of Bute, and George Grenville. Stuart was appointed prime minister in 1762 by George III, who had grown frustrated with the previous Newcastle-Pitt administration.[3] Faced with the challenges of paying for the Seven Years' War, Stuart introduced a tax of four shillings on every hogshead of cider and perry made in Britain, which became known as the Cider Tax.[4] It was extremely unpopular in western England, where most

British cider was produced, and there were several riots over its provisions. Stuart agreed to resign as prime minister the month after the bill was introduced in March 1763.[5] He was replaced by Grenville, who, like Stuart, was determined to bring Britain's debt levels in check.[6] Grenville enforced the Cider Tax, which was not repealed until 1766, and introduced two new taxes on the British North American colonists.[7]

The first of these taxes was commonly referred to as the Sugar Act of 1764, while the second one was referred to as the Stamp Act of 1765. Some thirty years earlier, Parliament had passed the Molasses Act of 1733, which placed a six-pence-per-gallon levy on molasses imported from non-British colonies.[8] The purpose of this tax was not to generate funds but to encourage British molasses production in the Caribbean. Many British North American colonists were in the habit of trading lumber, horses, fish, and other foodstuffs with sugar producers across the Caribbean regardless of their nationality. They saw this new tax as a nuisance but one that could be easily sidestepped by exchanging smuggled goods with French and Dutch sugar producers, since Britain did little to enforce the Molasses Act at that time.[9]

But the newly created Sugar Act, or the American Duties Act, was a different proposition.[10] First, it created a new tax on white sugar but reduced the tax on molasses to three pence per gallon on the grounds that it would be easier to persuade errant colonists to pay a smaller tax on molasses.[11] Second, it restricted trade among colonists in the Americas by requiring British colonists to only sell goods like lumber to Britain. Third, and most importantly, it stated that all money raised by the tax would be used to enforce the Navigation Acts in the Americas. Many mainland colonists saw the new tax as evidence that Parliament was favoring the British sugar-plantation owners in the Caribbean, an argument made by Stephen Hopkins in his two-part series "An Essay on the Trade of the Northern Colonies," which was published in the *Newport Mercury* in winter 1764.[12] Nevertheless, like the Molasses Act before it, the Sugar Act could still be sidestepped with the use of honey and maple syrup available in North America or smuggled sugar from other European islands in the Caribbean.[13] Petitions and letters were written against the Sugar Act, but there was little in the way of violent action.

By contrast, the passing of the Duties in American Colonies Act, or the Stamp Act, on March 22, 1765, would become a watershed moment for supporters and detractors of the British Crown alike. The Stamp Act was enforced via the application of "certain stamp duties, and other duties, in the British Colonies and plantations in America".[14] Wills, marital records, and birth certificates were not legal unless they received a seal or stamp of authority from a recognized Stamp Tax distributor. Newspapers could not be sold unless they were printed on stamped paper. Wallpaper needed to have an official stamp pasted on before it was sold. The money collected would be used to "defray the expences of defending, protecting, and securing [the British North American colonies]; and for amending such parts of the several acts of Parliament, relating to the trade and revenues of the said colonies and plantations." The Molasses Act had largely failed because the British Empire lacked the infrastructure to enforce the tax. The Sugar and Stamp Acts were intended to raise the funds needed to create that infrastructure. Money would now be spent on customs officials to monitor smuggling in coastal communities.[15] British naval vessels would be dispatched to apprehend colonial vessels returning from the Caribbean. Finally, any colonists caught resisting the new taxes would be required to travel to Halifax, Nova Scotia, for trial without a jury in the newly formed vice admiralty court for North America.[16]

Rhode Island's unique responses to the Stamp Act reflect its particular position within the British Empire in the 1760s. Despite the best efforts of the Newport Junto, Rhode Island was still a chartered colony with a locally elected governor who, like his legislature, was opposed to the Stamp Act. The governor and the legislature in Connecticut, the other remaining chartered colony, also opposed the Stamp Act.[17] What made the Stamp Act crisis in Rhode Island different from the Stamp Act crisis in Connecticut was the presence of the Newport Junto, a civilian group that vocally supported the law. By contrast, most British North American colonies were royal colonies with governors who supported the Stamp Act and legislatures that did not. Consequently, any discord over the Stamp Act in Rhode Island was between the locally elected government and the Newport Junto, all long-standing sparring partners. The resulting violence in Newport in late summer 1765 followed channels that were established long before the passing of the Stamp Act. As Allen Mansfield Thomas noted in 1996, "the Newport Stamp Act riots were far from being a specific response to British imperialist policy."[18] Once again, Rhode Island was trying to tear itself apart by the roots, the very act that the Newport Junto had hoped to prevent with their petition in 1764 for the colony to come under the direct supervision of the British Crown.

These tensions primarily manifested themselves in two forms during the months prior to the Newport Stamp Act riots in August 1765. The pamphlet war between Providence resident Stephen Hopkins and Newport resident Martin Howard predated the passing of the Stamp Act, but it took on an additional vehemence in spring 1765. In turn, agitation between the Newport Junto and Rhode Island's newly formed Sons of Liberty chapters continued to accelerate. The Stamp Act riots in Newport would not be as violent as the ones in Boston, but this was a far-more-intimate struggle, as much for Rhode Island's soul as its place within the British Empire.

The feud between Hopkins and Samuel Ward had divided many Rhode Island colonists in the 1750s and early 1760s. Hopkins's championing of a mercantile future for Rhode Island crashed against Ward's vision of an agricultural Eden. Their campaigns divided towns and, in some cases, forced families to choose sides. It is clear, however, that this feud was coming to an end by the time of the Stamp Act crisis. Both Hopkins and Ward saw British taxation as a common cause and, perhaps, recognized that infighting among British colonists would only weaken them. Three years after the Stamp Act crisis, Josias Lyndon would successfully run for governor on a platform that promised to unite the Hopkins and Ward supporters.[19]

The end of Hopkins-Ward feud left space for a new one between Hopkins and Martin Howard, the most vocal member of the Newport Junto. Their political rhetoric against one another in the mid-1760s grew increasingly acerbic, though it should be noted that their relationship often resembled an inverse mirror reflection. Both men were born in Rhode Island and active in legal and civic affairs in their respective communities of Providence and Newport. Both represented Rhode Island at the Albany Congress in 1754.[20] Hopkins contributed to the newly formed Providence Library Company, while Howard was the librarian at the Redwood Library.[21] In many ways, their relationship formed a microcosm of the larger challenges facing individual British North American colonists during this period as relations between them gradually disintegrated until the outbreak of war in 1776 forced a final decision.

Hopkins published the pamphlet *The Rights of the Colonies, Examined* on November 30, 1764, while Howard published *A Letter from a Gentleman at Halifax to his Friend in Rhode Island* on January 20, 1765.[22] These pamphlets were written in response to the Sugar Act in 1764 and to rumors that Parliament might pass an additional Stamp Act. Consequently, they can be read as a blanket airing of these men's views on parliamentary taxation on the British colonies.[23] Hopkins stated, "British subjects in America have equal rights with those in Britain ... [and] possess them as an inherent, indefeasible right, as they and their ancestors were freeborn subjects, justly and naturally entitled to all the rights and advantages of the British constitution."[24] His objections to the Sugar and Stamp Acts were predicated first on the argument that because he was a British subject, he was

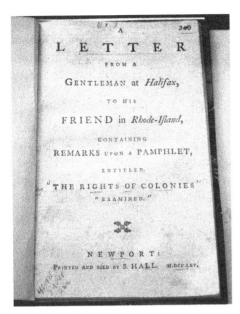

The pamphlet, *A Letter from a Gentleman at Halifax, to his Friend in Rhode Island*, by Martin Howard, published in January 1765. (*FIC.1993.11, collection of the Newport Historical Society*)

entitled to all the rights and privileges thereof, and, second, on the argument that he was not receiving those rights and privileges, which included the right to have a voice in parliamentary deliberations about colonial taxation because he lived in North America.

In turn, Howard stated that "our personal rights, comprehending those of life, liberty, and estate, are secured to us by the common law, which is every subject's birthright, whether born in Great Britain, on the ocean, or in the colonies."[25] His support for the Sugar and Stamp Acts was predicated first on the argument that because he was a British subject, he was entitled to all the rights and privileges thereof, and, second, on the argument that he was receiving those rights and privileges to which he was entitled in North America. In his view, this did not include a right to vote in parliamentary elections because that fell into the category of political rights, which were not, necessarily, a birthright privilege. The distinctions between the rhetoric of Hopkins and Howard were representative of the distinctions between most British North American colonists in the 1760s. Howard and other Loyalists continued to believe that their rights were untrammeled through the end of the American Revolution. By contrast, Hopkins and the other proponents of revolution against Britain would come to believe in the mid-1770s that the only way to preserve their rights and privileges was to break completely from the United Kingdom.

Stephen Hopkins's *The Rights of the Colonies* was published in the same month as Massachusetts colonist James Otis's pamphlet *The Rights of the*

British Colonies Asserted and Proved.[26] Bernard Bailyn comments that Hopkins's arguments were "intellectually a less ambitious and a less complicated effort than Otis'... but [they] display more typically the central convictions and the surrounding confusions of the early objections to England's new colonial policy."[27] Overall, Hopkins intended less an exploration of British political rights and more a discussion of trade within the colonies. In addition to placing taxes on molasses and white sugar, the Sugar Act mandated that British colonists could trade only within the British Empire. This interrupted their long-standing practice of trading with the Spanish, French, and Dutch colonies in North America, which he believed would have a deeply negative impact on the British colonies and British interests.[28] Therefore, if New England merchants turned to smuggling, it was the natural result of bad British policy and so should be exonerated.[29] Hopkins's emphasis on trade was consistent with his political activities during the past two years when he and other Rhode Island merchants had objected to the Newport Junto's campaign for domestic textile production in New England. This same emphasis on trade would play a central role in motivating Rhode Island merchants to join the colony's Sons of Liberty chapters in 1765.

Hopkins's *The Rights of the Colonies* offered its defense of the rights of British colonists as a simple statement of fact. By contrast, Martin Howard's *Letter from a Gentleman at Halifax* was a detailed exploration of the evolution of British common law and its resulting protections for British subjects.[30] Howard believed that British common law saw personal and political rights as distinct entities: "I fancy when we speak or think of the rights of freeborn Englishmen, we confound those rights which are personal with those which are political."[31] Howard believed the right to "life, liberty, and estate" was a personal right that traveled across the Atlantic with individual British colonists. Political rights were, by contrast, granted to political entities rather than the individuals within those entities. Individual colonies had the right to appeal to Parliament and the Crown. Had Parliament and the Crown intended individual colonists to have the right to parliamentary representation, it would have been specified in the original charters and mandates used to create the North American colonies.

Hopkins, Otis, and other advocates for the British colonies built their argument for parliamentary representation for colonists on the grounds that British subjects deserved representation regardless of where they lived in the empire. The first generation of colonists in Rhode Island had, presumably, had parliamentary representation before they left Britain, and so their descendants had inherited that same right in North America. Howard questioned this argument by examining the full extent of suffrage within Great Britain, asking, "is the Isle of Man, Jersey, or Guernsey represented? What is the value or amount of each man's representation in the kingdom of Scotland, which contains near two millions of people, and yet not more than three thousand have votes in the election of members of Parliament?" Contrary to the arguments of Hopkins and Otis, suffrage was not equally distributed throughout the United Kingdom. Furthermore, as Howard noted, similar to the British colonies, the right to vote was tied to landownership, which left many more British subjects without direct representation despite living in the United Kingdom rather than in one of the colonies. Consequently, a "worthless freeholder of forty shillings per annum can vote for a member of Parliament" while a "merchant, though worth one hundred thousand pounds sterling, if only in personal effects, has no vote at all," an observation that appears particularly targeted toward the many merchants who opposed the Newport Junto in 1764 and 1765.[32]

Interestingly, Howard did not address the most infamous way in which direct parliamentary representation was curtailed during most of the early modern period. Many British subjects lived in parliamentary districts known as "pocket" or "nomination" boroughs where, at best, there were either too few political representatives for the district's population in the House of Commons, or, at worst, the district's elected political representatives were controlled by landowners or peers within the House of Lords.[33] Since it seems likely that Howard was aware of this system, he may have wanted to avoid adding another controversial topic to his pamphlet. In any event, the plight of British subjects in pocket boroughs would have been meaningless to a man who believed that "the freedom and happiness of every British subject depends not on his share in elections but upon the sense and virtue of the British Parliament, and these depend reciprocally upon the sense and virtue of the whole nation," an argument designed to take the reader back to John Locke's vision of a sociopolitical contract between government and governed that informed British law and British colonial law.[34]

The topic of British subjects who resided in Britain and yet did not have direct parliamentary representation provided Martin Howard with the opportunity to raise additional questions about the motives of his colonial political opponents. Since thousands of British subjects on both sides of the Atlantic lacked political representation, why were Stephen Hopkins, James Otis, and their counterparts not calling for universal reform of suffrage for British subjects? What made British colonists in North America more deserving of direct representation than their (white male) counterparts in Scotland, the many pocket boroughs, or without landholdings across Britain? If these were arguments designed solely for the benefit of the men making them, then Howard believed they needed to be identified in this fashion.

Stephen Hopkins's and Martin Howard's published writings in 1764 and 1765 were deeply personal exchanges between two Rhode Island colonists whose long-standing geographic and cultural propinquity added fervor to their dismissals of one another. Given their prior shared histories as Rhode Island's representatives to the Albany Congress in 1754, it seems likely these were arguments that emerged long before the imperial crisis began in the mid-1760s.[35] James Otis responded to Howard with the pamphlet *A Vindication of the British Colonies, against the Aspersions of the Halifax Gentleman* in 1765. Otis's words, however, pale in comparison with the ones used in Hopkins's columns in the *Providence Gazette*.[36] Hopkins accused Howard of being a foreigner incapable of understanding British ways and customs. He had "the insolence of a haughty and imperious minister, the indolence and half-thought of a *petits-maitre*, the flutter of a cox-comb, the pedantry of a quack, and the nonsense of a pettifogger . . . [and] we want no foreign codes, nor canons here."[37] Many of the activities organized by the various chapters of the Sons of Liberty in 1765 were built on earlier commemorations of the foiling of Guy Fawkes's plans to blow up Parliament in 1605. Brendan McConville writes that "faith in the Protestant prince, and a related fear that the crisis amounted to some kind of popish or Jacobite plot, explain much of the imperial crisis's chronology."[38]

For his part, Martin Howard lectured Stephen Hopkins on the dangers of too much adherence to ancient Roman practices in the modern age of the eighteenth century, writing that "in a word, my dear sir, the belly of a sow pickled, was a high dish in ancient Rome; and I imagine . . . this will become a capital part of a Rhode Island feast, so fond you seem of ancient customs and laws."[39] This comparison was intended to suggest that Howard was the true Englishman while Hopkins was too wedded to the garish excesses of the European continent. Eighteenth-century garden historian Mark Laird has identified a similar dichotomy in Horace Walpole's *The History of the Modern Taste in Gardening*, which contrasted "the 'natural' forms created by English landscape gardening of the eighteenth centuries" with "the 'formality' of the European gardening styles" that were largely abandoned in Britain in the seventeenth century.[40] British patriots looked to the future, while degenerate continentals were permanently rooted in the past.

The accusations made by Hopkins and Howard were intended to convey a lack of patriotism and lack of modernity respectively. They also suggest

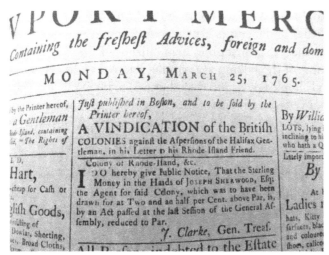

Advertisement for "A Vindication of the British Colonies," March 25, 1765, *Newport Mercury*. (*Collection of the Newport Historical Society*)

that neither man was fully comfortable with the political and cultural ramifications of being simultaneously from Britain and Rhode Island in the modern age of the eighteenth century. In many respects, Hopkins and Howard represented two sides of the same coin, which, again, highlights the intimate nature of the Stamp Act crisis in Rhode Island.

Howard's interactions with Hopkins via the printed page were only one part of his efforts to defend parliamentary taxation. His other activities were closer to home. As the Stamp Act crisis accelerated, relations between Howard and his opponents in Newport cooled even further.[41] The Newport Junto was an unusual entity at a time when most organized support for Parliament came from royally appointed officials rather than individual colonists.[42] Governors like Francis Bernard in Massachusetts, William Tryon in North Carolina, and Francis Fauquier in Virginia could issue proclamations in support of the Stamp Act, but they lacked the ability to influence opinion in daily exchanges used by eighteenth-century political organizations like the Newport Junto. This also suggests that the Newport Junto may have come into existence because its members recognized that their colony did not have a royally appointed governor and so felt a need to fill the resulting vacuum.

By contrast, opposition to parliamentary taxation began with individual colonists and then moved to the colonial legislatures. The first such organization was the Boston-based group known as the Loyal Nine, which emerged in spring 1765.[43] Its members were John Avery, Thomas Crafts,

John Smith, Henry Wells, Thomas Chase, Stephen Cleverly, Henry Bass, Benjamin Edes, and George Trott, whom Edmund and Helen Morgan describe as neither "the most prominent citizens of Boston, nor . . . the men who did most of the talking against the Stamp Act. In general, they were artisans and shopkeepers, and they shunned publicity."[44] The gap between the more subversive activities of the Loyal Nine and the formal opposition mounted by colonists like James Otis and Samuel Adams was probably a deliberate one in order to present a more moderated tone to Massachusetts Governor Francis Bernard and Parliament in the early response period to the Stamp Act.[45] By mid-summer, the Loyal Nine had evolved into the larger Sons of Liberty, who organized chapters in multiple British colonies and who labored to cloak their activities with a veneer of respectability whenever possible.

Most surviving information about the members of the Sons of Liberty chapters founded in Newport and Providence comes from the documentary project known as the "Stamp Act Notebook" created by Rhode Island colonist Ezra Stiles, which remains one of the most complete sources available on the Stamp Act crisis.[46] It is also a document written by a man who supported the protest movement against the Stamp Act and was an ardent resident of Newport, where he was the minister for the Second Congregational Church between 1755 and 1776, and so needs to be read in this light.[47] Section 3 opened with a list of all colonists known to Stiles as supporters of "Liberty" and all colonists known to be supporters of the "Crown."[48] Rhode Island had the most extensive lists of names in both categories, and the ones Stiles recorded consisted largely of Newport residents rather than representatives of the colony as a whole. The best-known figures on Stiles's list were merchants William and Samuel Vernon, William Ellery, Henry Channing, John Collins, and Robert Crook, and Rhode Island politicians Metcalf Bowler, Josias Lyndon, and Henry Ward (one of Samuel Ward's younger brothers), while lesser-known figures included silversmith Jonathan Otis and laborer John Spooner. Stiles's support for his home community is further demonstrated by the statement that "the Committee of the Sons of Liberty [in Newport is] so respectable that no Jacobite Tory or other Episcopalian durst reproach them as a body," a reminder that this particular Sons of Liberty chapter was composed entirely of Newport's most upstanding members of society, regardless of what their opponents may have said about them.[49]

The comparatively high ratio of merchants identified among Newport's Sons of Liberty may have stemmed from the contested debate over domestic textile production in Rhode Island in 1764 and early in 1765. The Newport Junto had championed home textile production as a way of expanding agriculture and landed estates in Rhode Island. By contrast, Newport's merchants who joined the sons of Liberty in summer 1765 wanted to expand the colony as a mercantile hub within the British Empire. The Vernon and Ellery families were, with one exception, among the most active opponents of Parliament in Newport.[50] Similar to the members of the Newport Junto, men in both families were active participants in Newport's civic life, whether serving in local and colonial government, the judiciary, or the Redwood Library.[51] Unlike the members of the Newport Junto, both families were eager to expand Newport's trade in imported fabrics in the years immediately following the close of the Seven Years' War in 1763. The advertisement for "an assortment of Checks, Broad Cloths [and] Calamancoe" that appeared on the front page of the August 20, 1764, edition of the *Newport Mercury* alongside the first O.Z. letter advocating in favor of home textile production was listed by the Vernon brothers.[52] While the remaining three merchants on Stiles's list—Henry Channing, John Collins, and Robert Crook—were not quite as well connected as the Vernon and Ellery families, they were equally active during this period, particularly Crook, who later helped Samuel Vernon and William Ellery organize the Stamp Act riots in Newport.[53]

Most members of the Newport Junto and the Sons of Liberty engaged with politics at the town and colony levels, but Metcalf Bowler, Josias Lyndon, and Henry Ward all had lengthy political careers in Rhode Island. Given Samuel Ward's roots in Newport, it is unsurprising that all three were affiliated with Ward's campaigns for the governorship in the 1750s, but, like Ward, they bonded with Stephen Hopkins's supporters over a distrust of parliamentary taxation in the 1760s. The positions of speaker and clerk for the Rhode Island General Assembly were both elected positions, and in most cases, the men elected were allied with whichever political faction had gained the governor's office. Bowler remained in the speaker's position even after Hopkins wrested the governorship back from Ward in 1767.[54] For his part, Lyndon was successfully elected clerk in 1728 and held the office until 1768, when he became Rhode Island's governor, though he returned to the office of clerk in 1770 when he stepped down from the governorship.[55] Henry Ward, the last political figure Stiles identified as a member of the Newport chapter of the Sons of Liberty, was, like his father and brothers, involved in Rhode Island politics. Thomas Ward, Samuel and Henry's brother, was Rhode Island's secretary of state between 1740 and 1760, and following his death, Henry Ward was elected to the same position until 1797.[56]

Two other men identified by Stiles as members of the Newport Sons of Liberty were Jonathan Otis and John Spooner. Otis was a cousin of the Massachusetts-based Otis family. Like Paul Revere in Boston, he was a trained silversmith who could be considered part of the very upper levels of the artisan classes. His marriage to Catherine Coggeshall in 1745 connected him with one of Rhode Island's oldest families.[57] Stiles described Spooner, by contrast, as "from among middling and lower Life, and united in himself the whole Confidence of the plebians."[58] Scholars continue to question whether the Sons of Liberty only welcomed members from elite levels of colonial society or whether its membership lists reached across socioeconomic classes. Edmund and Helen Morgan argue that, much like the relationship between the Loyal Nine and Samuel Adams and James Otis in Boston, the individual chapters of the Sons of Liberty consisted of elite members of colonial society who relied on carefully selected men like John Spooner to serve "as the intermediary between the Sons of Liberty and the lower classes," which made it possible for them to "seldom appear in the actual work of destruction [while] directing the show from behind the scene."[59] The presence of Spooner's name on one of Stiles's lists suggests he was aware of these efforts to reach out to men like Spooner who possessed the necessary social skills and connections to link the different social classes when needed.[60] John Webber, another figure who emerged during the Newport Stamp Act riots in an ostensibly similar role, will be discussed at greater length in chapter 4.[61]

Stiles's "Stamp Act Notebook," the pages of the *Newport Mercury*, and Rhode Island legislative records can be used to trace evolving responses to the Stamp Act in Newport in spring and early summer 1765. The announcement in the February 11, 1765, edition of the *Newport Mercury* that copies of Howard's *Letter from a Gentleman at Halifax* pamphlet in the *Newport Mercury* could be purchased from printer Samuel Hall created an immediate response from the Rhode Island General Assembly.[62] Joseph Wanton Jr., Rhode Island's deputy governor in 1765, attempted to persuade the legislature to launch an investigation into Howard's pamphlet. While some colonists wanted it labeled as libel or publicly burned by the local hangman, others eventually persuaded Wanton to drop the investigation into the pamphlet on the grounds that it would be unwise for the colony to become too deeply embroiled in what was still only a series of political exchanges between Rhode Island colonists.[63]

Newport Mercury editor Hall found himself as the primary target for the Rhode Island government throughout this period, perhaps because he was seen as more vulnerable than Martin Howard and the other members of the Newport Junto who were connected to many of Rhode Island's oldest families. Just before he was voted out of office in spring 1765, Governor Stephen Hopkins summoned Hall to be questioned by Rhode Island's Superior Court. Little information survives about this exchange, but the fifteenth O.Z. letter published by the Newport Junto on March 18 as part of their campaign in support of domestic textile production in Rhode Island was accompanied by a note expressing O.Z.'s concern about this latest turn of events. According to O.Z., Hall had been questioned "without any kind of warrant or legal process," and consequently, "Judge Jeffries, the Star Chamber, the Spanish Inquisition rush into our minds, and fill us with apprehensions."[64] But the extent of any actual threats against Hall at this time is unclear. Edmund and Helen Morgan note that "a printer who refused to cooperate was apt to regret it, for the Sons of Liberty might also be the leaders of the legislative assembly," which was certainly the case in Rhode Island.[65] The March 18 O.Z. letter was the last one published under that name in the *Newport Mercury*, and a wide array of columns reporting on political campaigns against the Sugar and Stamp Acts appeared in successive issues, many accompanied by editorial comments endorsing their political stances, which were either written by Hall or dictated to him.

One such example is the decision to republish an essay decrying the Sugar Act from the *South-Carolina Gazette* on the front page of the March 18 edition of the *Newport Mercury* with an editorial note commenting, "The petitions and representations of New York, Rhode Island, &c are much to the same effect with the above, most exceeding it in length and pathos."[66] Two weeks later, the April 1 issue of the *Newport Mercury* reprinted three appeals submitted by the colony of Virginia to the British government with the editorial comment that "it must necessarily afford [our readers] peculiar Pleasure and Satisfaction to observe the energetic and spirited Manner in which they are wrote."[67] A column from the April 22 edition of the *Newport Mercury* reported on a pamphlet from London that objected to the Sugar and Stamp Acts as evidence that the colonies had support overseas as well.[68] This same time frame also saw advertisements for James Otis's *A Vindication of the British Colonies, against the Aspersions of the Halifax Gentleman* pamphlet in the *Newport Mercury*.[69] Then as now, advertisements for saleable goods were a revenue source for newspapers, which raises the question of who was paying for these advertisements of a pamphlet that had been published in Boston and was for sale in that community.

The array of columns objecting to parliamentary taxation with their carefully constructed editorial approval published in the pages of the *Newport Mercury* in spring 1765 would suggest that Samuel Hall was toeing the party line laid down by the Rhode Island legislature. Hall did, however, continue to accept columns from the Newport Junto in the weeks following the Newport Stamp Act riots in late August 1765. Perhaps he was able to persuade the Superior Court that his personal stance was less editor endorsing the Newport Junto and more printer of a paper that happened to offer a wide range of political views. Hall's success in this arena would prove short-lived, but it did make the *Newport Mercury* a distinctive publication in a time of hyperpartisan newspaper publication. This is particularly evident in the March 18, 1765, issue of the *Newport Mercury*, which placed the O.Z. letter and its explicit concerns about the "Star Chamber, Judge Jeffries, and the Spanish Inquisition" next to the column from the *South-Carolina Gazette* describing the Massachusetts petition objecting to the Stamp Act. The April 29 issue featured a column describing successful efforts to raise hemp in Pennsylvania, which was included "to oblige some Gentlemen in Newport, who were desirous of being acquainted with the Manner of raising Hemp in that Province."[70] Given how many of the earlier O.Z. letters had extolled the virtues of growing hemp in Rhode Island, it is likely that they were the "Gentlemen in Newport" in question.

A column from June 10 suggests that the Newport Junto were deliberately provoking the Sons of Liberty in Rhode Island. It was common practice for newspapers to include speeches from political leaders in the other colonies or in Britain. Nevertheless, the full text of a recent speech given by "His Excellency Governor Bernard of the Massachusetts-Bay" describing "three Improvements which this Country was capable of making profitable to itself and convenient to Great Britain: I mean Pot-ash, Hemp and the carrying Lumber to the British Market" can only have come from the Newport Junto.[71] Reprinting Bernard's speech was an endorsement of a royal governor in neighboring Massachusetts and a portrayal of the colonies as little more than providers of raw goods for the British Empire. It also supported the Newport Junto's ongoing campaign in favor of the Rhode Island textile industry. Since Hall also included a column praising the current arguments against the Stamp Act, it seems unlikely that the inclusion of Bernard's speech was his submission.

Commentary from both sides quieted during the summer, although groundwork was being laid for explosions in late August. Ezra Stiles's notes on this period largely documented correspondence between Rhode Island residents and supporters in other colonies and in London.[72] A little over a week before the Newport Stamp Act riots, the *Newport Mercury* reported on an August 13 town meeting in Providence that had ended with the participants voting on instructions for their representatives in an upcoming meeting of the Rhode Island General Assembly. The arguments made during this meeting were largely constructed on Stephen Hopkins's arguments in *The Rights of the Colonies, Examined*.[73] First, they recommended that the Rhode Island government encourage Parliament to "postpon[e] the Introduction of the Stamp-Act... until the Colonies may have the Opportunity to be heard in Defense of such just Rights." Second, they asked for "an Address of Thanks" for "those Gentlemen who distinguished themselves at the last Session of Parliament, in Defense of Liberty and the Colonies; in particular to General *Conway* and Colonel *Isaac Barré*."[74] Similar meetings were held in other Rhode Island communities in early August, but this was the most extensive gathering reported in the *Newport Mercury*.

The town of Providence's instructions were eventually presented at a meeting of the Rhode Island General Assembly held in East Greenwich in September 1765.[75] By that time, the Newport Stamp Act riots had taken place, and several of the members of the Newport Junto had fled for England, including Martin Howard. Unlike Massachusetts and Virginia, where objections to the Stamp Act were vigorously discussed in the colonial legislatures, Rhode Island did not take any overt action until after the Stamp Act riots had taken place in Newport. An unidentified Providence colonist, who was probably Stephen Hopkins, submitted a petition late in 1764 to King George III asking him to interfere on Rhode Island's behalf in the implementation of the Stamp Act. David Lovejoy notes that addressing the petition to the British monarch rather than to Parliament was a deliberate attempt to remind the British government that the colony's original agreements were made with the Crown, since "as far as the petition is concerned it would seem that Parliament had nothing to do with the colony."[76] Joseph Sherwood, Rhode Island's agent in London, informed Hopkins in spring 1765 that the petition had, instead, been directed to the secretary of state since issues relating to trade and commerce were managed by the Board of Trade and Parliament.[77] In any event, nothing came of this petition, which was probably ignored by Parliament and George III alike.

The only direct mention of the Stamp Act in the Rhode Island colonial records prior to the end of August was the assembly's discussion of an invitation from Samuel White, speaker of the Massachusetts House of Representatives. White and the other members of the Massachusetts legislature believed the Stamp Act posed a more direct challenge to the British North American colonies than the earlier Sugar Act.[78] Consequently, they called for the colonial legislatures "to consult together on the ... difficulties to which they are, and must be, reduced by the operation of the acts of Parliament, for levying duties and taxes on the colonies."[79] This meeting eventually became the Stamp Act Congress, held in New York in October 1765. The congress was attended by delegates from Massachusetts, Rhode Island, Connecticut, New York, New Jersey, Pennsylvania, Delaware, Maryland, and South Carolina. Edmund and Helen Morgan note, "New Hampshire declined but formally approved the proceeds after the congress was over. Virginia, North Carolina, and Georgia were prevented from participating, because their governors refused to convene the assemblies to elect delegates."[80] Governor Tryon's refusal to allow North Carolina to send delegates to the Stamp Act Congress will be discussed in chapters 4 and 5.

Unlike the colonial government in neighboring Massachusetts, Rhode Island's governor and legislature were in agreement that the Stamp Act needed to be opposed. This allowed the Rhode Island assembly to focus on matters other than the Stamp Act in spring and summer 1765. Assembly members debated whether to divide Providence into two separate communities and discussed Governor Samuel Ward's request for Rhode Island to be "reimburse[d] for the expenses they were at for ordnance, stores, &c, for the use of the crown" during the French and Indian War.[81] Nevertheless, the assembly was deeply aware that the implementation of the Sugar Act in Rhode Island waters in 1764 and 1765 was a preview of challenges to come from the Stamp Act. It also discussed the efforts of the naval schooner HMS *St. John* to disrupt the smuggling of sugar in Newport Harbor and the resulting attack on the *St. John* from some Newport residents.[82] Finally, the assembly heard testimony from Ward documenting that "several inhabitants of this colony [had been] lately impressed and detained on board [HMS *Maidstone*] contrary to law."[83] The Rhode Island colonial government was united in its efforts to resist the strictures imposed by the Sugar and Stamp Acts. The only internal challenge faced by either the governor or the assembly was from the political activities of the Newport Junto. They were prepared to push back against any immediate behavior they perceived as placing restrictions on their economic and political interests. This last theme would reappear during the Newport Stamp Act riots late in summer 1765 and the burning of HMS *Gaspee* in 1772.[84] By that time, the Stamp Act had become a clear and present danger to the people of Rhode Island that needed to be addressed in the immediate moment.

Chapter Four

The Stamp Act Riots

COLONIAL POWER STRUCTURES UNDERWENT multiple changes in the decades prior to the Stamp Act crisis. Massachusetts became a royal colony in 1691, when King William III granted its second charter. As with the other royal colonies, the Massachusetts governor was now appointed by the king, and Governor Francis Bernard had held his position since summer 1760. Like Massachusetts, North Carolina was a royal colony, but William Tryon had only just received his appointment when the Stamp Act crisis began in 1765. Rhode Island was still a charter colony with the right to elect its own governor, who, at that time, was the recently elected Samuel Ward, who had only just wrested the governor's office from his long-time rival, Stephen Hopkins. The legislatures in Massachusetts and North Carolina composed resolves expressing their frustrations with the Stamp Act with the full knowledge that both their respective governors and the British Parliament would be unmoved by these appeals.[1] By contrast, Rhode Island's status as a chartered colony in which both the governor and the legislature opposed the Stamp Act created something of an echo chamber at the executive level. The presence, however, of the Newport Junto in Rhode Island made the fight over the parliamentary taxation a far more intimate one than in the other British North American colonies.

Colonial responses to the Stamp Act boiled over into violence in late summer and early fall 1765.[2] Full-scale riots broke out in Boston and Newport in August, while communities in New Hampshire, Connecticut, New

York, Pennsylvania, Maryland, Virginia, and both Carolinas experienced a wide range of public demonstrations in the following months. The riots in Boston and Newport directly targeted the bodies and houses of the men believed to be representing the interests of Parliament, though motivations for these riots differed. By contrast, Governor Tryon made multiple overtures to the North Carolina General Assembly as he struggled to avoid riots like the ones in Boston and Newport. His actions helped keep violence in check during the long summer and fall of 1765, but they also set the stage for his relationship with the assembly in the years following the Stamp Act crisis.

Some common themes appear throughout the responses to the Stamp Act in Massachusetts, North Carolina, Rhode Island, and the other colonies. Newspaper columns reporting the growing violence of the Stamp Act crisis took pains to document local commitment to the enterprise of the wider British Empire and its monarch, George III. Descriptions of local protests in newspapers and Ezra Stiles's "Stamp Act Notebook" emphasized the civility of the demonstrators, with an occasional hint that perhaps, in other less-well-run communities, events may have gotten out of hand.[3] These efforts were part of a larger strategy designed to cloak colonial protests with as much respectability as was available to their chroniclers. Pauline Maier writes that "almost immediately after the outbreak of mob activity, radicals undertook a painstaking elaboration of resistance strategy. Colonists consciously retreated from mere ad hoc violence to an ordered opposition," a pattern that continued to cycle throughout most colonial activities in the late 1760s and early 1770s.[4] But the question of whether the same colonists were part of these cycles of violence and orderly resistance is still being considered by scholars.

Early responses to the newly announced Stamp Act were primarily organized by colonists in Virginia, Massachusetts, and New York. Patrick Henry introduced a debate on condemning the Stamp Act to the floor of the Virginia House of Burgesses in spring 1765, which eventually led to the passing of some of Henry's Virginia Resolves.[5] The Massachusetts House of Representatives briefly raised the question of whether individual colonies could pass their own tax laws in lieu of the parliamentary tax, though nothing came of this proposal.[6] Governor Bernard urged his colonists toward a moderated response, and it appeared for a time in spring 1765 that Massachusetts colonists would accept the Stamp Tax. Unfortunately for Bernard's peace of mind, news of the "spirited assertion of rights that New York had sent to Parliament" following the passage of the Stamp Act on March 22 resulted in many Massachusetts colonists becoming "ashamed of their own moderation."[7]

Determined to retake its position as the primary organizer of colonial responses to Parliament, the Massachusetts House of Representatives issued a circular letter to the other colonial assemblies on June 8, 1765, inviting them to send delegates to a meeting in New York in October to discuss the Stamp Act.[8] A letter to the *Boston Gazette* on July 8, 1765, encouraged Massachusetts colonists to defend their rights and be wary of "Cur'sd Prudence of interested designing Politicians!"[9] Governor Bernard encouraged his colonists to accept the new tax, as Parliament retained the right to pass laws governing all British subjects.[10] The Massachusetts House responded by arguing that Parliament did not have the right to assess internal taxes, that is, taxes placed on goods that had not been imported to North America, which, in turn, rendered the Stamp Tax illegal, as the duties were placed on documents created in the colonies. These debates continued during summer 1765 in many of the colonial capitals but rarely seemed to move past hypotheticals and legal dicta. The Stamp Act was not scheduled to take effect until November 1, so for the moment its threats were largely abstract.

While the colonial legislatures debated the legality of the Stamp Act, other arguments emerged in Boston's streets and taverns. The members of the Loyal Nine wanted action and answers rather than theoretical debate.[11] It was unclear what the effects of the Stamp Act would be on the local mercantile community, and Boston was a port town whose economy depended on the open flow of goods. It was possible that local justices might be persuaded to refuse to issue legal documents on stamped papers. It was, however, highly unlikely that customs officers, who received their appointments from the Crown, would do likewise with the clearance papers necessary for trading vessels to travel between colonial ports. By early August, the Loyal Nine and their carefully cultivated contacts in the Massachusetts colonial legislature were ready to move forward as Boston's newly formed Sons of Liberty chapter.

Boston had long been home to disputes between the residents of the North and South Ends. These altercations often spun out from activities on November 5, or Pope's Day, when Protestant Anglo-Americans celebrated the end of Guy Fawkes's efforts in 1606 to destroy the British Parliament and bring England back under Catholic rule.[12] The hope now was that these long-standing rivalries could be harnessed in service of a different cause. Ebenezer Mackintosh, a shoemaker from Boston's South End and the probable leader of the Loyal Nine, began his preparations late on the night of August 13.[13] By early morning the following day, an effigy of Andrew Oliver had been hanged on Newbury Street "in the most public part of the town, together with a boot, wherein was concealed a young imp of a devil represented as peeping out of the top."[14] Oliver was both cousin to Lieutenant Governor Thomas Hutchinson and the appointed Stamp Tax distributor in Massachusetts. The image of a boot referred to John Stuart, the Earl of Bute, who had authored the equally unpopular Cider Tax in Britain in 1763 and who was an adviser to George III.[15] Governor Bernard urged his council to respond to the hanging of Oliver's effigy, but it only passed the matter on to Suffolk County Sheriff Stephen Greenleaf. He refused to summon any officers on the grounds that he would be unnecessarily endangering his men. By early evening, a large crowd of men had cut down the effigy and taken it to Oliver's house, where it was ceremoniously beheaded and the house attacked. Oliver and his family retreated for protection to Castle William, a fortified structure on Castle Island in Boston Harbor, where they were soon joined by Governor Bernard.[16] For his part, Hutchinson roused Sheriff Greenleaf later that night, and the two men ordered the mob around Oliver's house to cut down the effigy of Oliver and disperse. The crowd refused to do so and marched on to Fort Hill, an elevated area in Roxbury that would later be fortified during the Siege of Boston in 1776.[17] Once there, they burned the effigy to the ground but largely left the neighborhood surrounding Oliver's house alone.

The events of the following morning set a pattern that would be repeated in many of the colonies in late summer and fall 1765. Andrew Oliver received a delegation of visitors at Castle William who encouraged him to resign his position as Stamp Tax distributor. Oliver pointed out that the Stamp Act would not be effective until November 1 and, in any event, he had yet to receive his formal commission. Oliver's visitors urged him to write to Parliament to ask for permission to resign as a gesture of good will. Once Oliver had agreed to this, he ceased to be a target, as would other Stamp Tax distributors after him. Nevertheless, other events in Boston continued to escalate, and crowds of angry colonists were again chasing through the narrow Boston streets by August 26.

This time, the ire of the crowds was aimed at three new targets: William Story, the deputy registrar for the Admiralty Court; Benjamin Hallowell, the customs comptroller; and Lieutenant Governor Hutchinson. Pauline Maier notes that the testimony from Hutchinson and Bernard and the "mob's peculiar interest in its victims' papers indicate that it was inspired by a group of merchants who feared that they had been named in a set of recent depositions about smuggling."[18] Edmund and Helen Morgan speculate that the attack may have been related to land claims made by the New Plymouth Colony on the Kennebec River in Maine, though there is no im-

Engraving of the Boston Stamp Act Riots, from Edward Sylvester Ellis, *The Youths' History of the United States from the Discovery of America*, New York: Cassell & Company, c. 1886–87. (*Library of Congress*)

mediate evidence connecting this group with the men rioting in Boston that night.[19] Links between political and economic interests during the American Revolution are well documented and, in this case, political concerns may have been used as cover for economic ones.[20]

The August 26 riots began with the lighting of a bonfire on King Street, near where the Boston Massacre would occur five years later. Once the crowd was fully established, two groups headed out, one to attack Story's house and one to attack Hallowell's house. Ebenezer Mackintosh then united the two groups, and they turned their attention to Hutchinson's house in what turned out to be one of the most violent attacks on civilian property in the period before the Revolution.[21] A letter sent by Hutchinson on August 30 to London barrister Richard Jackson described the attackers as a "hellish crew [who] fell upon my house with the rage of devils" and forced Hutchinson "to retire through yards & gardens to a house more remote."[22] When he and his family eventually returned to their house, they found "nothing remaining but the bare walls and floors." Wainscoting was stripped from the walls, doors were broken into splinters, and the slates had begun to be removed from the roof. Nearly all the family's possessions, including furniture, portraits, silver plate, and clothing belonging to the Hutchinsons and the servants they employed were also carried off, along with some £900 in currency. Much to Hutchinson's amazement, his ruined house became a tourist attraction in the coming days, as colonists from around the Boston area flocked to see its remains. Robert Blair St. George writes that "the sense of awe they shared at witnessing the creation of an instant social ruin was an expression of a particularly colonial antiesthetic that saw in popular violence a sublime source of liberating pleasure."[23] The presence of tourists around houses attacked during political riots would become a pattern in other communities as well.

Hutchinson also noted that the crowds had not left "a single book or paper in [the house] & have scattered or destroyed all the manuscripts & other papers I had been collecting for 30 years together." The purpose of this destruction was probably eradicating evidence of smuggling or land claims, but for Hutchinson it was a dual blow. Like Ezra Stiles in Rhode Island, he was interested in the history of the New England colonies. He had spent years building up his collection of source materials in preparation for writing a multivolume history.[24] Now, both the past he had collected and his future in Massachusetts were coming to a rapid close.

Unlike most of the men who served as royal governors in the British North American colonies, Lieutenant Governor Hutchinson was, like Martin Howard, a "native of this colony." His family's roots in New England dated back to the founding period, and Massachusetts was his home. Consequently, his letter to Richard Jackson also expressed his concern for "the wretched state we are in. Such is the resentment of the people against the stamp duty" that it was highly unlikely that the Massachusetts courts would enforce the Stamp Act once it took effect in November. In that case, Parliament would probably order the British military to enforce the law. And if that happened, mourned Hutchinson, "there seems to be a danger of a total lasting alienation of affection." Such concerns were also voiced by royal governors in the other colonies. Many had questioned the wisdom of the Stamp Act as they feared the impact, both economic and psychological, that the tax would have on their colonies. They also believed they had little choice but to enforce it when possible. Ezra Stiles mourned that "the basis of Alienation will never be healed" from the Stamp Act crisis.[25] These writings remind us that if Hutchinson and Stiles came to the American Revolution on very different political sides, they, like thousands of other British colonists, shared a common colonial heritage. If a revolution did come, it would carry losses for both sides.

Governor Bernard called for a meeting of the council on the morning of August 27 to investigate the attack on Hutchinson's house. There were also rumors that a mob of men planned to pull down the customhouse. Sheriff Greenleaf issued a warrant for Ebenezer McIntosh's arrest, and he was taken into custody. According to Edmund and Helen Morgan, the word "went around that unless McIntosh was released, not a man would appear to defend the custom-house."[26] Greenleaf released McIntosh, and there were no further efforts to investigate who had taken part in the attack. Events in Boston largely calmed down at this point. It remains unclear, however, whether this was owing to the Massachusetts House's efforts to tamp down further violent outbreaks or whether the mere threat of more violence was enough to quell additional retaliatory actions against the men who had attacked Hutchinson's house.

By early fall, the arrival of November 1 and the implementation of the Stamp Act were looming on the horizon. The Massachusetts Resolves were passed by the legislature on October 29. This document stated that since the "Inhabitants of this Province pay their full Proportion of Taxes ... *here*, it is unreasonable for them to be called upon, to pay any Part of the Charges of the Government *there*."[27] Governor Bernard closed the port of Boston and the courts, arranged for companies of militias to guard Boston between October 31 and November 6, refused the offer of any British troops, and retired to Castle William with the intent of remaining there until Boston grew calmer. The Sons of Liberty organized decorous parades on November 1 and November 5, or Pope's Day, which ended by celebrating "the union of the South End and the North End ... with all the decorum of a church supper."[28] These actions created a stalemate in which all the involved parties—Governor Bernard and Lieutenant Governor Hutchinson, resigned Stamp Tax distributor Andrew Oliver, and the various customs officials—passed responsibility and, probably, the newly arrived stamps, among themselves. Bernard agreed to open the port of Boston in December, which was heralded as a great success by the Sons of Liberty. By that time, all of them were awaiting news of the promised parliamentary debate on repealing the Stamp Act.

News of the riots in Boston traveled quickly down the New England coast. The colony of Rhode Island had taken no actions against the Stamp Act. There were, however, rumors in Newport that treatment similar to the attacks on the homes of Andrew Oliver and Thomas Hutchinson would be meted out to the members of the Newport Junto. According to a letter sent by Thomas Moffat to Joseph Harrison on October 17, he and Martin Howard contacted Governor Samuel Ward, their one-time political ally, to ask for assistance. Ward agreed to mediate on their behalf with Samuel Vernon and William Ellery, the leaders of Newport's Sons of Liberty chapter. There is no evidence that this happened, and Moffat appealed directly to Vernon on August 26. In response, Vernon accused the Newport Junto of "brand[ing] the merchants of Rhode Island as smugglers which accusation alone Justly deserves death."[29] The Newport Junto had demonstrated no interest in the safety of Newport's merchants, and now they would show no interest in the safety of the members of the Newport Junto. Similar to the Boston Stamp Act riots, economic interests were also driving tensions in Newport.

However fruitless, these efforts to defuse the situation in Newport speak to the specific elements that created the Stamp Act crisis in Rhode Island. This was a quarrel among people of the same community. Martin Howard published a statement in the *Newport Mercury* on August 26 that opened with the reminder that "he is a Native of the Colonies, and has a heart as warmly attached to their true Interest as any man whatever."[30] Unlike many of the governors and colonial officials who had received their appointments through Parliament and the king, Howard was from North America. His entire career had been committed to the welfare and betterment of Rhode Island. Nevertheless, Howard, like Thomas Hutchinson, knew his time in New England was coming to a close. He ultimately chose to finish his letter by throwing down yet another gauntlet. "If his Person and Interest become the Objects of popular Revenge for these Sentiments," wrote Howard, "he thinks he shall never lament the Cause, whatever may be the Consequences." Revenge would not be long in coming.

With knowledge of the attack on Oliver's house on August 14 fresh in their minds, Martin Howard, Thomas Moffat, and John Robinson, the customs collector in Newport who was also a member of the Newport Junto, made arrangements to spend the night of August 26 on HMS *Cygnet* in Newport's harbor.[31] Our knowledge of what happened after that in Newport is pieced together from a letter sent by Newport resident William Almy to Boston resident Elisha Story on August 29; an account of the riots published in the *Newport Mercury* on September 2 that may have been written by Thomas Moffat; and a letter sent by Moffat to James Harrison on October 16.[32] All three accounts agree that the protests were initially constrained but exploded the following day. Sheila Skemp notes that Howard, Moffat, and Robinson's decision to take refuge on the *Cygnet* may "have been the reason for the relatively benign atmosphere prevailing on the night of the twenty-seventh" rather than the "good will of the crowd."[33] Whether the turn toward violence on August 28 was a premeditated decision remains unclear, *particularly* since two of the primary accounts of these events were composed by one of their targets.

The first major event on the morning of August 27 was a parade that traveled from the docks to the Parade and through the streets surrounding the Colony House. This route would have taken the marchers past the houses of Martin Howard and Thomas Moffat. The account published in the *Newport Mercury* on September 2 noted that "the whole was conducted with moderation, and no Violence offered to the Persons or Property of any Man."[34] This peaceful atmosphere may have been too decorous for Samuel Vernon, William Ellery, and Robert Crook, all of whom wanted revenge on the Newport Junto. Thomas Moffat claimed in his letter to Joseph Harrison that they "shew'd some uneasines Jealousie and fear least the rabble should not assemble." In order to draw further attention, they sent out "strong Drink in plenty with Cheshire cheese and other provocatives to intemperance and riot." Shortly afterward, a set of gallows was erected in front of the courthouse. Later, they would be used to hang effigies of Howard, Moffat, and Augustus Johnston, who had agreed to serve as Rhode Island's Stamp Tax distributor.

Effigy hanging was a popular means of publicly displaying anger in the early modern world. Robert Blair St. George notes that "the use of comical or parodic effigies to mock an individual represented an inversion of established norms."[35] They could also be used to send a visual message to communities with varying levels of literacy. Andrew Oliver's effigy was accompanied by the standard symbolism of the imperial crisis: an image of a boot as a reference to the Earl of Bute. The men who created the Oliver effigy were angry with his position as the Stamp Tax collector but not necessarily with him. By contrast, the effigies of Martin Howard, Thomas Moffat, and Augustus Johnston were accompanied by representations of their past activities in Rhode Island, although Moffat's effigy did include a boot. William Almy's letter to Elisha Story carefully documented the statements written out on the labels attached to the effigies. Moffat's effigy warned, "It is too late Martinius to Retract, for we are all Aground," while the label on Howard's effigy described him as "That fawning, insidious, infamous miscreant and paracide Martinius Scriblerius."[36] This particular title was originally coined for English philologist Richard Bentley by his adversaries in the early eighteenth century, but Howard's enemies were clearly taken with the similarity to his given name.[37] A label attached to the gallows informed readers that the "Person who shall Efface this Publick Mark of Resentment will be Deem'd an Enemy to liberty, while the second announced that the three men had "an Heriditary Indefeasible Right to a Halter, Besides we Encourag'd the Growth of Hemp you know." This last statement was a pointed reference to the Newport Junto's earlier arguments in favor of hemp production in Rhode Island in 1764. The Newport Junto's advocacy for home textile production was still seen as evidence of their support for the British Empire in 1765. Arguments in favor of home textile production would not become part of the Revolutionary movement until 1766 at the earliest.[38]

Tempers simmered down in the afternoon of August 27, only to boil over the next day when "the chief ring leaders of yesterdays spectacle rushd into the streets with a chosen band of Ruffians at their heels having their faces painted and being prepard and furnishd with broad axes and other tools of desolation."[39] The crowd traveled first to the Howard family home, which they very nearly tore down to the ground. Then they continued on to do much the same at Thomas Moffat's house around the corner. In 1772, Martin Howard would submit to the Rhode Island General Assembly an inventory of damages during the attack that totaled just over £320. The items listed included four family portraits; a "jappanned tea-table and tea board" and other pieces of furniture; a "shagreen set of knives and forks, almost new"; and, like the Hutchinson home, a number of books and papers.[40] The crowds then moved on to the Johnston family home, where Augustus Johnston briefly confronted them before joining Howard, Moffat, and John Robinson on the *Cygnet*. Following Johnston's departure, family friends managed to persuade the crowd that Johnston was willing to resign his position as Stamp Tax distributor and so forestalled an attack on his home.[41]

Accounts of the final stages of the Newport Stamp Act riots grow ever more confused after this point. By August 29, it appeared that the riots were winding down. Augustus Johnston successfully returned to his home, while Martin and Annie Howard and Thomas Moffat were making plans to travel to Britain on the next available ship.[42] By that time, Samuel Vernon, William Ellery, and Robert Crook appear to have had some regrets about the unspooling of the riots and the resulting impacts on the reputation of Newport's Sons of Liberty chapter. A sailor named John Webber, who was possibly of Irish heritage and who had only just arrived in Newport a few days before the Stamp Act riots, was presented to the town by Ellery and Vernon as the primary instigator for the more violent parts of the riots.[43] Shortly afterward, Ellery and Vernon arranged to have Webber arrested and imprisoned on the *Cygnet*, where Johnston, Howard, and Moffat had all taken shelter during the attacks on their houses. At this point, the crowd threatened to attack the homes of Ellery and Vernon, and Webber was released. The following day, Johnston, who was still Rhode Island's attorney general, had Webber arrested for a second time, but he was released shortly afterward in an effort to restore peace to Newport's streets. By contrast, the laborer John Spooner, whom Ezra Stiles had described as being "as important as any Man of the Committee, as they without him would not have had so intirely the Confidence of the Populace," is not mentioned in the descriptions of the Newport riots.[44] The long-standing political and economic tensions between the Newport Junto and the Sons of Liberty suggest that the presentation of Webber as the instigator of the Newport riots was a useful cover for Vernon, Ellery, Crook and the ever-useful Spooner, since Webber was not a Newport native and so an easy scapegoat. There is, however, also a hint that the Sons of Liberty knew they were unable to control Webber.

Martin and Annie Howard and Thomas Moffat left for London a few days later. Both Howard and Moffat described the events of the Stamp Act crisis in Rhode Island for Parliament in October. Henry Seymour Conway, the secretary of state for the Southern Department and an advocate for repealing the Stamp Act, noted that Howard's and Moffat's testimonies were given "with knowledge and without passion or prejudice and had, I believe, great weight in persuading the repeal of the Stamp Act."[45] During his time in London, Howard submitted the first of many requests to the colony of Rhode Island for repayment for financial losses sustained during the riots. This first request indicated that while he and Moffat held no ill will toward their erstwhile neighbors, they did still hold them responsible for their actions. Governor Ward told Conway on June 25, 1766, that "if any application of that kind should be made to the Assembly, I doubt not but they will take it into serious consideration."[46] Later that fall, however, Ward informed Joseph Sherwood, Rhode Island's colonial agent in London, that Rhode Island would only compensate Howard and Moffat for their losses if Parliament reimbursed Rhode Island for money spent during the French and Indian War. Not surprisingly, neither of these things ever happened.

Conway became the secretary of state for the Northern Department in May 1766 and was replaced by Charles Lennox, 3rd Duke of Richmond, who informed Governor Ward on May 23, 1766, that he could "depend on my punctuality in laying your letters . . . before the King."[47] Like Conway, Lennox supported the repeal of the Stamp Act and eagerly conveyed this support to the American colonists with whom he was in regular contact. At this time, Lennox also recommended Martin Howard for the position of chief justice in North Carolina, which suggests a man trying to remain neutral in the affairs of the colonies.[48] Whatever the reasons for his commission, Howard was elated by the promotion and immediately began laying plans for his return to North America.

An additional matter to be wrapped up in winter 1767 was a formal proposal of marriage from Martin Howard to Abigail Greenleaf, the twenty-four-year-old daughter of Sheriff Stephen Greenleaf in Massachusetts. A decade earlier, Newport Junto member Peter Harrison had asked Greenleaf to oversee the delivery of the 751 books purchased for the Redwood Library from London to Newport.[49] While it is unknown exactly when or how Howard and Abigail Greenleaf became acquainted, it seems likely that her father's connection to the Redwood Library played a role in their courtship.[50] Howard arrived in Boston that spring and commissioned a portrait of himself in his judicial robes from John Singleton Copley.[51] Howard and Greenleaf were married at the home of John Wentworth, the last royal governor of New Hampshire, on August 26, 1767.[52] Shortly afterward, the Howards, including Annie, took up residence in New Bern, North Carolina.

The Stamp Act had been repealed for nearly a year when the Howard family arrived. The Stamp Act crisis had also played out in very different ways in North Carolina than it had in Massachusetts and Rhode Island. Multiple colonists had objected to the Stamp Act, and there were demonstrations in some of the coastal communities in the Cape Fear River region. Unlike Governor Bernard in Massachusetts, Governor Tryon had actively worked to defuse tensions in North Carolina. New York colonist William Smith later praised Tryon's skill and diplomacy during the Stamp Act crisis, though he also noted Tryon's vulnerable position in North Carolina.[53] Tryon first arrived in the colony in fall 1764 as lieutenant governor.[54] He had been promised the position of governor once Arthur Dobbs retired. Dobbs, despite having promised to retire, remained in office for another year. His abrupt death due to a seizure in spring 1765 allowed Tryon to finally ascend to the governor's office, but the delay had weakened him in the colony.

William Tryon's uncertain position was not the only challenge facing him during his first year in North Carolina. Edmund and Helen Morgan note that "most colonies chose to regard [the Sugar Act] as a regulation of trade, which it was, rather than a revenue measure, which it also was."[55] The only colonies that openly described the Sugar Act as both trade regulation and revenue generator were Massachusetts, New York, and North Carolina. The ship carrying the Tryon family from Britain reached the mouth of the Cape Fear River on October 9, 1764, and Tryon traveled up the river to Wilmington ten days later on the barge belonging to HMS *Viper*.[56] The North Carolina General Assembly informed current Governor Dobbs on October 31 that it would not "fail to take into Consideration what your Excellency has been pleased to recommend ... to Encourag[e] and secur[e] the Commerce and Interior Improvement of this Province."[57] Nevertheless, it remained concerned by the "new Taxes and Impositions laid on us without our Privity and Consent, and against what we esteem our Inherent right, and Exclusive privilege." As Tryon settled into his new office, he was primarily interested in expanding the executive powers of the governor and the role of the Anglican Church in North Carolina. These were actions likely to meet with opposition in a historically fragile colony whose commitment to religious toleration dated back to its founding in the early 1660s. Since he would need the support of the assembly to achieve these goals, Tryon embraced a willingness to choose his battles as he approached his new position, a strategy that would remain in place until the end of his tenure in North Carolina in 1771.[58]

News of the New England Stamp Act riots reached the southern colonies in early September. Prior to the passing of the Stamp Act, Governor Francis Fauquier of Virginia had recommended against parliamentary taxation of the North American colonies.[59] He also prorogued the Virginia House of Burgesses early in summer 1765 following their debates on the Virginia Resolves. Virginia colonist George Mercer was in London in March 1765 when the Stamp Act was initially passed by Parliament. He accepted a position as Stamp Tax distributor for Virginia and returned to North America two days before the law was scheduled to take effect on November 1. Mercer's arrival in Williamsburg was met by a large group of colonists who demanded his immediate resignation, which eased tensions in Virginia. When a similar crowd of colonists approached the Charleston home of Caleb Lloyd, Stamp Tax distributor for South Carolina, he took refuge in Fort Johnson on the Ashley River on October 20.[60] A few days later, Lloyd was joined by George Saxby, the newly arrived Stamp Tax distributor for both Carolinas and Bermuda. Lloyd and Saxby later informed Parliament that angry mobs of men had hanged Lloyd in effigy and attacked his house. When the group of men threatened to launch further attacks on Lloyd and Saxby's family members, both men agreed to resign their positions, which also eased tensions in South Carolina.

The first response in North Carolina to the passing of the Stamp Act was the publication of Maurice Moore's pamphlet *The Justice and Policy of Taxing The American Colonies, in Great Britain, considered*.[61] At that time, Moore was in his early thirties and had served as an associate justice for the North Carolina Superior Court for the past three years. Similar to James Otis and Stephen Hopkins, Moore argued that the Stamp Act was illegitimate because the North American colonies did not have direct representation in Parliament. Like Hopkins, Moore rooted the bulk of his arguments in the particular history of his home colony. Since it would have been difficult to persuade British subjects "to leave their native country, wherein they enjoyed every right and liberty an excellent constitution could afford," the Carolina Charter drawn up by John Locke in 1663 had promised them "an enjoyment of those rights and liberties in Carolina," including the right "to be taxed only by their own consent."[62] Furthermore, the Carolina Charter sanctioned the creation of a colonial legislature that had the power to pass laws for the colony's inhabitants. Parliament argued that all British subjects were "virtually represented" by its collective body of parliamentary members.[63] According to Moore, the creation of this assembly made virtual representation in Parliament impossible for North Carolina colonists because "such a grant would have been extremely absurd; for no set of people can be represented at one time in two distinct and independent assemblies." This argument would appear to have been in direct contradiction to long-standing British policy that colonial laws "could not be contrary or repugnant to the laws of England," though this particular counterargument does not appear to have been made by Tryon or anyone else in response to Moore.[64]

The appointment of Martin Howard as North Carolina's chief justice in 1767 made him and Maurice Moore colleagues for a number of years, and there is no evidence that this was not a cordial relationship. William Price notes certain similarities between the two men, commenting, "Howard and Moore shared a fundamental conservatism. They loved order and dreaded any assault on it."[65] Years later, the Regulators would appeal to Howard's sense of order, and this appeal will be discussed in chapter 7. By spring 1766, however, Governor Tryon had wearied of discussions about the Stamp Act. Since Moore directly represented colonial opposition to the Stamp Act, Tryon suspended Moore from his position as associate justice "for his intemperate zeal and behaviour in his opposition to the Act of Parliament imposing Stamp duties in America."[66] Moore was replaced by Edmund Fanning for the next two years. Tryon finally returned Moore to the bench in 1768, at the beginning of the Regulator Rebellion, though there are no immediate connections between these two events.[67]

The first chapter of the Sons of Liberty was organized in the Cape Fear region early in fall 1765.[68] Prominent members included Maurice Moore's brother, James Moore; John Ashe, the speaker of the North Carolina General Assembly; Moses John De Rosset, the mayor of Wilmington; Cornelius Harnett, the chairman of North Carolina's chapter of the Sons of Liberty; and Hugh Waddell, the commander of the Rowan and Mecklenberg militia companies. By that time, the Board of Trade was also searching for a Stamp Tax distributor for North Carolina. Their first choice, Henry McCulloh, a wealthy London merchant and land speculator in North Carolina, declined the position. Their second choice was McCulloh's nephew, physician William Houston. The letter informing Houston about his new post arrived in Wilmington in early November 1765 and was intercepted by De Rosset, who ordered Houston to come to Wilmington from his home in Duplin County to retrieve the letter in person. While De Rosset and the other Sons of Liberty were waiting for Houston to retrieve his letter, small demonstrations broke out in Wilmington, Cross Creek, and New Bern in which effigies of Houston were hanged. Another demonstration took place in Wilmington on October 31, the night before the Stamp Tax was scheduled to take effect, but property damage was limited during all of these events.

William Houston arrived in Wilmington on November 16 and was almost immediately confronted by a crowd of approximately three hundred to four hundred colonists led by John Ashe. The *North-Carolina Gazette* reported that the crowd asked Houston whether he intended to carry out his office. Houston said he would be "very sorry to execute any Office disagreeable to the People of the Province."[69] He was then asked to resign from his position in writing. The *North-Carolina Gazette* further reported that they "placed him in an Arm-Chair, carried him first round the Court House, giving three Huzzas at every Corner, and then proceeded with him round one of the Squares of the Town, and sat him down at the Door of his Lodgings." Later that night, a bonfire was lit in the streets of Wilmington where crowds of colonists gathered to consume massive amounts of alcohol and cheered their success. Nevertheless, the *North-Carolina Gazette* was careful to note that the entire proceedings were "conducted with great Decorum, and not the least Insult offered to any Person," a concern undoubtedly prompted by reports of less genial protests in other colonies. In addition, the crowd ordered Andrew Steuart, the *North-Carolina Gazette's* editor, to not use the official stamped paper for his press.[70] Steuart agreed to these demands, with the caveat that he wanted witnesses to testify he had done so under threat from the Sons of Liberty since this would place him in direct opposition to Governor Tryon and Parliament.

The protests in Wilmington and the other coastal communities in October and November sent a dual message to Tryon. Like other royal governors in British North America, he was facing opposition from many of his colonists over the Stamp Act. The almost lighthearted nature of the November 16 demonstration suggested, however, that a lighter touch might prove productive. Like Governor Fauquier, Tryon had already prorogued the North Carolina General Assembly. This put a stop to any formal debates on the Stamp Act in the colony as well as preventing the assembly from sending delegates to the Stamp Act Congress in New York in October 1765. But some two days after the November 16 demonstration in Wilmington, Tryon invited fifty leading colonists from Bladen, Brunswick, and New Hanover Counties to dine with him and express their concerns in person.

These conversations were reported by the *North-Carolina Gazette*, which was still being published by Andrew Steuart in Wilmington, albeit on unstamped paper. Tryon reportedly began the evening with assurances that he would "exert his interest and influence in England in endeavouring to promote the prosperity of this colony by every means in his power consistent with his duty to his King and country."[71] Biographer William Nelson collectively described Tryon's efforts as a "tempting smorgasbord of self-serving proposals."[72] First, Tryon took pains to describe the violence that had taken place in other colonies and assessed his sincere hope that similar violence would not occur in North Carolina. Next, he told his guests he planned to appeal to Parliament for a reprieve since the Stamp Act's requirement that all fees be paid in hard coin would pose particular challenges in a colony where hard currency was rarely used. But, noted Nelson, if Parliament persisted in expecting North Carolina to pay its share of the Stamp Act, Tryon "generously offered to pay himself the whole duty arising on any Instruments executed on stampt paper; on which he should have any perquisite or fee."[73] This offer was not made by any other royal governor during this period, and it provides further evidence of Tryon's recognition of the challenges facing a historically fragile colony with little in the way of trade available to it.[74]

In the same article describing Tryon's efforts to appease his colonists, Steuart recorded their response. All the men present remained adamant that "every view of this Act confirms us in our opinion, that it is destructive of these Liberties which, as British Subjects, we have a Right to enjoy in common with Great Britain."[75] Furthermore, they believed that "the submission to any part of so oppressive and (as we think) so unconstitutional attempts, is opening a direct inlet for Slavery, which all Mankind will endeavor to avoid."[76] Consequently, they refused to pay any stamp duties, no matter how small, and reminded Tryon that "the Office of Distributors of the Stamps is so detested by the People in general that we dont think either the person or Property of such an Officer, could by any means be secured from the resentment of the Country," a not-so-veiled threat against anyone who tried to collect the stamp duties in North Carolina.

A temporary, albeit enforced, peace lasted from the time of this exchange in late November 1765 to the middle of January 1766. Since neither stamps nor stamped paper had arrived in North Carolina from London, the law could not be utilized even by colonists who supported the tax. Tryon closed

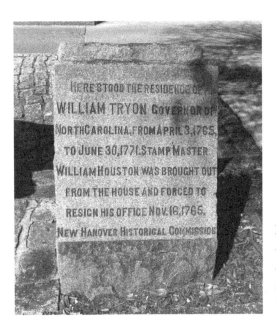

A marker at the site of governor William Tryon's residence in Wilmington, North Carolina, where William Houston was forced to resign as Stamp Master. (*Author's Photograph*)

ports in the Cape Fear region as a way of punishing the colonists who had advocated against the Stamp Act but did not otherwise push the issue. This period of détente ended when two ships, the *Dobbs* from Philadelphia and the *Patience* from the West Indies, arrived in the Cape Fear River. Trading vessels were required to file clearance papers before leaving port with fresh cargoes, and the Stamp Act further required that these papers be processed with the stamp duties, which necessitated an additional payment from shipmasters. Since the other colonial ports had either not received their stamps or were not allowing clearance papers to be processed by the Stamp Act distributors, neither ship's papers had the necessary stamps. Captain Jacob Lobb and HMS *Viper* were still patrolling the North Carolina coast in 1766, and Lobb seized both the *Dobbs* and the *Patience*, as well as another trading vessel, the *Ruby*. Shortly afterward, another British naval vessel, the *Diligence*, arrived with North Carolina's stock of stamps and stamped paper. The Sons of Liberty openly pledged to disrupt the enforcement of the Stamp Act in any way possible. Merchants in Wilmington and the other coastal towns refused to sell supplies to the British naval vessels. A small boat came into Wilmington to buy supplies for the *Viper* and *Diligence*, only to have its crew arrested and the boat dragged through the streets, while further armed colonists seized the customhouse in Brunswick.

The standoff ended on February 20, when members of the Sons of Liberty met with Captain Lobb on the *Diligence*. Lobb was forced to agree that since no ship could have its clearance papers processed with the necessary duties in British North America, all three vessels should be allowed to unload their cargoes and leave North Carolina without stamped papers. Moreover, Lobb and the other officials agreed to swear they would not enforce the Stamp Act in North Carolina. Andrew Steuart's article describing these negotiations in the *North-Carolina Gazette* again congratulated the participants on their excellent behavior. It noted that "few instances can be produced, of such a number of men being together so long and behaving so well... the whole affair [was] conducted with decency and spirit, worthy of the imitation of all the sons of Liberty throughout the Continent," a remark that echoed similar descriptions in other accounts of colonial activities during the Stamp Act crisis.[77]

The *Diligence* then returned to Britain, and the Stamp Act crisis effectively came to an end when news of the repeal arrived in North America in April. At that time, tensions between Governor Tryon and his colonists began to ease, though there was one final turn of events that would have lasting effects on North Carolina. Tryon had long desired a larger residence for his family than was available to him in Wilmington. Now he was also uneasy about remaining much longer in the area. The coastal communities north of the Cape Fear region joined Tryon's efforts to persuade the North Carolina General Assembly to approve funds for the construction of a governor's mansion in New Bern, a little over a hundred miles north of Wilmington. This decision would soon become one of the core motivating factors for the Regulator Rebellion, but for the moment, peace had arrived in North Carolina.

The experiences of the colonies of Massachusetts, Rhode Island, and North Carolina during the Stamp Act crisis were shaped by each colony's individual blend of power structures prior to the passing of the Stamp Act in 1765. Massachusetts experienced the Stamp Act crisis as a battle between the locally elected colonial legislature and the royal government represented by Governor Francis Bernard and Lieutenant Governor Thomas Hutchinson. The Stamp Act crisis in Massachusetts ended with both parties still in power, although groundwork had been laid for drastic and violent change. Rhode Island experienced the Stamp Act crisis as a battle between a locally elected government and the Rhode Island colonists who sought to shift the balance of power toward the British monarch and Parliament.[78] The Stamp Act crisis in Rhode Island ended with the locally elected government in place and their opponents either gone from the colony or deeply weakened, though there would be a resurgence of Loyalist power during the British occupation of Newport in the middle of the American Revolution. Finally, while North Carolina experienced the Stamp Act crisis as a dispute between the locally elected colonial legislature and the royal governor, William Tryon, it was a dispute in which both sides sought to find some form of common ground. The Stamp Act crisis ended in North Carolina with both sides in place and a sea of unresolved issues about the lengths to which appeasement might take them in the coming years.

Chapter Five

The Regulator Rebellion Begins

EUROPEAN SETTLEMENT IN NORTH CAROLINA followed the coastline, and the first English traders did not reach the interior Piedmont region in the late seventeenth century. Fur trader Abraham Wood described one such expedition in a letter that noted "when they lost sight of those hills they see a fog or smoke like a cloud from whence rain falls for several days on their right hand as they travel still towards the sun setting."[1] Wood hoped to establish trade networks with the Native American peoples the English called the Tomahattans, who lived in fortified villages along the many creeks and rivers threading through the region.[2] In time, reports of good farmland and a "great store of game, all along as turkeys, deer, elk, bear, wolf, and other vermin, very tame" drew English Quakers, Methodists, and Baptists, Scots-Irish Presbyterians, and German Moravians to the Piedmont in the 1730s and 1740s.[3] Two decades later, treaties between the Catawba tribe and the governors of North and South Carolina, Georgia, and Virginia in 1763 would bring even more European colonists to the region while laying the groundwork for the Regulator Rebellion.[4]

The first European settlers in the Piedmont region established farms that ranged from pure subsistence to small-scale production for the local cash economy. By contrast, the new settlers who moved to the region in the early 1760s were land speculators, attorneys, and merchants who had very different ambitions for North Carolina's newly formed Orange, Rowan, and Anson Counties.[5] They also had the connections to North Carolina's colonial government to bolster their claims to power.[6] The North Carolina battles over differing socioeconomic models for British communities echo the tensions between the Newport Junto and their antagonists in Rhode Island. The first letter from the Junto in the *Newport Mercury* on April 23, 1764, had made the case that when "simplicity of heart, and mutual confidence, is changed to licentiousness of manners, and universal distrust . . . a superior force is necessary . . . to regulate and keep it within bounds."[7] The Newport Junto believed that greater parliamentary and Crown control over Rhode Island would create a colony whose government was informed less by partisan interests and more by the needs of its inhabitants. A similar faith in better "regulation" of political and social systems infused the efforts of the North Carolina colonists who called themselves Regulators. They also hoped to transform their British colony into one whose government was informed less by partisan interests and more by the needs of its inhabitants. Concerns about the Regulators' home region were the spark that ignited the start of the Regulator Rebellion in 1768, but the wider movement was further fueled by unease over the lack of available currency for paying rising local and parliamentary taxes; concerns about North Carolina's broader political system; and, finally, Governor William Tryon's cultural and political agendas in the late 1760s.

The colonists who joined the Regulator movement believed that political and legal actions were rooted in social contracts between leaders and the communities they governed and that, in turn, such contracts provided the governed with legitimate channels for voicing concerns when needed.[8] Many of the Regulators were eligible to vote for representatives to the General Assembly and to run themselves, but they lacked the personal and political connections that wealthier, often slave-owning, assembly representatives from eastern counties used to advance their own initiatives. Instead, the wider Regulator movement utilized the mediums, both legal and extralegal, available to them. Like the members of the Newport Junto and the Sons of Liberty during the Stamp Act crisis, individual Regulators wrote petitions and published pamphlets explaining their positions, utilized the North Carolina court system, and, at times, turned to more-violent forms of expression. In turn, Tryon and the General Assembly utilized the options available to them, as the governor issued proclamations defining their positions, established new laws expanding their jurisdiction within the colony, and, ultimately, executed seven of the Regulators on treason charges following the Battle of Alamance.[9] Collectively, their writings demonstrate that both sides—the Regulators, and Tryon and the General Assembly—believed the other to be "unawed by the Laws of their Country" and that this belief legitimized their respective course of actions during the Regulator Rebellion, which took place in a period of rising tensions between British politicians and North American colonists.[10]

The colonists who joined the Regulator movement hoped their actions would help North Carolina address three separate but interlocking areas of concern: currency scarcities in British North America, the intricacies and corruption found in North Carolina's government and judiciary, and Tryon's efforts to reshape North Carolina into a political and cultural entity that more closely resembled neighboring Virginia. Some of these concerns were unique to North Carolina's particular circumstances while others reflected broader colonial tensions in British North America in the 1760s. Currency, whether specie or paper money, was extremely scarce in North America.[11] British law required that taxes—the ones created by individual colonies and the newly imposed Townshend duties that replaced the repealed Stamp Tax—be paid in currency, rather than the barter systems commonly used in the colonies. The petition submitted by the Regulators on October 4, 1768, further noted that the primary means of obtaining currency in the backcountry was by trading their livestock, which placed their livelihoods in further jeopardy. Parliament's Currency Act of 1764 prevented individual colonies from printing new currency and threatened royal governors with loss of their positions and a £1,000 fee if they violated the law.[12] Governor Tryon and the General Assembly repeatedly petitioned Parliament to exempt North Carolina from this requirement owing to the colony's cash-poor economy, but to no avail. Wills Hill, Lord Hillsborough, the newly appointed secretary of state for the colonies, instructed Tryon on April 16, 1768, that the same penalties would apply to North Carolina if the colony printed additional currency.[13]

The second area of concern raised by the Regulators was North Carolina's political and judicial systems. Similar to the other royal colonies, the governor and council were positions appointed by the British monarch, though the governor could recommend members for his council. This council formed the upper house of the General Assembly, while the lower house members were all elected by property-owning white men. North Carolina's chief justice was appointed by the Crown, but the colony's two associate justices were appointed by the governor. Additional government positions were allocated by the individual counties.[14] While many of these lower positions were elected offices, they generally went to families with good social and political connections, and, consequently, the Regulators rarely appeared in their ranks. What concerned the Regulators was how North Carolina paid the salaries of the men who held most of these positions. The colony did not generate enough revenue to fully pay for civic infrastructure. The governor, his council, the members of the lower house, the chief justice, and the two associate justices were the only positions to receive full salaries. As a way of supplementing their minimal pay, locally appointed sheriffs were entitled to commissions based on a percentage of the tax money collected, generally between 5 and 8 percent of the initial tax assessment.[15] Similarly, attorneys, registrars, and clerks were allowed to collect a percentage-based fee for services such as notarizing a land sale.

The many abuses of this system made up the backbone of the Regulators' objections to the colonial North Carolina government. There were almost no rules governing how much of a percentage could be collected on taxes and fees. Likewise, the return of the collected money to the colony was equally unregulated. Nothing prevented a corrupt government official from claiming that a colonist had not paid his taxes or fees, which then allowed the official to garnish a second payment.[16] The Regulators acknowledged that Governors Arthur Dobbs and William Tryon had made some efforts to address these problems. The General Assembly under Dobbs passed laws to stop government corruption, including one in 1755 that required sheriffs to account for the money collected with the treasurer for their districts. William Smith carefully documented Tryon's efforts to address these issues in North Carolina as part of his campaign to present Tryon to the people of New York as a responsible, caring governor.[17] Smith had access to Tryon's letter book and so would have read letters like the one Tryon sent to the Earl of Shelburne on July 4, 1767, documenting that "the Treasurers have hitherto shewn so much ill judged Lenity towards the Sheriffs that . . . [they] have embezzled more than one half of the Publick Money ordered to be raised and collected by them."[18]

The North Carolina documentary record suggests that while Tryon recognized the weight of the problem, he was unwilling to push the assembly on the issue. Many assembly members were either sheriffs or clerks or were related to sheriffs or clerks, and therefore unlikely to support such legislation.[19] Tryon's reluctance to press them further may have stemmed from the lingering effects of his uncertain first days in North Carolina, or it may reflect his failed efforts to negotiate terms for a mutual agreement between governor and legislature during the Stamp Act crisis. The assembly members also appeared to have adopted the strategy of simply waiting out Tryon's attention span. By 1768, Tryon had turned to North Carolina's lack of currency as a solution to the Regulator Rebellion rather than addressing the colony's internal problems. And by that time, Tryon's power was also challenged by the rising tensions of the imperial crisis.

Finally, the Regulators were concerned by Tryon's growing efforts to model North Carolina on the neighboring colonies of Virginia and Maryland, where the Anglican Church had been the only recognized church for decades in the mid-eighteenth century.[20] By contrast, the Fundamental Constitutions of Carolina created by John Locke in 1669 was still being used in North Carolina, where religious congregations ranged from Moravian to Presbyterian to Quaker to Baptist to Jewish.[21] Tryon, however, had argued in his first address to the assembly that the Anglican Church needed official recognition and support from North Carolina.[22] The resulting Orthodox Clergy Act provided salaries and glebes from tax revenues, plus certain payments for conducting marriages and funerals.[23] Tryon reluctantly agreed to allow the various dissenting faiths to continue practicing their religions in North Carolina. But many colonists, including the Regulators, resented paying taxes to support the Anglican Church when they themselves were not members of it.

Finally, Tryon and the General Assembly finalized plans in 1766 to locate the colony's capital in New Bern on the Neuse River and to build a home for the governor's family in that community. The building would also serve as a meeting place for the assembly, so they were able to justify using colonial taxes to pay for the edifice.[24] The resulting construction was colloquially known as "Tryon's Palace" and cost the colony nearly £15,000.[25] In 1766, the assembly created the first taxes to pay for the governor's mansion, with a two-pence-per-gallon levy on rum, wine, and distilled liquors, as well as an annual poll tax of eight pence, to be collected for two years.[26] Many of the Regulators were infuriated when Orange County Sheriff Tyree Harris announced in February 1768 that the taxes to pay for the governor's mansion would be collected "at five designated localities, and those who did not attend with money in hand to pay up would have to pay an extra fee of two shillings eight pence."[27] In 1769, the assembly approved an additional poll tax of two shillings and sixpence, to be collected for three years. Similar to the Townshend taxes, these new payments had to be made in cash and, again, currency shortages were one of the causes of the Regulator Rebellion. Furthermore, the men assigned to collect these taxes were the same ones who were already abusing the perquisites available to them as fee collectors. William Smith would later note that the palace was "raised in an unfortunate manner" that fed the anger of the Regulators owing to "the unskillful policy of the Assembly," which, presumably, was a reference to the assembly's willingness to turn a blind eye to such practices.[28]

Tryon's Palace, completed in 1770, served as the residence of Governor William Tryon and his family as well as the capitol of North Carolina. (*Author's Photograph*)

The written documents issued by the Regulators, Governor Tryon, the General Assembly, and other North Carolina officials between 1766 and 1771 point to each group's respective search for the legitimacy needed to support its actions. These documents fall into two predominant categories: proclamations issued by Tryon and the assembly, and petitions and pamphlets issued by some of the Regulators. David Zaret writes that while "rulers had ceremonies, priests, printers, assize judges, and more for sending political messages . . . highly ritualized forms of collective behavior afforded a limited opportunity for crowds to send messages to local and national rulers."[29] Similar to proclamations, petitions were highly ritualized, and petitioners were expected to demonstrate their deference to authority alongside their concerns. It is not surprising that Tryon and the members of the assembly were familiar with the use of public proclamations to support governmental actions. But the fact that the Regulators utilized carefully worded petitions to express their grievances demonstrates that members of this movement were equally knowledgeable about the English political process.

Unlike the Newport Junto and Sons of Liberty, whose members are easily traced back to the same groups of families, the Regulators were a far more amorphous group who ultimately encompassed a wide range of colonists from Orange, Rowan, and Anson Counties. Written documents composed by individual Regulators and by Tryon suggest the evolution of two centers within the larger Regulator movement, one working within the legal and political systems, and the other surging into ever-more-violent protests. They shared a cause, but their moments of convergence were infrequent until the final stages of the Regulator Rebellion. Nevertheless, both centers were portrayed by Tryon and the other North Carolina officials as a single, united group more interested in violence than in civil disobedience.

Carole Watterson Troxler's *Farming Dissenters: The Regulator Movement in Piedmont North Carolina* lists the names of 920 men she identified as having connections with the Regulator movement at some point between 1766 and 1771.[30] The fluid nature of the Regulator movement meant most participants came and went as interest and availability allowed. Most names appear only once, whether as signatories to petitions to the North Carolina colonial government; called out in Tryon's proclamations condemning the Regulators' actions; or in legal documents. But several Regulators' names appear repeatedly and in multiple capacities. Some were considered the primary instigators for the Regulator Rebellion by the North Carolina colonial government, others were larger landowners in Orange, Rowan, and Anson Counties who drew on their socioeconomic positions to support the Regulators' cause.

The Sandy Creek watershed laces through the acres of farmland southwest of Hillsborough, the county seat for Orange County since it was founded in 1754. Today, North Carolina Highway 62 follows the trail used by Native Americans and European settlers to move trade goods through the southern backcountry.[31] Markers along Highway 62 indicate the location of the Battle of Alamance, which brought the Regulator Rebellion to a close in 1771, as well as the home sites for Regulator leaders James Hunter, Herman Husband, and Redknap Howell.[32] Hunter's farm was some eight miles southwest of the Alamance battlefield.[33] He was a literate man who was active in local political affairs prior to the Regulator Rebellion and probably helped compose the four petitions submitted by the Regulators between 1768 and 1770, although he is not listed as a signatory on these petitions.[34] He did, however, sign the "Regulators' Advertisement No. 11," sent by eight of the Regulators to Governor Tryon in spring 1768.[35] The order book for the expedition sent to suppress the Regulator movement in spring 1771 noted that a contingent of the North Carolina colonial militia had "marched Five Miles to James Hunter's, the General of the Rebels . . . His dwelling House, Barn &c- though mean, burnt down."[36] Since Hunter was a prosperous farmer prior to the Regulator Rebellion, this description suggests he experienced a financial downturn during the final stages of the Regulator movement.

Herman Husband is the best-known colonist associated with the Regulator Rebellion and the one whose actions are the blurriest within the historical record. He was born to an Anglican family in Maryland and briefly joined a Presbyterian congregation before joining the Quaker church.[37] Husband first traveled to North Carolina in the 1750s and received approximately twenty land grants from the North Carolina colonial government between 1753 and 1762 along Sandy Creek, Abbot Creek, Muddy Creek, and the Alamance and Rocky Rivers.[38] These activities placed him in the planter class, albeit on a smaller scale than either the McCulloh or Granville families.[39] Husband was best known during the Regulator Rebellion for publishing pamphlets about the Regulators' plight, which drew attention to the wider movement in the other British colonies. He appears, however, to have seen his role in the Regulator movement as an auxiliary position rather than an active member. This perception is reinforced by Husband's decision to flee the region just before the Battle of Alamance on the grounds that his Quaker faith made it impossible for him to take part in a violent altercation. Husband continued to see himself as a political agitator long after the Regulator Rebellion and helped instigate the Whiskey Rebellion in western Pennsylvania in the 1790s.[40]

Redknap Howell's farm was about twenty miles south of the Alamance battlefield.[41] Like James Hunter, Howell's name does not appear on the Regulator petitions, but he did sign the "Regulators' Advertisement No. 11." Governor Tryon would later use a letter sent by Howell to Hunter as a pretext for ordering the militia expedition to Orange County in spring 1771.[42] Howell made other contributions to the Regulator movement. Arthur Palmer Hudson described him as a "person of spirit and energy, with a good education, [who] was probably the author" of at least four of the ballads connected with the Regulator movement.[43] Herman Husband's pamphlets publicized the Regulators' concerns in the other British colonies, but satirical ballads like Howell's were necessary recruiting tools in a society where literacy rates varied widely.

There was also a handful of larger planters whose names became associated with the Regulator movement. Thomas Person, who was elected to the General Assembly in 1769 and 1770, first went to North Carolina in the early 1760s as a surveyor for the Granville Grant.[44] Similar to James Hunter, Person preferred to serve as a guiding voice behind the scenes, and it is likely that his more-established financial position as a landowner with thousands of acres helped with these efforts. Person was not present at the Battle of Alamance, but his name was on the list of Regulators for whom Governor Tryon refused to consider pardons.[45] While Howell Lewis and

John Pryor are best described as Regulator sympathizers rather than active participants, Henry Eustace McCulloh commented that "the madness of the people must be great indeed, to trust such wretches as Herman Husband and Christopher Nation as their representatives but it is a comfort, that these violent mad fits seldom last long."[46] Finally, like Husband, three members of the Hamilton family—Ninion, Ninion Bell, and Matthew—were involved in land speculation and, like Redknap Howell, were active participants in the more-violent moments of the Regulator Rebellion.[47]

A group of North Carolina colonists formed the Sandy Creek Organization in August 1766 to "mutter and grumble under any abuses of power until such a noble spirit prevails in our posterity."[48] They acknowledged the eastern North Carolina colonists who had led the fight against the Stamp Act as their inspiration while offering a prophetic caution: "Those Sons of Liberty (who has just now redeemed us from tyranny) . . . would soon corrupt again and oppress if they were not called upon to give an account of their Stewardship." In time, the North Carolina assembly members would prove more interested in protecting their rights from parliamentary overreach than in investigating corruption at home. In 1766, however, the members of the Sandy Creek Organization were hopeful that they could bring about change in North Carolina. Their first move was to ask local officers and vestrymen to consider their concerns about the Orange County government. This request was immediately dismissed by Edmund Fanning, the county registrar and commissioner for the town of Hillsborough. At that time, Fanning was a relative newcomer in Orange County. A Yale graduate with connections to Governor Tryon, he was eager to rise in North Carolina society by any means possible. Redknap Howell later described Fanning's time in Orange County in a ballad noting, "When Fanning first to Orange came/He looked both pale and wan/. . . But by his civil robberies/He's laced his coat with gold."[49]

Two years later, a group of people who called themselves the Sandy Creek Association met on April 4, 1768. The minutes from this meeting suggest a movement in flux. The concerns raised by the original members had attracted interest beyond the Sandy Creek watershed, and there were also colonists from the Haw River region in attendance. Perhaps in recognition that they needed a more-encompassing name for themselves, they used the term "Regulators" to describe themselves and their intentions for the first time at this meeting.[50] It is also likely that the legal and extralegal centers for the Regulator movement emerged at this time. Members of the Sandy Creek Association had submitted requests to Edmund Fanning for "an Account [on] How the [tax] Money was applied" and to "Show us Law for the

Customary fees that have been taken for Deeds Indentures Admrs &c," and these requests would have come from the newly emerged legal center. Fanning dismissed these requests as well. Around this same time, a mare that belonged to an unnamed colonist was seized by Orange County Sheriff Tyree Harris in lieu of unpaid tax money. Here, the extralegal center for the Regulator movement stepped up. Harris was attacked by a group of Regulators in Hillsborough on April 8, and they repossessed the mare. Fanning, in turn, arrested Herman Husband and William Butler, another prominent Regulator, on April 30.[51] Their rescue on May 3 by a group of Regulators resulted in another ballad condemning "those murdering traitors/[who] went to oppose the honest men/That were called the Regulators."[52]

These actions laid the groundwork for the two centers of the Regulator movement and the North Carolina colonial government throughout the Regulator Rebellion, which would occur and recur in the coming years. By spring 1768, the Regulators' resistance efforts had been brought to the attention of colonial officials in New Bern. Governor Tryon issued two proclamations against the Regulators, one dated April 27 and the other May 17, 1768. Both described the Regulators as having "Confederated together to oppose the just Measures of Government," which, in turn, was deemed "Subversive of that Security Derived to every Individual from a Submission to Order and Good Government."[53] These statements touch on the core breaking point between the Regulators and Tryon. All parties involved agreed on the need for "Order and Good Government." However, the Regulators did not believe they had "Good Government," which, in their eyes, justified their actions.

For his part, Tryon took pains to announce he had consulted with his council and was now "Command[ing] all Officers Civil and Military to take all Lawful Means for Suppressing" the Regulators. Tryon also needed to affirm that he was following the letter of the law. William Smith emphasized Tryon's efforts to appeal to the Regulators, observing in his later history that "to countenance an Example of so much Submission, the Gov. enforced them with a Promise that he would consider Grievances, and encouraged their Hopes of Impunity." Furthermore, "the Gov's Measures began to spread a generous Tenor among [those] who had hitherto indulged in a criminal licentious."[54] It should be noted, however, that the historical record in North Carolina suggests this was an overly optimistic portrayal of Tryon's approach, as there is no evidence the governor introduced measures in the assembly to address the Regulators' concerns.

Spring and summer 1768 were active months for the Regulator movement and the North Carolina government. After Herman Husband and

William Butler were released from the Hillsborough jail on May 3, Governor Tryon called on the colony militia to provide additional protection for government officials in Orange County. Relatively few North Carolina colonists were willing to join the Regulators, but many sympathized with their cause. Tryon struggled to find men willing to join the expedition to Hillsborough, finally noting that "[m]ore than a fifth of [the resulting militia force] were commissioned officers including eight generals and seven colonels."[55] Tryon released his next proclamation concerning the Regulators on October 3, 1768; it explained that there were "divirs Dissolute Outragious and Disorderly Persons" who have "Committ[ed] many Acts of Violence contrary to Law."[56] This proclamation differentiated between the men instigating these actions and the colonists described as the "Misguided Multitudes." Thirteen named men—Peter Craven, Malachi Fyke, Solomon Gross, Matthew Hamilton, Ninion Hamilton, Ninion Bell Hamilton, Herman Husband, James Hunter, Isaac Jackson, William Moffat, Christopher Nation, John Oneal, and William Payne—would be subject to the full penalties under the law for their actions. Other colonists could receive pardons if they laid down their arms and "implored his Majesty's Gracious Clemency." This suggests that Tryon was willing to distinguish between the leaders of the Regulator movement and ordinary North Carolina colonists but saw no differences between the leaders even as two centers, one legal, one extralegal, were increasingly emerging from the movement.

The following day, October 4, 1768, saw the submission of the first of four Regulator petitions. This one was signed by men from Orange and Rowan Counties and addressed imbalances in the North Carolina tax code and concerns over the lack of currency in the colony. Early modern petitions were required to follow a carefully structured narrative intended to demonstrate the petitioners' deference to authority and desire to draw their leaders' attention to a problematic situation. Traditionally, petitioners did not advocate any particular solution. The opening paragraph stated that the document was a "humble petition" from "true and lawful subjects of His Majesty King George, the Third."[57] The petition was signed by twenty-nine men, none of whose names appeared in Tryon's April 27, May 17, or October 3 proclamations, which, again, suggests the growing presence of two centers within the Regulator movement, though it is possible the petition writers were advised by James Hunter. The petitioners were writing to document that they were being "Continually Sqez'd and pressed" by government officials in regard to both "their fees" and "the laying on of Taxes," and with "Iniquitious Appropriations and Wrong Applications." They believed a petition to the governor would resolve the issue "through his Spirited Behavior and upright Conduct in Conjunction with the Honourable Judges." The petitioners suspected that some "Publick Officers" were corrupt, but they believed in Governor Tryon, the "Honourable Justices," and the overall North Carolina political and judicial system. Their statement simultaneously flattered Tryon and the justices but also challenged them to address the petitioners' concerns.

A consistent belief in social and political contracts appears throughout the written documents from members of the Regulator movement. They hoped to improve North Carolina society through their actions, but they also recognized that this was a reciprocal relationship. With the issue of "Iniquitious Appropriations" addressed, the petition reminded the governor of the challenges posed by the lack of legitimate currency in the colony. Taxes were required to be paid in cash, but the petitioners argued that "money is very scarce ... [and we must] Purchase it at ten times its Value." Despite these challenges, the petitioners acknowledged that "the Contingencies of Government Must be Paid, and which we are Willing to Pay." If the governor and other officials responded to their requests, "Labour and Industry [would] prevail over Murmuring Discontents," which could only help the financial state of the colony. Demonstrating their familiarity with the political process, they detailed plans to submit one copy of the petition to the "Assembly by our own Representatives" and a second copy to the assembly by another person who is not named in the petition.

The men who wrote the October 4 petition interspersed their concerns with observations detailing the specific challenges facing ordinary colonists in North Carolina. Commenting on their efforts to pay the common tax, the petition notes that "yea their Wives Petticoats [must be] taken and sold to Defray ... in Pity to your Poor Petitioners do not let it Stand any Longer to Drink up the Blood and Vitals of the Poor Distressed." This vivid image was an unusual reference to the Regulators' wives and daughters, who were rarely mentioned in the political activities of their husbands, brothers, and sons. Marjoleine Kars theorizes that "they played roles now invisible to us: encouraging or dissuading their men from action, participating in crowds that pressured officials at local courthouses and in Hillsborough, taking over the management of their farms ... and nursing the wounded after the Battle of Alamance."[58] A later passage described the dangers posed to colonists who lose their "only Horse to raise Bread or Only Cow to give Milk." Dire poverty, if not outright starvation, awaited such "helpless families," and surely the worthy gentleman of the colony would not want such a fate for their "poor petitioners." This writing undoubtedly reflected the voices of the Regulators and their families, but it also served an additional purpose. David Zaret notes that petitions needed to portray "grievance as an apolitical conveyance of information principally by emphasizing *deferential, juridical*, and *spontaneous* attributes of the grievance."[59] Petitions should not appear overly premeditated, and these passages suggest that the Regulators were recording their laments as they were spoken when the petition was composed. The phrases, as richly colloquial as the cadences of a Shakespearean play or a psalm in the King James Bible, tapped equally into a common English literary heritage.

Spring and summer 1768 also saw the composition of an undated letter, known as the "Regulators' Advertisement No. 11," to Governor Tryon from eight Regulator leaders who included James Hunter and Redknap Howell. This second document was intended to provide Tryon with a record of recent events in Orange County. Like the petition, the "Regulators' Advertisement" is deferential to Tryon's office as governor. Nevertheless, its authors are confident that once Tryon read their narrative, he would instantly agree that the recent "disturbances had their source in the corrupt and arbitrary Practices of nefarious & designing men who . . . have been using every artifice [and] practicing every Fraud to squeeze and extort from the wretched Poor."[60] The problem was not the actions of the Regulators but rather the actions of county government officials like Edmund Fanning and Tyree Harris that were forcing otherwise law-abiding men into violence. The "Regulators' Advertisement No. 11" was duly delivered to Tryon, but it is unclear if he read it.

A second Regulator petition was submitted to Tryon and the assembly on November 11. Its authors identified themselves as "the Inhabitants of Orange County Bordering on Cumberland as likewise the Inhabitants of Cumberland Bordering on Orange."[61] It was signed by 144 men, none of whom was named in Tryon's earlier proclamations and none of whom had signed the petition from the previous month. They asked Tryon, the council members, and the assembly to consider creating a new county "where Johnson and Orange meet Cumberland," because they "live[d] at so great a Distance from the Several Courthouses" that it was difficult for them to serve on juries, vote in elections, and attend general musters. They suggested boundaries for the new county and noted that there was a precedent for their request, as other new counties had been created for the same reason. They likely used formal language in their petition in order to legitimize their concerns, especially since Tryon and the assembly had not responded to their previous petition.

There is no record of a response to either of these first two petitions from Tryon or the General Assembly, but the issues raised by the hundreds

The Regulator Rebellion Begins

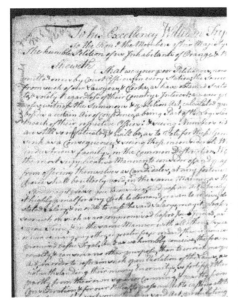

"The Humble Petition of Us the Inhabitants of Orange County Bordering on Cumberland," November 11, 1768, from North Carolina General Assembly Session Records, Colonial (Upper and Lower Houses), Box 3, November–December 1768, Lower House Papers Petitions Rejected or Not Acted on, Bills Folder, State Archives of North Carolina. (*Author's Photograph*)

of men identifying as Regulators were beginning to gain traction in North Carolina. The General Assembly passed a law in late fall 1768 allowing colonists to pay some of their taxes with "certain commodities" rather than currency. When Tryon called for an election for the assembly's lower house in fall 1769, Regulators Herman Husband, Christopher Nation, Thomas Person, and John Pryor—the first two of whom were listed in Tryon's proclamations from spring 1768—all successfully ran for office. With forty-five of the seventy-seven seats occupied by new members, colonists across western North Carolina hoped for new laws and better regulation of the colony's government and tax collection. This time, they could be certain that their next plea for help could be brought to the floor of the assembly, so they began work on crafting the petition, which was presented by Husband on October 27, 1769, although his name was not among the signatories.

The first Regulator petition in October 1768 had focused on the difficulty of paying taxes in a colony with little currency, while the second had exposed the challenges caused by distant county seats, but both petitions took pains to demonstrate that these concerns were little more than suggestions. The third petition, by contrast, was a very different document. Yes, the opening passages once again described the document as a "humble petition" from "true and faithful subjects to his Majesty King George," but this was the only linguistic similarity to be found among them.[62] With one exception, the third petition was carefully divided into separate paragraphs, each containing an individual issue or suggestion. The writing was crisp and clear, with little of the colorful language that had peppered the first petition. Most strikingly, the document swung back and forth between a comprehensive list of the petitioners' concerns and a list of suggestions for alleviating those concerns. Finally, the petition was signed by forty-nine men, none of whose names can be found on either of the first two petitions or on Tryon's many proclamations condemning the leaders of the Regulator Rebellion, though it is possible the terse professionalism of the third petition was the result of suggestions from James Hunter and Christopher Nation.

The third petition opened by addressing the long-standing issue of payment for nonsalaried colony officials. North Carolina allowed colony officials to keep a percentage of the fees they collected to supplement their salaries, and colonists deplored the "heavy Exertions, Oppressions, & Enormitys committed on [them] by Court Officers in every Station." The lawyers and clerks who charged the fees were free to run for the House of Representatives and, once elected, had no interest in curbing the resulting abuses. The petitioners presented a solution: they asked the governor and the assembly to consider an Act "to prevent . . . all & every Lawyer & Clerk whatsoever from offering themselves as Candidates at any future Election of Delegates," which would prevent them from creating legislation designed to benefit only themselves.

The following paragraph proposed an additional law "to allow Clerks of the Courts, Crown, &c certain yearly stated salarys, instead if perquisite," which would provide them with enough pay to not need the supplemental income provided by the percentage of the fees. This proposal aligns with the Regulators' assertion that they were not opposed to paying taxes and fees; they only wanted them to be better regulated. The petitioners not only stated that the various fees placed an economic burden on their families, but they also emphasized that any government official who supported unregulated fees was "blind to & solely Regardless of their Countrys Interests," once again demonstrating that they sought justice for the whole colony, not just themselves.

The third paragraph addressed a multitude of concerns connected to tensions between colonists in the eastern and western parts of North Carolina. The petitioners asked the governor to repeal "the Act prohibiting Dissenting Ministers from Marrying according to . . . the ceremonys of their Prospective Churches," a direct reference to Tryon's efforts to have the Anglican Church recognized as the official church for the colony. Most of the western colonists were members of the dissenting faiths, and they wanted all marriages conducted in those churches to be recognized. Once again, the petition relied on precedent for justifying its requests, as it reminded the governor that this is a "priviledge these stand enstituted to, by the Act of Toleration . . . a priviledge granted even to the very Catholics in Ireland." In this case, at least, the law was on the side of the Regulators.

The third paragraph included some additional requests, perhaps since the petitioners hoped to preserve the momentum gained by demonstrating that their petition was supported by parliamentary decree. They asked for an Act to "divide the several Counties within this Province into Proper districts," a topic also addressed in the second Regulator petition. Furthermore, they recommended that each district have a collector designated for the "several Taxes laid, & to be laid, by Law, who shall be accountable" and "effectually prevent the Sherrifs from robbing, & plundering the Country." The Regulators sought a tax structure that better reflected the economic standing of the individual colonists. Colonists in eastern North Carolina, they argued, often had "Estates consist[ing] chiefly in slaves," but "to us in the frontier, where very few are possessed of slaves," paying the same taxes "is with Submission, very grievous, & Oppressive." Frontier colonists often owned acreages similar to their eastern counterparts, but without enslaved people that land was far less economically productive, a point that would remain an issue in the South well into the nineteenth century.

The last point in the third paragraph asked that "Notes on the imperishable Commoditys, of the produce of the Province [be] lawful Tender . . . throughout the Province," and this topic was further elaborated on in the next paragraph. Once again, finding enough hard currency to pay colony and imperial taxes was an ongoing problem throughout British North America. Would not, implored the petition, "pot Ash be a fine Article, to Answer the British Markets?"[63] North Carolina colonists lived "in a Country [so] abounding with wood" that their "very ashes [are] now thrown away." Allowing them to use potash to pay their taxes would solve the tax problem and "render Voyages to Liga, Narva, & Dantzrick; from Great Britain, for that useful commodity needless." Once again, the Regulators who composed these petitions had conducted research to justify their requests. This point also highlighted their larger argument that the issue was not that they were unwilling to pay taxes but rather that those taxes and fees needed to be regulated and payable with goods available to them in the North Carolina backcountry.

Finally, the October 27, 1769, petition asked to have the "yeas, & Nays, inserted in the Journal of your House" and transmitted to the various counties so "we may have an Opportunity, to Distinguish our friends from our foes among you, & to Act accordingly," a suggestion demonstrating the Regulators' desire to actively monitor the votes conducted in the assembly so they could respond in future elections. If the assembly would grant them such "Just, wholesome, & necessary Laws," they would "heal the bleeding Wounds of the Province" and "cause joy, Gladness, Glee, & prosperity. diffusely to spread themselves thro every Quarter." And, in turn, suggested the third petition, if the assembly supported all of the residents of North Carolina, so would the residents of North Carolina, including the Regulators, support the assembly. This conclusion, however inadvertently, echoes a point made by Martin Howard in his *Letter from a Gentleman at Halifax* pamphlet: "the freedom and happiness of every British subject depends not on his share in elections but upon the sense and virtue of the British Parliament, and these depend reciprocally upon the sense and virtue of the whole nation."[64] These arguments demonstrate that Howard and the Regulators alike believed in the power and protections of the British political system, though the Regulators also took pains to issue warnings to political leaders who betrayed such contracts.

The phrasing and the organization used in this third petition present modern historians with a number of questions. Traditional protocol called for petitioners to portray their grievances "as a neutral conveyance of information that eschew[ed] prescribing solutions."[65] The Regulators' earlier petitions had followed the prescribed format, so this third petition was a deliberate, premeditated break with protocol. The hope, most likely, was that the five Regulators now serving in the assembly would be able to contextualize these suggestions with their own testimony. "[T]he Inhabitants of Granville County" would later submit a petition to the General Assembly on December 10, 1770, noting that "it is not the County of Orange alone that have Great and Just Cause to Complain of those Grieviances but Every County in the Said Province."[66] Support for the Regulator movement's concerns appears to have been on the rise in North Carolina. They also may have believed they had nothing to lose. Even though five men who openly presented themselves as supporting the Regulator movement were now serving in the assembly, the legislature had not addressed their core concerns for several years. Perhaps the petitioners believed that breaking the unwritten rules for submitting petitions with a collection of "Just, wholesome, & necessary" laws was the only way to attract the attention of the remaining assembly members.

Unfortunately for the Regulators, the October 27, 1769, petition hit a roadblock forged by the growing imperial crisis. The Townshend duties on a variety of imported goods were being imposed throughout British North

America, and the first wave of British soldiers had arrived in Boston.[67] Uneasily remembering the protests against the Stamp Act, Tryon dissolved the assembly before its members were able to address all the issues before them, much as he had dissolved the assembly in 1765 so its members would be unable to choose delegates for the Stamp Act Congress in New York. Other British colonial legislatures were introducing debates suggesting boycotting the goods taxed by the Townshend Acts, and Tryon feared that his assembly would join these efforts.[68] The dissolution of the North Carolina legislature means historians will never know how the remaining seventy-two members would have responded to this petition. It does, however, speak to the increasingly intertwined nature of the Regulator Rebellion and the imperial crisis in the late 1760s. Tryon faced two primary challenges in 1769: first, his assembly's impatience with rising parliamentary oversight and, second, the Regulators' impatience with how their colony was run. The ability to present the third Regulator petition before the assembly in fall 1769 could have defused growing internal tensions in North Carolina. Instead, Tryon chose to dissolve the assembly, knowing this would deprive its members of a legitimate forum for discussing their concerns about parliamentary taxation. Challenges from restive (and well-connected) assembly members were a greater threat to Tryon's authority than the Regulators. This belief, coupled with most assembly members' lack of interest in addressing the Regulators' concerns, would inform his actions for the next two years.

Herman Husband, Howell Lewis, Christopher Nation, Thomas Person, and John Pryor were all reelected to the assembly in March 1770. Once again, Tryon refused to call the assembly to order, so there were no opportunities for the Regulators to present a petition directly to the legislature. By that time, they had been actively pursuing changes in North Carolina's political and legal systems for three years. They had submitted petitions, there had been court trials, and there had been violent exchanges between individual Regulators and local government officials. Tryon had called out colonial militias against the Regulators and had issued a series of proclamations condemning their actions. Tempers were rising on all sides and would explode at a meeting of the Hillsborough District Superior Court in September 1770. First, though, the publication of Husband's pamphlet *An Impartial Relation of the First Rise and Cause of the Recent Differences in Publick Affairs* added another document to the Regulator Rebellion's paper trail.

Pamphlet writing played a central role in the imperial crisis of the 1760s and the Revolutionary movement that emerged from it in the early 1770s.

Bernard Bailyn notes "the pamphlet had peculiar virtues as a medium of communication ... highly flexible, easy to manufacture, and cheap," while providing more page space than was available in broadsheets and newspaper essays.[69] The pamphlets published, respectively, by Stephen Hopkins and Martin Howard in 1764 and 1765 in response to the Sugar and Stamp Acts are typical examples of the genre.[70] By contrast, both Husband's *An Impartial Relation* and his later 1771 pamphlet, *A Fan for Fanning, and A Touchstone to Tryon*, read more as documentary record of the Regulator Rebellion than full-throated defense of the movement's causes and concerns.[71] Husband further observes that "the task of an Historian is a difficult one" owing to "an aptness in Men to inform us, not of the facts as they are in themselves ... but of the impressions made upon their minds."[72] The self-presentation of Husband as disinterested historian was intended to reassure readers that his pamphlets were "impartial relations" of the Regulator Rebellion. It also offers a read on Husband himself. The publication of *An Impartial Relation* a year before the Regulator Rebellion ended at the Battle of Alamance suggests Husband had always seen himself as historian/journalist rather than participant, which may, in turn, explain why he appears as a rather tenuous figure within the Regulator movement.[73]

Husband's portrayal of the Regulator Rebellion as a historical event in motion makes his pamphlets a very different source base from the ballads, court trials, letters, petitions, and proclamations that make up the rest of the documentary record for the Regulator Rebellion. Nevertheless, a sense of taking part in a larger event infused the Regulator Rebellion in its final years. The original Sandy Creek Association began in 1766 as an organization with little consequence beyond the forests and creeks of North Carolina. By now, however, the full-blown rebellion was sweeping onto the stage of the imperial crisis as its participants reached outward for assistance and guidance alike.

Chapter Six

The Regulator Rebellion and the Imperial Crisis

THE FINAL COLLAPSE OF THE REGULATOR REBELLION in 1771 spiraled outward from the Hillsborough District Superior Court Riots in September 1770. The Regulators' struggle to have Edmund Fanning tried on extortion charges in 1769 and the ongoing testing of their relationship with the North Carolina judiciary, coupled with the use of ever-more-draconian measures by Governor William Tryon and the General Assembly, suggests both sides were experimenting with different approaches. The legal and extralegal centers of the Regulator movement were active in this period, though the latter was growing increasingly dominant. Tryon remained suspended between the Regulator Rebellion and the imperial crisis. This period also saw the rise of other players in the North Carolina colonial orbit, some of whom would become advocates for independence in the mid-1770s.

With the exception of the universal lack of currency in the British North American colonies, the Regulators' concerns were rooted in colonial North Carolina's lopsided political system. Property-owning Regulators could elect representatives to the General Assembly and hold political office, but they were often outvoted by their wealthy, slave-owning counterparts from eastern North Carolina.[1] These frustrations accelerated after the end of the French and Indian War in 1763 when the sons and nephews of wealthy eastern families moved to the Piedmont region in the mid-1760s to engage in land speculation, open businesses, and establish new societal structures, which, in turn, facilitated their rising political, legal, and economic authority in Orange, Rowan, and Anson Counties.

The men appointed by the British Crown to serve as North Carolina's governors came, like all royal appointees, from a small pool of well-connected families in Britain and the British colonies. Tryon, who was North Carolina's governor between 1765 and 1771, received his initial posting as the colony's lieutenant governor through his wife's family connections to Wills Hill, the Earl of Hillsborough.[2] Tryon, a career military officer and politician, was eager to establish himself in his new home, but his early months in the colony were racked with uncertainty. His appointment as lieutenant governor came with the promise that the current governor, Arthur Dobbs, was on the verge of retirement, but Dobbs met Tryon's arrival in North Carolina in 1764 with the announcement that he planned to remain in office for at least another year. Dobbs's abrupt death from a seizure in spring 1765 meant Tryon could finally ascend to the governor's office but, by that time, his authority was being tested by the Stamp Act crisis. These challenges accelerated Tryon's desire to build connections with the equally ambitious North Carolina colonists whom he saw as his most likely allies in the colony. Some of these families would remain loyal to the Crown during the Revolution, but others joined the rising Patriot cause and so created a new ruling class in North Carolina.

Samuel and Elizabeth Henderson moved to North Carolina from Virginia in the early 1740s and settled in Granville County. Similar to other wealthy families in this period, the Hendersons engaged in land speculation on a massive scale.[3] Their son, Richard Henderson, served as his father's deputy when Samuel Henderson became the Granville County sheriff. Richard Henderson continued his legal training in the 1750s, when he studied law with his mother's cousin, John Williams, before moving to Hillsborough, where they set up a legal practice in the early 1760s.[4] Governor Tryon saw Richard Henderson as an ally worth cultivating and recommended him for an appointment as one of North Carolina's two associate justices for the Superior Court in 1768.[5] During the American Revolution, Henderson fought in the Granville County regiment, one of the North Carolina state militias, and later served in the North Carolina state legislature.

The McCulloh family came to North Carolina in 1739, when London merchant Henry McCulloh received grants for over a million acres of land in exchange for rebuilding North Carolina's failing quitrent system.[6] Charles Sellers notes that "this first grant was typical of the McCulloh land-grabbing procedure. The patents ... were made out to 'divers persons, then and now unknown' but were actually for the benefit of McCulloh."[7] He remained loyal to Britain during the Revolution, and McCulloh family lands were confiscated by the North Carolina state legislature during the war.[8] His son, Henry Eustace McCulloh, traveled to North Carolina with his family in 1739 before returning to London in 1747 and studying law at Middle Temple, one of the four Inns of Court.[9] After Henry Eustace McCulloh returned to North Carolina in 1761, he was a land agent for his father. Governor Tryon appointed the younger McCulloh as North Carolina's agent in 1767, which sent him back to London.[10] By that time, McCulloh had also befriended Edmund Fanning, who, with Tryon, were the men most hated by the Regulators.

Edmund Fanning came from a Long Island family wealthy enough to send him to Yale and to Harvard for his legal training. In 1760, Fanning moved to North Carolina, where he was public registrar for Orange County, represented Orange County in the North Carolina Assembly, and joined the local militia, becoming a colonel in 1767. William Powell notes that "to his equals (or his 'betters') Fanning was kind, hospitable and considerate" but "to his inferiors, and he regarded most of the residents of Hillsborough and the surrounding area in that category, he was cruel and domineering."[11] Fanning's actions soon caught the eye of the newly arrived Governor Tryon. When Associate Justice Maurice Moore launched a campaign against the Stamp Act in 1765, Tryon retaliated by replacing Moore with Fanning for the next two years. This pattern of patronage between Tryon and Fanning set in the 1760s continued for the next few decades.[12]

The early stages of the Regulator Rebellion had consisted largely of confrontations between Fanning and the extralegal center of the Regulator movement. Fanning refused to meet with the Sandy Creek Association to discuss its concerns in 1766 and 1767. He had Herman Husband and William Butler arrested on April 30, 1768, for "being guilty of Traterously and feloniously Conspiring with others in stirring up an Insurrection" and encouraging Orange County colonists to turn from "their Natural Obediences to our said Lord the King and Excite them to act in open Rebellion to his Government & Laws."[13] The Regulators' march on Hillsborough on May 3 was celebrated in one of Redknap Howell's satirical ballads, which included the line, "To see Ned Fanning wade Eno [river]/Brave boys you'll all admire."[14] A series of letters between Fanning and various members of North Carolina's colonial government document his rising outrage as the Regulators, frustrated by Fanning's refusal to respond to their concerns, staged increasingly violent demonstrations against him in 1768.[15]

These demonstrations were organized by the extralegal center of the Regulator movement, but there is also evidence that the legal center was equally active during this period. The records for the March 1769 session of the Hillsborough District Superior Court include an extortion charge brought against Edmund Fanning in his capacity as the public registrar in Orange County. At that time, Herman Husband, Christopher Nation, Thomas Person, and John Pryor were all newly elected members of the General Assembly. The first two Regulator petitions had been submitted to Governor Tryon, along with the "Regulators' Advertisement 11." Tryon had sent a letter on June 21, 1768, to the "Inhabitants on the South Side Haw River in Orange County" that acknowledged he had "received by the Hands of Mess.[rs] Hunter and Howell a Petition and other Papers." After reading through their concerns, Tryon was ready to have "every Officer who has been guilty of Extortion or illegal Practices" prosecuted in court.[16] The next step for the Regulators was to bring the relevant accusations to court.

The issue for many of the Regulators was not that they were destitute but that managing land in North Carolina was nearly impossible. The "land-grabbing practices" of wealthy families like the McCullohs had been in place since the 1720s.[17] The creation of the Granville District in 1744 had complicated matters further by opening up thousands more acres of poorly managed land in the North Carolina interior.[18] Some colonists already settled in the Granville District hoped that residence would be enough to claim ownership to the lands they were already farming, while others sought formal grants from Lord Granville's agents.[19] Regulators like Herman Husband, Thomas Person, and the Hamiltons were also involved in land speculation, albeit on a far smaller scale than the McCulloh or Henderson families. These activities brought them in direct contact with the iniquities of North Carolina's political and legal systems. Attorneys, registrars, and clerks were allowed to collect a percentage-based fee for their services, which included notarizing land sales, collecting taxes, and processing wills.[20] Many of the Regulators believed that Edmund Fanning, like other county registrars in North Carolina, was abusing his position by elevating the fees he collected on land sales between Orange County residents. Now they needed to find colonists willing to accuse Fanning of charging extortionate fees on a recent land transaction in Orange County in court.

Adam Moser and Henry Bray were not among the hundreds of men who signed the Regulators' four petitions. They also do not appear in Tryon's many proclamations condemning the extralegal members of the Regulator movement. The absence of Bray's and Moser's names in the other

Regulator documents suggests that, like Howell Lewis and John Pryor, they were more fellow travelers than active participants in the Regulator movement. Moreover, Bray's land adjoined land belonging to Joseph Brantley, who, along with several other members of his family, had signed the Regulator petition submitted November 11, 1768.[21] On October 9, 1769, Herman Husband sold Bray 480 acres he had received as a grant from the Granville District.[22] The frequent appearance of Bray's name as a witness to land sales between men who are identifiable as Regulators suggests a scenario in which Bray noticed Fanning taking higher and higher percentages of transactions and brought his concerns to the Regulator leaders. Braced by Tryon's promise to prosecute "Extortion or Illegal Practices," the Regulators had reason to hope a court case based on a recent land sale between Bray and Moser would result in charges against Fanning.

The Edmund Fanning extortion trial remains one of the most fascinating and puzzling episodes to emerge from the Regulator Rebellion. Fanning was charged with "demand[ing] receiv[ing], and have[ing] of one Adam Moser the sum of six shillings proclamation Money for and as a fee for Registering a Deed from one Henry Bray and Sarah his wife to the said Moser for Two Hundred Acres of Land lying in Orange County" in the Hillsborough District Superior Court on March 22, 1769.[23] There are no surviving documents from the trial, but the record book notes that Fanning received a juried trial.[24] The jury's verdict stated that Fanning had "Unlawfully Unjustly and Extorsively" demanded six shillings from Moser when "in Truth and in Fact there was no such Fee due to the said Edmund Fanning." The members of the jury plainly agreed that Fanning had abused his office by demanding six shillings from Moser as payment for registering the land purchase. Fanning's conviction however, is not in the record book where the other convictions from that day are listed. Neither is the punishment that was assigned to Fanning.

William Lawrence Saunders noted in 1886 that popular tradition holds that Fanning was "fined [only] a penny and costs" by Associate Justice Richard Henderson, but Saunders offers no evidence for this tradition.[25] One possibility is that Henderson was wary of issuing a harsh sentence to a man whose allies included Governor Tryon and the powerful McCulloh family. Fining Fanning only a penny and costs may have been intended as a deliberate insult to the Regulators, who probably helped bring the original charges against Fanning. Both centers of the Regulator movement would have been equally frustrated by this failure to bring about any form of lasting change in the North Carolina legal system. The third Regulator petition, composed six months later, explicitly recommended that North

Carolina create a law allowing "Clerks of the Courts, Crown, &c certain yearly stated salaries, instead of perquisite" as a way of addressing these challenges.[26] Unfortunately, owing to his concerns about the Townshend Acts, Tryon would refuse to call the assembly to order in fall 1769, the third petition was never heard, and the matter continued unaddressed for another year.

The Fanning trial also gave birth to a series of letters that encapsulate the Regulators' frustrations with North Carolina's colonial elite. Fanning appears to have been dismissed from the Hillsborough District Superior Court with little more than a slap on the wrist. Nevertheless, the jury's conviction was still rankling him months later. Henry Eustace McCulloh had been in place in London as North Carolina's colonial agent since 1767. Fanning wrote McCulloh in spring 1769 to ask for legal assistance. McCulloh gleefully responded in 1770 with a letter announcing that "no Man's opinion can have equal weight & authority [to] that of the Attorney-General of England." [27] William de Grey, first Baron Walsingham, became Britain's attorney general in 1766.[28] McCulloh further added that he had obtained "J.M's father Opinion, which I think sufficiently strong," which appears to be a reference to John Morgan, a barrister at the Inner Temple at that time.[29]

De Grey sent a letter to John Morgan on April 22, 1769, documenting that Fanning had been told "he was legally entitled to 6s and odd Pence at least for every Deed whatever" and that Thomas McGuire, North Carolina's attorney general had told de Grey "that all Registrars were entitled to demand Fees to the amount of 8 shillings and 7 pence on any Deed."[30] Based on this information, de Grey concluded that "Mr. Fanning did actually intend to take less than he conceived himself Entitled to . . . and [since] he may be said to have acted with the approbation of the Justices, &c therefore tis Incumbent on the Judges before whom this matter is depending to give all the relief they can to Mr. F." Morgan finished assembling his findings on the matter on August 4, 1770, and it is likely this was the document that accompanied the letter written to Edmund Fanning by Henry McCulloh that same day.

John Morgan opened by quoting from the 1748 Act of Assembly "passed in the province of No. Carolina for regulating the several Officer's Fees within that province."[31] Morgan noted, "[It is] lawful for the several Officers within this province to take & receive . . . such Fees only as appointed by this Act. If any Officer shall Demand, Extort, Exact, or receive any other or larger Fees than what is particularly mentioned in this Act . . . such Officer shall for every such Offense . . . forfeit the Sum of Five pounds." Morgan and de Grey's goal was to assess whether Fanning was actually guilty of using his office to extort from the residents of Orange County. Only lawful fees could be collected and that if a government official collected more than the legal fees, he should be charged five pounds. If Fanning was guilty, then the court that convicted him had been downright negligent since they apparently only charged him a single penny and his legal costs. However, since de Grey's research had indicated Fanning was entitled to either "6s and odd Pence" or "8 shillings and 7 pence" per transaction, both he and Morgan concluded that Fanning had been wrongly charged and that he should move for a new trial as soon as possible, though there is no evidence this ever occurred.

Henry McCulloh, provincial agent for North Carolina in London and friend to Fanning, drew on his personal and professional connections to obtain legal counsel for Fanning from de Grey and John Morgan. These connections do not, however, entirely explain why the "Attorney-General of England" and a barrister at one of the Inns of Court became involved with an affair from one of the poorest British colonies in North America in which the amount of money declared extortionary was relatively small. De Grey and Morgan appear to have concluded that the British Empire benefitted from a legal outcome that supported the North Carolina colonial government as a political institution within that larger empire. For the past century, British monarchs, Parliament, and colonial officials had labored to create the infrastructure necessary for running their expanding empire. The Lords of Trade and Plantations created by King William III in 1696 had been designed to assess colonial legislation, nominate governors and other high officials for royal colonies, and correspond with those same governors about their individual colonies.[32] The imperial crisis meant these systems were increasingly being tested by Britain's colonists, and, as a result, channeling the support of men like de Grey and Morgan was mutually expedient.

This system obviously benefitted the British government and its expanding empire, but its channels could also be used for the political and economic benefit of individual colonists. The colonies needed agents like Henry McCulloh to represent their interests in London, but wealthy families then drew on the connections gained by their sons' labors.[33] The colonists who took part in the Regulator movement were frustrated by Edmund Fanning's political connections to Governor Tryon and the wealthy McCulloh family that fueled Fanning's near exoneration during his trial.[34] Yet the documentary record also demonstrates that many, if not all, of the Regulators understood the patronage system underpinning their own political world. They might lack the connections needed to appeal to officials in London, but they had the right to claim a reciprocal relationship with individual members of their local government. Petition writing, the conduit used most often by ordinary British subjects, was a hallowed tradition, but it also came with no guarantees of success.

The first three Regulator petitions were directed to "His Excellency William Tryon Captain General Governor and Commander in Chief" and "the Honourable members of his Majestys Council and Gentlemen of the Assembly."[35] The intent was for them to be presented to the North Carolina legislature and discussed by that body. By 1770, however, Tryon had repeatedly dismissed the assembly as a means of avoiding discussing the Townshend Acts, and none of these first three petitions had ever made it to the floor for discussion. The Regulator Rebellion was not a response to the imperial crisis, but, once again, the imperial crisis was inadvertently helping to fuel the Regulator Rebellion.

It was clear that petitioning Tryon and the assembly was a dead end. Consequently, the fourth, and final, Regulator petition was addressed to Chief Justice Martin Howard and Associate Justices Josiah Henderson and Maurice Moore.[36] This new petition identified the Regulators' concerns and explained their actions, but unlike the October 27, 1769, petition, it did not suggest enacting specific laws. Instead, it was a direct appeal to Howard. The Regulators believed he would "wish us all the success imaginable and heartily concur with us" if he knew "what we did was from motives to promote Justice detect Extortion &c: for the publick good." Furthermore, the petitioners assured Howard that their actions had always been conducted within the confines of the law and, if anything, the "only crime with which they can charge us is vertue in the very highest degree." The Regulators had seen corruption and ill government and had struggled to address those wrongs. A shared belief in social contracts between the governed and those who govern runs through the writings of both Howard and the Regulators. They may also have been aware of Howard's support for the older agricultural economies in the face of challenges from the new mercantile elite in Rhode Island and seen him as a possible champion for their concerns.

More importantly, unlike Richard Henderson and Maurice Moore, Martin Howard was an outsider in North Carolina. His nomination and eventual appointment as chief justice both took place in London. Like Howard, Henderson and Moore received their appointments from King George III, but they were both nominated by Tryon, who had a long history of presenting the sons and nephews of his political allies for government positions. Howard, by contrast, had no reason, political or economic, to preserve the endemic corruption in North Carolina's political and legal systems. One of Henderson's descendants would complain in the early twentieth century that "the Regulators had [long] been ingratiated by Chief Justice Howard's leniency and considerate attitude."[37] This sense of respect for Howard but not Henderson or Moore would be further reinforced by an episode in spring 1771, some two months before the Battle of Alamance.

Orange County was the acknowledged epicenter for most Regulator activities, but many Regulators also lived in neighboring Rowan and Anson Counties. The Salisbury court in Rowan County was scheduled to hold its session in March 1771, but it was canceled by Governor Tryon, who feared more riots like the one that had disrupted the court session in Hillsborough six months earlier. Rowan County residents John Frohock and Alexander Martin wrote Tryon on March 18 to voice their concerns about the canceled court session and to document their conversations with the Regulators encamped near Salisbury prior to the start of the court session.

The Frohock family was well established in Rowan County. John Frohock was the county clerk, while family members Thomas Frohock and William Frohock served, respectively, as the clerk for the Salisbury Superior Court and the Rowan County sheriff. One of the Regulator ballads opened with the line "Says Frohock to Fanning" and closed by noting that "now we've got rich and it's very well known / That we'll do well enough if they'll let us alone."[38] This reputation would seem to suggest a less-than-cordial welcome for Frohock and Martin in the Regulators' camp. Nevertheless, the men were civilly received, and the Regulators were willing to have their voices recorded. They had come "with no Intention to disturb the Court or to injure the Person or property of any one, only to petition the Court for a redress of Grievances against Officers taking exorbitant Fees."[39] After Frohock and Martin told the Regulators that "the court session had been canceled because the Judges did not think it prudent to hold one at Salisbury under the direction of Whips and Clubs," they responded that "there would have been no danger for the Chief Justice to have held a Court, but as to the Associates they were silent."

This statement reinforces the decision to target the fourth Regulator petition toward Chief Justice Howard. Don Higginbotham and William Price note that "there is actually considerable evidence that [Howard] was respected by various—even conflicting—elements in the colony," which clearly included the Regulators.[40] The abuses perpetrated by North Carolina's system of tax collection had long been overlooked by the assembly, and both Moore and Henderson had family members serving in that same assembly. There may also have been another element present during these conversations. John Murrin has documented growing tensions between eighteenth-century Anglo-American justices and attorneys.[41] Local justices of the peace generally gained their positions through informal apprenticeships rather than any legal formal training, while attorneys were increasingly expected to attend university before practicing law. The Regulators' primary courtroom attacks on legal officials were generally on university-trained attorneys like Edmund Fanning. Howard, ever the traditionalist, probably presented himself in North Carolina as the quintessential English justice of the peace, closely embedded within his local community and committed to the welfare of that same community. This often-overlooked exchange between John Frohock, Alexander Martin, and the Regulators speaks to the complexities and nuances that infused the Regulator Rebellion and the wider Anglo-American world in the final decades of the eighteenth century. The Regulator Rebellion was the product of endemic corruption in colonial North Carolina, but it also reflected the tensions that emerged alongside the Industrial Revolution and the resulting disruptions to social, political, and economic systems.

The two centers of the Regulator movement, one legal, the other extralegal, largely functioned as parallel entities in the early years of the Regulator Rebellion. The hundreds of men who signed the Regulator petitions between 1768 and 1770 hoped to bring about solutions for their concerns within preexisting political systems. The men whose names appeared on Tryon's proclamations condemning the instigators of more-violent interactions seemingly had less faith in the political process, though James Hunter is thought to have contributed to the Regulator petitions. Nevertheless, the decision to present the fourth petition at a quarterly meeting of the Hillsborough District Superior Court in 1770 was probably made by men from both of the centers. It is unclear, however, whether men from both groups planned the disruptions that would bring the court to an abrupt close.

The Hillsborough District Superior Court session was scheduled to open on Saturday, September 22, 1770, with Associate Justice Henderson as the sole justice presiding. All surviving accounts agree that the court proceeded without issue on its first day. The crowd that filled the courtroom on the morning of Monday, September 24, 1770, was a completely different matter. Henderson noted that "the House [was] filled as close as one Man could stand by another; some with Clubs, others with Whips and Switches, few or none without some weapon!"[42] One of the Regulators, whom Henderson identified as "Fields," told Henderson that he "spoke for the whole

The Edmund Fanning marker in Hillsborough, Orange County, North Carolina. (*Author's Photograph*)

body of the People called Regulators" and that they wanted "to see Justice done, and Justice they would have."[43] Fields and the other Regulators asked for a jury to be chosen among themselves rather than the "Jurors appointed by the Inferior Court." This led to a debate within the court chambers, and the Regulators left the building when the wider audience present "cried out 'Retire, Retire, and let the Court go on." At this point, John Williams, Henderson's former legal partner and the deputy attorney general in Hillsborough, approached the Regulators, who "fell on him in a most Furious Manner with Clubs and sticks of enormous size." When Williams took shelter in a nearby store, the Regulators attacked Edmund Fanning. Once he had fled the scene, Henderson struggled to regain order in the courtroom.

At this point, James Hunter approached Henderson's bench to reassure him "that no Man should hurt [him] on proviso, I would set and hold this Court to the end of the Term." Henderson publicly agreed to abide by this condition, but his letter to Tryon further noted that he made no "scuple at promising what was not in my Intention to perform." The court session continued, and the Regulators finished the day by escorting Henderson to his lodgings and allowing Fanning to return to his home. Late that night, Henderson "took an Opportunity of making my Escape by a back Way," which effectively ended the formal court as the session could not be held without a justice present. Later that night, Fanning was attacked again by Regulators who "entered his Mansion House, destroyed every Article of

Furniture," and, in an action reminiscent of the attack five years earlier on Lieutenant Governor Thomas Hutchinson's house during the Boston Stamp Act riots, "carried [his papers] into the Streets by Armfuls and destroyed" them. The attack on Fanning's house was followed by other attacks on the homes and businesses of other merchants in Hillsborough before the Regulators left the town on Wednesday, September 26.

The Hillsborough riots were described in increasingly sensationalized reports in newspapers ranging from neighboring Virginia to New York to Boston. The *New York Gazette* stated on October 5 that the Regulators pursued Fanning "out of town, and with a cruelty more savage than bloodhounds, stoned him as he fled," though there is no evidence that Fanning was stoned in the accounts from North Carolina, so it is possible this was an exaggeration. On October 25, the *Virginia Gazette* accused the Regulators of "leap[ing] the strong barrier of private property, and audaciously violat[ing] the laws of God and man." The *Evening Post* further noted on November 12, 1770, that after Justice Henderson fled Hillsborough on September 24, the Regulators "took from his chains a Negro that had been executed some time, and placed him at the lawyer's bar, and filled the judge's seat with human excrement" before holding a trial of their own.[44] Again, this incident was not described in accounts from North Carolina of the Hillsborough riots, so it may have been an exaggerated report. The sympathy expressed for North Carolina's political and legal officials in these reports demonstrates that most British North American colonists did not see connections between the events of the Regulator Rebellion and the unrest caused by the Stamp Act in 1765 and the Townshend Acts after 1767. Instead, the actions of the Regulators were routinely portrayed as an assault on law and order in the British colonies, though depictions of them would take on a more sympathetic tone in the coming year.

The report in the *Evening Post* noted, almost as an afterthought, that the Regulators finished their attack on the Hillsborough court with a trial of their own. It appears that the Regulators staged some kind of legal performance in the courtroom after Henderson's departure, but its purpose and meaning are unclear. Alonzo Thomas Dill contends that the docket demonstrates that the "Regulators . . . held a boisterous mock court [intended to] shock and alarm the staid east." Carole Watterson Troxler believes the resulting docket "is either the original docket of the district court . . . or a careful transcription, for its legal terms and abbreviations are consistently accurate." Rather than mock British legal procedures, the Regulators were commenting on trials that had already occurred. Wayne Lee adds that the events of September 1770 in Hillsborough were "definitely more

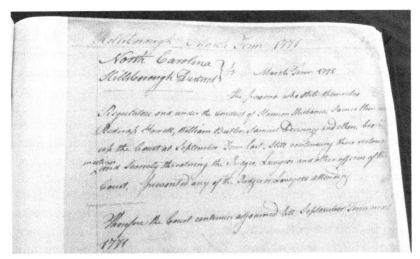

"North Carolina Hillsborough District Court Record," March Term 1771, from Hillsborough District Trial Reference and Appearance Docket Superior Court, 1768-1773, Part One, D.S.C.R. 204.323.1, State Archives of North Carolina. (*Author's Photograph*)

like a riot. But to say that it was a riot is not to say that it was chaotic or uncontrolled. Riots, too, had traditional forms, and the Regulators followed the 'script' almost line by line."[45] The blend of violent protest and careful manipulation of legal norms that characterized the Hillsborough riots suggests both the legal and extralegal centers of the Regulator movement were active players in these events.

The evidence suggests that the legal center was still a driving force within the Regulator movement. Nevertheless, Tryon continued to portray all the Regulators as lawless renegades, most likely because this was the most politically expedient option for him in the early 1770s. By that time, all the royal governors were taking pains to demonstrate they were capable of keeping their unruly colonists in check. Tryon reported to Lord Hillsborough on October 7, 1770, that the Regulators had "offered many Insults to the Dignity and proceedings of the Court" but that he would not "enter Minutely into their Savage Conduct" until after he had consulted with his council. Following this meeting, Tryon issued a proclamation on October 18 that stated "Outragious & disorderly persons" had "Opposed the Just Measures of Government ... in open Violation of the Laws of this Country."[46] Tryon further demanded that anyone responsible for the attacks in Hillsborough immediately make their confessions to their local justices. Interestingly, Tryon also claimed in the October 18 proclamation that the wrongdoers had drunk "Damnation to their Lawful Sovereign King George & Success to the Pretender."[47] This was likely hyperbole; the Regulators' loyalty to King George III and the Hanoverian succession was never in doubt. The Regulators swore their loyalty to the king in all the petitions, almost certainly adopting the standard form for the time, but nowhere did they propose overthrowing him in favor of one of his Stuart cousins. But casting the Regulators in the worst possible light helped Tryon plan more punitive actions against them.[48] Wayne Lee writes that "rhetorically framing the Regulator movement within the context of these fears eased the process of 'othering' and delegitimizing its participants," a tactic that would become increasingly familiar in the turbulent days of the early-to-mid-1770s.[49]

It is also clear that Governor Tryon's struggles with the Regulators were known beyond the environs of North Carolina. Massachusetts Governor Thomas Hutchinson, who was facing similar challenges from unruly colonists in Machias, Maine, which, at that time, was part of Massachusetts, wrote to Lord Hillsborough on November 30, 1770, that "there is danger of [the Machias settlers] being as troublesome as the Regulators in North Carolina."[50] Two months later, Hutchinson advised Tryon that "the best way of treating [rebellious colonists] is to make no concessions, to void all taunts of irritating language & to dispise their calumnies."[51] Tryon, however, had two groups of colonists to manage, the Regulators and the members of the North Carolina General Assembly. He had repeatedly frustrated the members of North Carolina's elite who wanted to use the assembly as a conduit for expressing their concerns about the Townshend taxes by dismissing that body. Placing all his attention on suppressing the Regulator Rebellion was an appeasement tactic. In the long run, a successful Regulator Rebellion posed a greater threat to the livelihoods of wealthy North Carolina families.

But Tryon was aware that any actions taken against the Regulators would happen in a period of rising tensions between British North American colonists and British government officials. The Regulators' actions in Hillsborough attracted unfavorable press in newspapers throughout the colonies, but their concerns were not entirely without sympathy. "Extract from a letter from Mecklenburg," published in the *Boston Chronicle* in 1768, had condemned the North Carolina poll tax levied to pay for "Tryon's palace" for requiring "a man that is worth £10,000 [to pay] no more than a poor back settler that has nothing but the labour of his hands to depend upon." It also praised the men who refused to join the militia forces rallied by Tryon to respond to the Regulators that same year.[52] The publication location for Herman Husband's first pamphlet, *An Impartial Relation of the*

First Rise and Cause of the Recent Differences in Publick Affairs, is unknown, but his second pamphlet, *A Fan for Fanning, and A Touchstone to Tryon* was published in Boston in 1771.[53] The willingness of a Boston printer to publish a pamphlet about an event in North Carolina suggests that Husband had carefully cultivated relationships with the Boston press during the years of the Regulator Rebellion in the hope of gaining wider support for the movement.

The final stages of the Regulator Rebellion took place concurrently with the event known as the Boston Massacre, when British soldiers under the leadership of Captain Thomas Preston fired on a crowd of Boston colonists and killed five of them on March 5, 1770. By the time Governor Tryon was trying to prosecute members of the Regulator movement in fall 1770, Preston was scheduled to go to trial on October 24, while the soldiers who had fired the shots were preparing for their trials in November. Neither Tryon nor Governor Hutchinson would have wanted to risk any course of action that might affect the outcome of their trials.[54] Furthermore, any life-threatening actions taken by Tryon against the Regulators that could not be demonstrated to have been sanctioned by North Carolina law could be portrayed as a second massacre in a newspaper editorial from one of the many colonial newspapers.

Tryon's next course of action was to appeal to North Carolina Attorney General Thomas McGuire for advice. McGuire determined that the Regulators' actions thus far could only be construed as a "Riot" and a "Misdemeanour, though of the highest Nature," neither of which were treasonous in North Carolina. McGuire recommended that Tryon convene the assembly "as soon as possible . . . to give the Representatives of the People the earliest opportunity of making such Laws and providing for the Vigorous Execution of them."[55] While this recommendation provided Tryon with a legal avenue toward rendering the Regulators' actions treasonous, McGuire's choice of language further underscores their concerns over legitimacy. Tryon, a royally appointed governor, would not issue such a decree. The assembly would enact the laws, and any resulting newspaper editorials could argue that the "Representatives of the People" had only the best interests of all North Carolina colonists at heart. Furthermore, having the bill passed by the locally elected members of the assembly would demonstrate that the Regulator Rebellion was a purely local affair and so could not be construed as rebellion against the British Crown and Parliament in the ways the Stamp Act riots had been five years earlier.

The next meeting of the assembly took place in December 1770 in the wing of "Tryon's Palace" in New Bern dedicated to colonial business. The summary of this meeting given to Tryon on December 10 briefly addressed the Regulators' concerns about abuses of fees for government transactions but ultimately concluded that the problem was due less to "a depravity of Morals among the Servants of the Publick" and more to "the Consequences of an inconsistent and Oppresive Fee Bill," a conclusion similar to the one reached by William de Grey and John Morgan when assessing Edmund Fanning's extortion charges. Furthermore, the assembly members assured Tryon that they were deeply concerned by the "late daring and insolent Attack made on the Superior Court of Hillsborough by the People who call themselves Regulators" and would be taking up "Measures at once Spirited and decisive" against its perpetrators necessary to provide Tryon with the legal grounds needed for pursuing the Regulators.[56]

The mutual zest expressed by Tryon and the assembly in fall 1770 speaks to the balancing act required for governors throughout the colonies during this period. The documentary record shows most assembly members supported all possible efforts to quell the Regulator Rebellion, whose primary target was the colonial government of North Carolina and its sanctioning of the policies that allowed government officials like Fanning to exploit their positions. There is evidence suggesting that Tryon and his predecessor, Arthur Dobbs, made some furtive moves in the direction of reforming North Carolina's political system and were immediately stonewalled by the assembly. Unfortunately for the Regulators, the acceleration of their movement in the early 1770s came at a moment when Tryon desperately needed common ground with an increasingly restive assembly. Supporting its concerns about the Regulator Rebellion also provided distraction from the Townshend Acts and so may have bought him a little more time.

The "Bill for preventing tumultuous and riotous Assemblies, etc." was initially proposed by attorney Samuel Johnston on December 15. It questioned "how far the Laws now in Force are sufficient to inflict punishments Adequate to such heinous offences." The new law, which would later be known as Johnston's Riot Act, covered every possible eventuality the assembly (and Tryon) could envision. "After the first day of February next," it stated, all "persons to the number of ten or more being unlawfully, tumultously and Riotously assembled together" who refused to leave after "being asked to peaceably disperse within an hour by either Justices of the Peace or Sheriffs" would be immediately arrested. If the justices and sheriffs needed help making these arrests, they could "command all his Majestys Subjects of this Province of age and Ability to be Assisting to them therein to Seize and apprehend such persons."[57] If any rioters were killed while being detained, the officers of the law responsible for their deaths would automatically be acquitted. Furthermore, it was also legal to arrest and try anyone who had previously threatened to attack officers of the law or prevented others from doing so prior to its taking effect on February 1.[58]

The new law also authorized the "Governor or Commander in Chief" to "Command that Necessary draughts be made from the different Regiments of Militia" and requested the necessary financial support from colony funds. Any man who opposed "any military Forces raised in Virtue of this Act" would be declared a traitor and treated accordingly. Once defendants were arrested, North Carolina justices were authorized to create courts of oyer and terminer. Rioters who confessed or were convicted by a jury would "suffer Death as in cases of Felony and be utterly excluded from his or their Clergy if found guilty."[59] This was an important distinction in the Anglo-American legal world. Many defendants had successfully escaped death by pleading benefit of clergy, which was traditionally tied to literacy, rather than actually proving that the defendant was a member of a clerical order.[60]

Johnston's Riot Act was modeled on the English Riot Act of 1715, but it went several steps further with its retroactive provisions and threat of treason charges.[61] Recognizing that they were breaking from legal precedent, Tryon and the assembly sought other means for conveying the new law's legitimacy. The final paragraph of the Johnston Riot Act ordered all inferior court justices to "Cause this Act to be Read at the Court House door the second day of each court for their Counties," while the "Minister, Clerk or Reader of every Parish" was required to read it to their congregations "once in three months at least, immediately after Divine Service." This decision set up an interesting tension. Tryon was upholding older oral traditions that maintained that laws were not legitimate until they had been publicly and verbally woven into the community. However, public dissent against the law would result in its immediate, and forceful, application in the North Carolina legal system.

Both the Regulators and Governor Tryon were rapidly running out of time in spring 1771. It was clear to both sides that the legal center of the Regulator movement had failed in its efforts to bring about reform in North Carolina. Now there was no choice for Tryon or the Regulators but to escalate the stakes further on the banks of Alamance Creek.

Chapter Seven

Imperial Crisis to Revolutionary Era

The Regulator Rebellion ended at the Battle of Alamance on May 16, 1771. Three weeks later, twelve Regulators were tried on treason charges and six hanged in Hillsborough. William Fitch wrote in 1906 that "the War of the Regulators was a revolution and the beginning of, and the Revolutionary War the ending of, one and the same war against oppression by the British government."[1] A closer look at the documentary record demonstrates, however, that the causes for the Regulator Rebellion were rooted in North Carolina's colonial government. The imperial crisis placed additional pressures on Governor William Tryon, but it was not the cause of the Regulator Rebellion itself.

Tryon's efforts to pursue the leaders of the Regulator Rebellion into every corner and hill of the Piedmont were driven equally by his need to find common cause with a restive General Assembly and his desire to crush the other challenge to his authority in the colony. The passing of Johnston's Riot Act in January 1771 was championed equally by Tryon and the General Assembly. Tryon's departure from North Carolina in 1771 shifted the colony's fragile political balance as his successor, Josiah Martin, would tangle far more directly with the assembly during his tenure as governor. Martin's efforts to investigate the Regulators' concerns were portrayed as yet another example of imperial overreach by an assembly eager to prove that the Regulators' plight did not warrant sympathy in the other British colonies. These tensions later informed North Carolina's rush to the American Revolution with the passing of the Mecklenburg Resolves, which ended the royalist government in the colony in 1775, the first colony to take such a step.

Johnston's Riot Act gave Governor Tryon and the assembly the legal apparatus needed to prosecute members of the Regulator movement to the full extent of the law, which now included treason charges and the death penalty. The law also allowed the colonial government to try anyone who had previously threatened "to assault beat or wound any of the Judges . . . or with force hinder or Obstruct any Sheriff." Even if the Regulators laid down their arms on the day the law took effect, they could still be prosecuted for their earlier actions. This provision placed the North Carolina government on the wrong side of British law, as it was far more stringent than anything created by Parliament at that time. London was three thousand miles away, but colonial laws were still subject to imperial review.[2] The North Carolina assembly might, in time, face penalties for passing such a law, but that was unlikely to happen until long after the crisis point of the Regulator Rebellion.

In turn, the Regulators were facing their own challenges. The movement's two centers, one legal, the other extralegal, had always functioned concurrently, but this became nearly impossible after the attack on the Hillsborough Superior Court. The legal center's efforts to have its concerns addressed in North Carolina's political and legal systems had made many in the colony sympathetic to the Regulators' plight. At the same time, the extralegal center was growing bolder, which risked alienating the legal center's more moderate supporters. In the eyes of the extralegal center, a more cautious approach had failed, and it was time for more drastic approaches. Wayne Lee notes that many Regulators simply ceased to recognize the North Carolina colonial government in the Piedmont in winter 1770–1771 and, instead, were conducting their own legal courts. This did not mean, however, that the Regulators intended to overthrow the colonial government in New Bern. Nevertheless, Tryon appeared determined to persuade the assembly that such a threat existed.[3] William Smith's carefully constructed narrative of this period described the Regulators as "advanc[ing] with waggon and arms to the number of 2200" in winter 1770–1771, which would "prove Near destruction" to New Bern.[4] Tryon had also just received an invitation to become the next governor of New York. Prompting a violent end to the Regulator Rebellion would help him wrap up loose ends in North Carolina before moving on to a new, and more prestigious, posting.

Identifying candidates for the governorships of the British North American colonies was an evolving game for the political elite. Moves between squares were propelled by a blend of family connections, sudden openings due to illness or death, and, occasionally, ability. If one position came open, the game pieces were reorganized, and, sometimes, a new player was allowed onto the board. Norborne Berkeley, the fourth Baron Botetourt, became Virginia's governor in 1768, only to die in office after a lingering illness in 1770.[5] Lord Botetourt's death was immediately seized upon in London by two parliamentary members who saw the new vacancy as a way to promote their protégé's careers and, by extension, their influence in North America. These men included Tryon's long-standing patron, Lord Hillsborough, and Granville Leveson-Gower, the second Earl Gower, who had a similar relationship with John Murray, the fourth Earl Dunmore, the royal governor of New York at that time.[6]

Lord Gower recommended Lord Dunmore as Virginia's royal governor since it was an advancement in both power and salary for Dunmore. Dunmore initially resisted the promotion on the grounds that the Virginia climate would be unhealthy for his wife and children.[7] Once the possibility of Dunmore's being repositioned in Virginia was on the table, Lord Hillsborough recommended Tryon as New York's governor. Tryon signaled that he was open to either post, but both Gower and Hillsborough agreed that placing Tryon in New York and Dunsmore in Virginia was the better plan. Hillsborough then recommended British army officer Josiah Martin as North Carolina's next governor. Martin was unable to take up his new position in North Carolina until August 1771, and Dunmore delayed moving to Virginia until September, though Tryon did move to New York in June immediately following the Battle of Alamance.[8]

During his final months in office, Tryon faced the habitual two challenges to his authority in North Carolina: the Regulators and the General Assembly's growing desire to respond more forcefully to the Townshend Acts. Now, his elevation to the governorship of a larger and more powerful colony meant his leadership skills were under ever greater scrutiny. If Tryon proved unable to handle unruly colonists while he was waiting to assume his new position, it was not impossible for another candidate to be brought forward as the next governor of New York. William Smith's enthusiastic commitment to portraying Tryon's tenure as governor in the best light possible suggests that Tryon confided some of these concerns to Smith after arriving in New York in 1771. Even then, Tryon's ascension to the governorship of New York remained in doubt until Dunmore finally conceded the position and moved to Virginia.

Following the Stamp Act riots outside his residence in Wilmington in 1765, Governor Tryon had campaigned for a new capital away from the restive Cape Fear region in southeastern North Carolina. New Bern, located some hundred miles north on the Neuse River, became North Carolina's capital in 1766. That same year, Tryon oversaw the creation of the building known as "Tryon's Palace" where his family resided and where the colony's official business was conducted. The new building cost nearly £15,000, and the General Assembly ordered a number of new colonial taxes to pay for the construction in the late 1760s.[9] These were levied in the same period as the controversial Townshend taxes, but they had a more direct impact on backcountry colonists, who rarely purchased the imported goods taxed by the Townshend Acts. By contrast, most assembly members came from the wealthy eastern families who were more directly impacted by the Townshend taxes.[10]

Diverging sources of anger over taxation in the colony provided Tryon with challenge and opportunity alike during the Regulator Rebellion. He was already placating the assembly by supporting its efforts to quell the Regulator movement's demands for internal reforms. But unrest in North Carolina due to the Townshend Acts was rooted in the eastern counties. It was unlikely that the Regulators would launch a full attack on New Bern, but the presence of even a handful of Regulators in the community could put pressure on their eastern neighbors to fuse their separate furies with North Carolina's colonial government and parliamentary taxation. Moreover, "Tryon's Palace" was the perfect symbol of government overreach to serve as a target for a newly created coalition of Regulators and rising Patriots. The best course of action available to Tryon was to keep the minds of eastern North Carolina colonists fixated on threats posed by angry Regulators. In this scenario, he could argue that his particular abilities as a military commander were necessary to protect them from these threats. This strategy worked for Tryon, but the assembly's immediate pivot back to expressing concerns about the Townshend taxes following the end of the Regulator Rebellion demonstrates that it was a short-lived alliance. Tryon's successor, Josiah Martin, who lacked such distractions, would have a far harder time controlling the North Carolina elite.

The assembly members who gathered in New Bern in December 1770 included Regulator Herman Husband. It is unknown how Husband responded to the first draft of Johnston's Riot Act when it was introduced on December 15, but it seems unlikely he was silent. Five days later, Husband was censored for being a "principal Mover and promoter of the late Riots and Seditions in the County of Orange and other parts of the

Province" and removed from the assembly.[11] The evidence used to expel him stemmed from a recent investigation into an open letter ostensibly published in the *North-Carolina Gazette* by Regulator James Hunter on December 14. It appears that Maurice Moore, one of North Carolina's two associate justices, had published an earlier letter accusing Husband and Hunter of inciting unrest in the North Carolina backcountry. Hunter's letter instructed Moore to "turn around, and view the many enormities, extortions, and exactions, daily practiced on us by Lawyer's clerks, registers, sheriffs, &c."[12] The group of legislators assigned to investigate the open letter argued that it was "a false Malicious and seditious Libel" on Moore and a direct challenge to the assembly itself.[13] Since Moore had composed a pamphlet criticizing the Stamp Act in 1765, it is likely Hunter was targeting Moore for his unwillingness to recognize the parallels between the Regulators' concerns and the overall unease with British taxes in North America.[14] In any event, censoring Husband removed a dissenting vote for Johnston's Riot Act from the assembly when it came up for a vote the following month.

The General Assembly expelled Husband but placed no restrictions on his movements. Tryon then arranged to have him jailed without charges in New Bern, an act prohibited by British and North Carolina law. It appears Tryon hoped that keeping Husband wrongfully imprisoned would encourage other Regulators to come to New Bern to break him out of the local jail. Johnston's Riot Act was now in full effect, and a rescue party could then be charged with treason. Tryon reported to the Earl of Hillsborough that he had "received Inteligence by Express [in late January] that the Insurgents were making preparations to come down to Newbern to release Husbands and to lay in the Town in Ashes."[15] At this point, Tryon's best laid plans began to fall apart. He called out the local militias to defend New Bern but, as Wayne Lee notes, eventually realized that most militia members would probably view "such a jailbreak as legitimate" since Husband had been imprisoned without charges.[16] Chief Justice Martin Howard promised Tryon he would put Husband on trial on libel charges, but a grand jury failed to find any evidence to support a libel charge against Husband. Based on this ruling from the jury, Howard chose not only to order Husband released from the New Bern jail but to order him released without probation charges. Husband was now completely free to resume his customary activities.

A disgusted Tryon further reported to Lord Hillsborough that while several Regulators had paraded through the town of Hillsborough on February 16 to celebrate Husband's release, they had scrupulously conducted these activities within the confines of the law.[17] He had failed to convict Husband, and there was still "no Evidence coming down from the back Settlements to prosecute the Insurgents agreeable to the Subpeonas sent to them."[18]

Tryon's next move was to organize a "Special Court of Oyer and Terminer" to be held in New Bern on March 11 in order to review the charges levied against the Regulators by Tryon and the General Assembly.[19] In early March, he had additional weapons, ammunition, and other supplies delivered to New Bern. The *South-Carolina Gazette* reported that "many strange tales daily arrive from North Carolina ... the Governor's sumptious palace is thought to stand in so much danger of being destroyed, that an entrenchment or barricade has lately been thrown up."[20] Tryon asked militia Captains James Hinton and Needham Bryan to submit "the whole Expense of Assembling your Regiment to prevent the Regulators Marching to Newbern" on February 27.[21] New Bern was now ready for a siege that never came. Again, keeping the community of New Bern on constant alert was a strategic move for Tryon.

The oyer and terminer court session to review the charges against the Regulators took place without interruption in March 1771. There is, however, evidence suggesting some local support for the Regulators' concerns. The *Virginia Gazette* reported that Craven County militia member Jeremiah Pritchet was court-martialed on March 12 for his earlier efforts "to breed a Mutiny at the last general Muster" owing to his being "disaffected to Government."[22] Pritchett was sentenced to 150 lashings in the town square. During his punishment, a "Bystander was overhead making a Proposal to pelt the Executioner with Eggs" who was then detained and, presumably, punished. By the end of the court session, sixty-two Regulators, including James Hunter and Herman Husband, had been indicted for "assembl[ing] together, in a riotous and tumultuous manner, barbarously insult[ing] and br[eaking] up th[e Hillsborough] Court" and for "publickly avowing their intention of Marching to Newbern and of carrying into execution by Force their hostile measures."[23] The first of these charges was valid, but there is no evidence for the second. Regardless, all sixty-two men would now have to stand trial at a second court of oyer and terminer. Since most, or all, of the indicted Regulators were in Orange County, Tryon decided to hold this court in Hillsborough rather than have them transported to New Bern. Conducting the second court of oyer and terminer in the North Carolina backcountry was less risky than moving the Regulators to New Bern, but it presented Tryon with the new challenge of identifying funds to pay for militia companies to march west to Hillsborough to protect the court.

The Governor's Council met on March 18, 1771, to discuss the funds needed to pay the militias during the court trials. As further evidence of Regulator plans to disrupt the peace in North Carolina, Tryon provided a copy of an intercepted letter sent by Redknap Howell to James Hunter on February 16. Since Herman Husband "was at liberty," wrote Howell, it is now "needless to raise the Country." He reported on Tryon's struggles to persuade individual militia members to join the search for the Regulators before adding "it's a pity to breed a civil war among ourselves . . . [but] if [Tryon] could have raised the Province on us he would have told another tale." Howell's letter points more to Tryon's need to take action rather than to any valid threats against the colony's safety. It is highly unlikely that the Regulators would have included plans for an organized uprising against the North Carolina government in an easily intercepted letter, though an absence of evidence does not automatically connote an absence of intent. Still, Howell's letter was slim evidence for justifying Tryon's claim that New Bern was in serious danger of being attacked by the Regulators. In any event, the council was equally eager to see the Regulator movement crushed and on March 18 agreed to provide the necessary funds for the expedition.[24]

The letter sent to Tryon by John Frohock and Alexander Martin detailing their questioning of the Regulators camped outside Salisbury was discussed in chapter 6.[25] Frohock and Martin feared the Regulators would stage a reprise of the attack on the Hillsborough District Superior Court on an upcoming court session in Salisbury. Their belief that mediation could avert such an attack demonstrates that most North Carolina colonists were aware of the efforts of the legal center of the Regulator movement. By the time Frohock and Martin's letter reached Tryon, the court session had been canceled, and it was clear there would be no Regulator attack on Salisbury. Moreover, Tryon had spent the late winter trying to bait the Regulators into an attack on New Bern. He informed Frohock and Martin on April 5 that their actions were "unconstitutional, Dishonorable to Government and introductive of a practice the most dangerous to the peace and happiness of Society."[26] Moreover, Tryon believed that a full-scale military invasion of Orange County would do more to stabilize the colony of North Carolina than any efforts at civic engagement with the Regulators. William Smith later noted that he believed the only way to address the challenges posed by the "people calling themselves 'Regulators'" was by "raising a Body of Militia and marching with all Expedition" to Hillsborough.[27]

It should be noted that this was a major change in approach for Tryon. Prior to winter and now spring 1771, he had been willing to entertain the Regulators' petitions and, treading in the footsteps of his predecessor, Governor Arthur Dobbs, consider their suggestions for better regulation of the North Carolina government. This willingness had created enough of an equilibrium in the colony for the Regulator Rebellion to continue into its third year, long after the ending point of North Carolina's earlier internal rebellions. But now that Tryon was weeks away from departing for his new position in New York, he believed that the colony's status quo needed to be changed, regardless of the costs. And, again, annihilating the Regulator Rebellion in 1770–1771 was a way to appease the assembly until Tryon departed for New York in June 1771.

Nevertheless, not everything went smoothly for Tryon and the assembly that spring. Despite various financial inducements, only fourteen hundred men signed up to join the expedition to Orange County, "approximately half the full militia strength of twenty-nine counties."[28] The failure to persuade many militia members to join the expedition speaks to the silent sympathy many North Carolina colonists held for the Regulator movement. Colonial militias had readily enlisted to protect North Carolina during the French and Indian War, and they would readily enlist during the American Revolution, but the Regulators posed little threat to the eastern counties where most of these recruiting efforts were conducted.[29] Tryon and the militias left the New Bern region on May 4, 1771, with plans to march to Hillsborough. Wary of inadvertently creating further support for the Regulators, Tryon discouraged individual militia members from provisioning themselves with supplies from local farms, but a May 13 entry in the *General Orders of the Army* record book suggests such incidents still occurred.[30]

Both centers of the Regulator movement remained active during this period, and, again, it is difficult to tell how closely they were working with one another. Assembly member Hugh Waddell, whom Governor Tryon had made a general, was assigned to recruit new militia troops from Bladen, Cumberland, Anson, Mecklenburg, and Rowan Counties in early May. Waddell's efforts to move toward Hillsborough were halted on May 10 when a group of approximately two thousand Regulators forced his troops back across the Yadkin River to Salisbury.[31] Shortly after Waddell's retreat to Salisbury, a group of Orange County farmers submitted a written "Address from inhabitants of Orange County" to Tryon. This statement began by assuring Tryon that they were willing "to suppress or remove any nuisance that may be an obstruction to good government."[32] This emphasis on "good government" suggests that the statement either came from the legal center of the Regulator movement or was informed by their writings. Nevertheless, if Tryon's intention was "to force us to submit to that Tyrany which has so long been Premeditated by some Officers of the Province," then they too would "contend for our just rights." Wayne Lee notes that "restrained, communicative violence (the 'careful riot') had cultural legitimacy and the Regulators carefully patterned their actions according to the traditional rules of violent protest."[33] The authors of the "Address" had documented their commitment to "good government." They were currently trying to reach a diplomatic resolution with Tryon. If these efforts failed, then a turn to measured violence to uphold their "just rights" was justifiable according to British political tradition. This same argument would later be used by advocates for the American Revolution. The irony of the Alamance campaign was that many of the men, Hugh Waddell included, who fought against the Regulators would later be Patriots.

The existence of two centers for the Regulator movement, one determined to work within existing political and legal systems, the other willing to commit violence if it would obtain its goals, has been discussed throughout this book. There is also evidence suggesting that three of the Regulators communicated regularly with both centers: Herman Husband, James Hunter, and Thomas Person. Husband and Hunter were initially present at Alamance Creek, though Husband, who identified as a Quaker, left the battlefield before it began on religious grounds. William Smith further described Hunter as "the General of the Rebel Army," an appellation that can only have come from Tryon.[34] David Caldwell, however, later recalled that Hunter refused to take command during the battle.[35] Hunter later escaped and did not return to North Carolina until a few years after the Regulator Rebellion had ended. Person was not present for the Battle of Alamance, though he was treated as if he had taken part in the battle. Tryon's troops later captured him, and he was imprisoned in Hillsborough.

Despite widespread evidence of legal and extralegal centers for the Regulator movement, Governor Tryon consistently refused to differentiate between them. In the long run, this helped sustain his depiction of the Regulator movement as entirely made up of ruffians bent on destroying the peace. Not surprisingly, Tryon's chronicler, William Smith, would later condemn the Regulators' "wicked Designs" on the North Carolina colonial government.[36] This same portrayal took hold in the years following the Battle of Alamance, as the Regulators' legal center has continued to be erased in North Carolina's cultural memory.

By the middle of May 1771, the Regulators and Tryon, Waddell, and the militias were settled into adjoining encampments along the Alamance Creek. Five men who identified themselves as Regulators sent a final petition to Tryon on May 15 asking permission to outline "a full detail of all our Grievances" in the hope this would prevent "the sad presaged Tragedy

The Alamance battlefield, Alamance County, North Carolina. (*Author's Photograph*)

of the warlike Troops marching with Ardour to meet each other."[37] Tryon appears to have ignored this petition. Regulators Robert Mateer and Robert Thompson, accompanied by Presbyterian minister David Caldwell, also traveled to Tryon's camp to meet with him.[38] Tryon took Mateer and Thompson as hostages and sent Caldwell back to tell the Regulators that if they surrendered their leaders, he would not attack. The Regulators refused this offer but did agree to exchange two of their prisoners for the seven men held captive by Tryon's men.

The planned prisoner exchange on May 16 was disrupted when Tryon ordered Robert Thompson executed and instructed the Regulators to "quietly lay down your arms, to surrender up your leaders."[39] They refused, and the first shots were fired a few hours later. The Regulators had a few moments of success owing to their familiarity with the local terrain, but they were quickly outgunned and forced to concede within a few hours.[40] One episode from the battle serves as a further illustration of Tryon's hysteria in March. The governor had transformed New Bern and his mansion into an armed fortress ready for attack from the Regulators. William Fitch notes, however, that when Tryon's troops left a cannon on the Alamance battlefield, "two brothers, McPherson by name, rushed up and captured the guns, but having no ammunition suitable were unable to use them."[41] Colonists who lacked ammunition for cannon during a battle would also have lacked the artillery needed to conduct a full military siege on a town. Scholars estimate that nine members of the militia were killed during the battle, while anywhere from ten to three hundred of the Regulators were killed. There also appears to have been a total of around 150 men wounded, but the records do not indicate which side these men came from.[42]

Tryon acted within hours of the end of the battle. Wayne Lee notes that "before Alamance, he had trod lightly, respecting the military potential of his enemy . . . acting as if, indeed, he was in a conventional war."[43] Now, Tryon "behaved as one suppressing a rebellion." First, he issued a proclamation offering pardons to all Regulators, except their leaders, which led to waves of men surrendering to him.[44] The following day he executed Regulator James Few on the battlefield without a trial, a decision condemned six months later by "Atticus" in the pages of the *Virginia Gazette*.[45] Next, Tryon ordered his troops to destroy as many of the Regulators' farms as they could locate in an effort to further weaken them. Then, on June 9, he condemned Regulator leaders Herman Husband James Hunter, Redknap Howell, and William Butler as outlaws and offered "One Hundred Pounds and one thousand acres of Land" for their capture.[46] Two days later, Tryon identified sixteen more men as ineligible for pardons owing to their actions during the Regulator Rebellion.[47] By then, Tryon was wrapping up loose ends as quickly as possible, as he would leave for his new position in New York within the month.

Chief Justice Martin Howard oversaw a second court of oyer and terminer on June 15 for the prisoners captured during the Battle of Alamance and in the days following it. The records for this trial have not been located, so it is currently impossible to know what charges were used against the accused men. William Smith commented only that the justices "found it difficult after the Battle in holding the court in Hillsborough."[48] None of the men tried in the days following Alamance included the four outlawed by Tryon on June 9, and few of them were on the list of men declared ineligible for pardons on June 11. Marjoleine Kars further notes that Tryon staged the executions for the best effect, sending soldiers "to clear the grove of trees and bushes so there would be more room and a better view for those compelled to watch," who included many of the families of the Regulators.[49]

At the last minute, Tryon pardoned six of the twelve condemned men. He identified them as James Stewart, James Emmerson, William Brown, Forester Mercer, James Copeland, and Hermon Cox in a December 14, 1771, letter to Lord Hillsborough.[50] None of these men's names appear in either the Regulator petitions or Tryon's prior correspondence about the Regulators, and it is unclear why they were charged or pardoned at the last

The Regulator monument in Hillsborough, North Carolina, marking the spot where six Regulators were hanged on June 19, 1771. (*Author's photograph*)

minute. The remaining six were hanged, but only four of their names have survived: Robert Mateer, James Pugh, Benjamin Merrell, and Robert Messer.[51] The following day, Tryon wiped the red dust of North Carolina from his shoes and departed for New York, leaving a colony in pieces.

Josiah Martin, Tryon's replacement, arrived two months later, on August 12, 1771. Unlike Tryon, whose position in North Carolina had come about via his wife's family, Governor Martin had acquired his new position via his own family connections. Martin's father, Samuel Martin, was an Anglo-Irish plantation owner based in Antigua who commanded the island's militia while also serving on Antigua's royal council.[52] Martin's early military career took him to North America during the French and Indian War, where he served at the Crown Point fortress on Lake Champlain. Visits to his uncle's estate in Long Island opened up further family connections and led to an appointment to the New York royal council in 1758.[53] Martin married his first cousin, Elizabeth, in 1761, but this marriage was against his father's wishes.[54] Like most wealthy eighteenth-century parents, Samuel Martin wanted his sons' marriages to bring additional alliances to the family. Martin continued to pursue other government positions in New York after the war, though these efforts were often curtailed by time spent in Antigua owing to his father's failing health. These collective efforts were rewarded in 1770, when Lord Hillsborough recommended that he become governor of the colony of North Carolina.[55]

Martin's four years in North Carolina were far more controversial than Tryon's tenure had been. Vernon Stumpf writes that "as the crown's representative, Governor Martin provided a convenient and accessible symbol of tyranny for the North Carolina Patriots by his actions, which further stimulated them to revolt."[56] Most of this anger stemmed from rising tensions between the colonies and British government, but the lingering aftermath of the Regulator movement also informed the General Assembly's many grievances with Martin.

British monarchs routinely issued royal governors with recommendations on how to best achieve the tenuous balance needed to govern their colonies while simultaneously supporting the Crown's interests. Martin's first set of instructions were written on February 6, 1771, some six months before he arrived in the colony. Their generic nature suggests these were instructions sent to all of the British royal governors, including Tryon in his new capacity as governor of New York. Martin was ordered to convene his council and administer their oaths promising to uphold King George III and his Protestant heirs, to regulate the numbers of representatives sent to the assembly, and to limit lotteries until "you shall have first transmitted to us by one of our principal Secretaries of State a draught or draughts of such act or acts."[57] Again, these are routine instructions providing information to the royal governors about implementing the systems needed to properly run their colonies.

By contrast, the instructions sent to Martin the following year were specific to his role as North Carolina's governor. They also came immediately to the point. The Crown had reviewed the "Act for preventing Tumultuous and riotous Assemblies," or Johnston's Riot Act, passed by the North Carolina assembly early in 1771.[58] British law explicitly stated that laws created in the individual British colonies "could not be contrary or repugnant to the laws of England."[59] Individual colonies could create laws to address situations such as interactions between indigenous peoples and British colonists since such interactions were not included in the British legal codes, but they could not make laws overriding British law. Johnston's Riot Act was modeled on the English Riot Act of 1715, but it went several steps further. George III and his advisers believed the provision making it "lawful for any one to kill and destroy such Offender and his Lands and chattels shall be confiscated to the King for the use of Government," coupled with retroactive provisions for crimes committed before the law took effect in February 1771, rendered Johnston's Riot Act "irreconcilable with the principles of the constitution, full of danger in its operation and unfit for any part of the British Empire."[60] The Crown and Parliament wanted greater control over colonial economic affairs, but they were willing to allow colonial governors to manage internal politics as they saw fit. Criticizing a law designed to curb unruly colonists placed George III and Parliament in a particularly difficult position.

The early 1770s were a tense time for the British Empire. The uproar over the Boston Massacre in 1770 had subsided, but there was little to suggest that colonial responses to the Townshend Acts would not, in time, turn to violence. Since Johnston's Riot Act was on the verge of expiring in 1772 and did "contain many useful and proper regulations for the preservation of the Public Peace of our said Province," George III allowed that repealing it might "have very fatal consequences and revive that seditious spirit (not yet wholly subsided amongst some of the Inhabitants)." Instead, he instructed Governor Martin that if North Carolina should pass a new law "for preventing tumults and riotous assemblies," it was his responsibility to ensure that "the said laws be framed as near as may be agreeable to the Laws of this Kingdom."[61]

Again, the persecution of the Regulators by the North Carolina elite was deeply ironic. "The most surprising thing," writes William Lawrence Saunders, is not that the Regulator Rebellion existed "but that it was so ruthlessly stamped out by . . . the people of the Eastern portion of the Province, a people whose own garments were already reeking with local rebellion and insurrection of every hue and grade."[62] The original writings of the Sandy Creek Association had predicted these challenges for the Regulators.[63] They knew their oppressors, and their interests, very well.

It is doubtful, however, whether George III and his advisers saw any differences between rabble-rousers among the Regulators and rabble-rousers among the members of North Carolina's coastal elite. It is not an accident that the actions of the Regulators in Hillsborough in 1770 closely resembled the actions of the mobs who had protested the Stamp Act in Boston, Newport, and Wilmington in 1765. Both groups drew their rhetoric from the same political traditions that allowed British subjects to comment on the laws governing them, and, in cases of extremity, violently oppose those laws. Furthermore, it is unlikely that British government officials were familiar enough with conditions on the ground in North America to draw distinctions between objections to the North Carolina colonial government and objections to parliamentary tax codes. Governor Tryon was all too aware of these distinctions, but it would not have benefited him to dwell on them in his letters to the Earl of Hillsborough since that would have exposed his alliance with an otherwise recalcitrant General Assembly during the final stages of the Regulator Rebellion. Josiah Martin's father had openly objected to the Stamp Act in Antigua, but all of his sons, who were either British politicians or military officers at the time, had supported it. There was nothing in Martin's record suggesting that he would distinguish between Regulators and proto-Patriots when he arrived in the colony, which was probably why Lord Hillsborough had recommended him for the position.[64]

Once he arrived in North Carolina, however, Governor Martin's approach toward restive colonists shifted. Tryon's hasty departure for New York in June 1771 had left dozens of men condemned as Regulators, their lands and goods forfeit to the North Carolina government and their lives in limbo. Surviving Regulators hoped that a new administration might look more kindly on their claims. Shortly after arriving, Martin received a "Petition from Orange-Guilford Counties" asking him to pardon Thomas Wellborn. His neighbors argued that Wellborn was a "man of Justice and Honest Integrity in his Dealing and Conversation Excepting the Late Insurrection and Rebellion.[65] That same year, he received other petitions from men involved with the Regulator Rebellion. These documents consistently vouched for the petitioners' commitment to rebuilding the peace in Orange, Anson, and Rowan Counties.[66] Curious to learn more about the Regulators' concerns and eager to build alliances with his colonists, Martin made plans to travel to the Piedmont region in summer 1772.

Following his late August return to New Bern, Martin sent Lord Hillsborough a detailed assessment. Lord Hillsborough almost certainly would have seen the Regulators in a negative light from Tryon's reports. Martin, however, argued, "I now see most clearly that the [Regulators] have been provoked by insolence and cruel advantages taken of [them] by mercenary tricking Attorneys, Clerks, and other little Officers who have practiced upon them every sort of rapine and extortion which [brought upon] . . . their just resentment." He then added that "my indignation [with these people] is not only disarmed but converted to pity."[67] Based on these experiences, Martin provided suggestions for how the North Carolina colonial government might now approach its backcountry residents. First, it was time to cease prosecuting the Regulators for their actions. Second, Martin recommended that North Carolina consider reforming the practices identified in his letter that had led the Regulators to begin rebelling against the colonial government in 1767. These recommendations were made after consulatation with Chief Justice Martin Howard, who noted on August 30, 1772, that while "it is not easy for me to say in what light the Legislature will view the Insurgents," he believed "it would be wiser to pass a General Amnesty without making any further stir concerning the criminality of the

Insurgents."[68] Furthermore, added Howard, a "cordial union can never take place until the victors forget to exult on the last years triumph at Alamance." Ending the Regulator Rebellion was a shared goal for Tryon and the General Assembly, but it was not a shared goal for Martin or Howard. Consequently, Martin's recommendations placed Martin and Howard, both men who had received their positions via royal command, in direct opposition to the locally elected assembly. In time, both men would pay for their support of the Regulators and for their support of the British Empire.

Martin's willingness to advocate for the Regulators demonstrates the evolution in his responses toward British North American colonists. Having decided the Regulators' concerns held merit, and convinced that his own training and background fitted him better for the job at hand than the colonial assembly, Martin proceeded to take action. A. Roger Ekirch writes that "such was his zeal for political reform while in the backcountry that Martin projected several sweeping changes in the structure of local government."[69] By 1775, he would approvingly note to the Earl of Dartmouth that he had "the satisfaction to find the people in the western parts of this Province withstanding for the most part steadily all the efforts of the factions to seduce them from their duty."[70] The vision of government presented by his administration resembles the world described in the Regulators' fourth petition to Chief Justice Howard in September 1770.[71] Both sides believed in a commitment to social contracts between subjects and leaders that emphasized the older relationships between landed gentry and agricultural laborers that had informed the actions of the Newport Junto in 1764 and 1765.

Days after the hangings of six condemned Regulators in Hillsborough, the Regulator Rebellion was being portrayed outside of North Carolina as an exemplar of the growing Patriot movement. Like the colonists who protested the Stamp Act in 1765, the Regulators had sought redress through petitions before finally taking up arms in desperation at Alamance. An open letter to Governor Tryon published in the *Massachusetts Spy* on June 27, 1771, under the pen name "Leonidas" asked how Tryon might "account for the acknowledged perfidy of *opening* on a people with a full discharge of artillery, while under the sacred bond of a treaty, the observation of which might have been expected by a Saracen?"[72] The most interesting of these letters is the one signed "Atticus," which appeared in the *Virginia Gazette* on November 7, 1771. Like Leonidas, Atticus condemned Tryon's actions and his character, noting how "pitiable, sir, is the pale and trembling impatience of your temper."[73] Leonidas is thought to have been a pen name for Herman Husband, whose second pamphlet was published in Massachusetts that same year.[74] Scholars have been been unable to identify the author of the Atticus letter, although William Fitch attributed it to Maurice Moore on the grounds that Moore's "sympathy for the 'Regulators' and for their distresses classed him as a "Regulator."[75] It is true that Tryon disciplined Moore in 1765 for his pamphlet opposing the Stamp Act by removing him from his position as an associate justice for two years, but this did not automatically make Moore a Regulator. If anything, Moore's involvement with having Herman Husband removed from the General Assembly would seem to suggest that Moore, like many of his fellow assembly members, was opposed to the Regulator Rebellion and so it is unlikely that he wrote the Atticus letter.

The Regulator movement ultimately provided a direct challenge to North Carolina's landed families in the eastern parts of the colony. Bent, as they were, on first "serving their own interests," the assembly was determined "to reject any real reform of [North Carolina's] tax structure" demanded by the Regulators.[76] Moreover, the Regulators had successfully forged, if not an alliance, then an accordance with Chief Justice Howard before seeking redress from the royal government embodied by Josiah Martin. These actions, coupled with the assembly's own rising commitment to the Revolutionary cause, necessitated a rebuke to the positive portrayals of the Regulator Rebellion in the press.[77] A letter published by "Phocion" in the *Virginia Gazette* and the *Massachusetts Spy* reminded Leonidas that "the passing compliment you pay to the Judges, Sheriffs, and Pettifoggers, has perhaps been furnished to you by some of our Renegadoes."[78] Furthermore, "large bodies of men assembling to commit acts of depredation on private property, and threatening even the government itself, must either receive a timely and severe check or they will soon destroy the Government." These issues would fully manifest themselves in the signing of the Mecklenburg Resolves in 1775. In the meantime, both the former Regulators and the North Carolina General Assembly hoped to gain the upper hand when it came to telling the story of their affairs on the public stage of the Anglo-American world.

Chapter Eight

Rhode Island and North Carolina: New Battles

THE YEARS BETWEEN THE PASSING of the Stamp Act on March 25, 1765, and the signing of the Declaration of Independence on July 4, 1776, were marked by stretches of quiet and flares of colonial violence. The early 1770s are often considered a period of "calm in the wake of the repeal of most provisions of the 1767 Townshend Acts."[1] Nevertheless, Rhode Island colonists attacked and burned HMS *Gaspee* on June 10, 1772, after years of harassing customs officials in Narragansett Bay. Months of wrangling between North Carolina Governor Josiah Martin and the General Assembly led to adoption of the Mecklenburg Resolves on May 31, 1775, which effectively ended the royal government in that colony. These actions placed Rhode Island and North Carolina in the vanguard of colonial efforts to politically sever the North American colonies from Britain. They also demonstrate that Rhode Island and North Carolina hoped for independence but not necessarily union, a point underscored by both states' later reluctance to ratify the US Constitution in 1787.

The burning of the *Gaspee* and the creation of the Mecklenburg Resolves were rooted in Rhode Island's and North Carolina's colonial pasts, even as these events pulled both closer to the coming Revolution. Rhode Island

and North Carolina shared common histories of struggling to preserve local control in the face of demands for a more centralized authority, whether from their own residents, neighboring colonies, or the British Empire itself. During the Stamp Act crisis, many Rhode Island colonists fought internal efforts to place it under greater imperial control, while North Carolinians resisted their royal governor's efforts to accommodate their concerns. A few years later, colonists on both sides of the Regulator Rebellion would question who had the authority to govern and adjudicate in North Carolina. These issues were left unresolved when Parliament repealed the Stamp Act in 1766 and the Battle of Alamance brought the Regulator Rebellion to a close in 1771.

The American Revolution and the years immediately following the war only deepened internal tensions in Rhode Island and North Carolina. Parts of both states were occupied by the British army in the late 1770s. At the same time, the war effort largely silenced Loyalists in Rhode Island and North Carolina who, like the Howard family, left the United States for other parts of the British Empire.[2] The war years also saw divisions within the communities of Regulators. Most remained loyal to the empire, but some of the Regulators did join the Revolutionary cause. This final chapter links the Stamp Act crisis and the Regulator Rebellion with the burning of the *Gaspee* and the creation of the Mecklenberg Resolves, before turning to the ratification debate for the Constitution. Once again, Rhode Island's and North Carolina's colonial pasts were shaping their futures. Pauline Maier notes that this was a common experience during the ratification period for the Constitution: "[H]ow a convention developed depended on the characters of the state, its history and traditions, the relative strength of the contenders, the strategies they took (which were reflected in the rules they adopted), and occasionally some outside event."[3] The questions raised in both colonies about the intersecting roles played by local and imperial interests and identities in the 1760s were becoming questions about the roles played by local and federal interests and identities in the 1780s.

News of the burning of the *Gaspee* off the Rhode Island coast in June 1772 reached London within the month.[4] An unknown London newspaper editor commented on July 18 that "the conduct of Rhode Islanders ... will be productive of much disturbance in America."[5] The author appears familiar with the individual British colonies, as the editorial carefully distinguished between them, noting that "the New Englanders are universally hated in America; and notwithstanding Boston asserts to be the capital of the colonies, the colonies would rather embrace the most certain destruction than acknowledge her for a mistress." Virginia willingly joined the war effort in 1776. Nevertheless, the question of how best to respond to Parliament was openly debated in many of the colonies. The conclusion of the editorial raised the issue at the heart of the colonial responses to the Sugar and Stamp Acts: "[I]t is a melancholy truth that in all disagreements between the parent state and her children they are more affected by views of private interest than by the prosperity of their country." Early British colonists had quickly developed the habit of running goods along the Eastern Seaboard, which gave them easy access to other European ports in the Caribbean. Much to the frustration of the unknown newspaper editor, these colonists were focused on their own financial success rather than the prosperity of the British Empire as a whole.

These tensions fully emerged on the Anglo-American stage with the creation of the first Navigation Act in 1651 by Oliver Cromwell.[6] Four decades later, the Navigation Act of 1696 granted Parliament the power to create vice admiralty courts to further enforce mercantile law in the colonies, though these courts were not implemented until decades later. Unfortunately for the British exchequer, colonial traders blithely ignored the Navigation Acts. Dutch, French, and Spanish merchants were eager to trade with British colonists without the expense and hassle necessitated by laws requiring all foreign goods to enter the British Empire in London to be logged and taxed before being resold into the colonial market.[7] Rhode Island's ties to the transatlantic slave trade and the sugar plantations made it particularly easy for ship captains engaged in the legitimate funneling of people and comestibles between New England and the Caribbean to pick up illegal goods from other European ports that could then be bartered or sold for high profits when they returned to their home ports.[8]

A two-part essay authored by Providence merchant and politician Stephen Hopkins was published in the *Newport Mercury* in early February 1764. If "Trade carried on by the Northern Colonies with the French and Dutch Sugar Colonies . . . [was] injurious to the British [sugar colonies]," argued the essay, the solution was not for Parliament to tax the mainland British colonies in order to prop up the Caribbean colonies.[9] Parliament disagreed. The British Empire was in debt from the recent Seven Years' War to protect the North American colonies, and it needed the income provided by legitimate, taxable trade goods. Furthermore, the goal was to enrich the empire as a whole, rather than the pocketbooks of individual traders. Consequently, the Sugar Act was passed two months later, on April 5, 1764.[10]

The new law halved the earlier tax on molasses and placed a nominal tax on white sugar, but its primary goal, like the Stamp Act the following year, was to "break the hold of local commercial influence over customs enforcements by . . . [shifting smuggling cases] to distant imperial Vice-Admiralty Courts, where local commercial influence had no sway."[11] The London-based commissioners of customs began placing officials in coastal communities in 1763 to monitor ships carrying contraband goods. The newly created Admiralty courts promised by the Navigation Act of 1696 would provide them with the necessary tools for prosecuting smugglers to the full extent of the law. Ostensibly, money raised from the Stamp Act the following year would be used to "defray the expences of defending, protecting, and securing the [British colonies and plantations]" from the possibility of attacks from foreign powers in North America.[12] Everyone knew, however, that the Stamp Act's primary purpose was to "direct the manner of determining and recovering the penalties and forfeitures therein mentioned." Colonial merchants could now expect to pay for their surveillance with their own tax money.

The Sugar and Stamp Acts created a maelstrom of responses in the mainland British colonies. With their business interests on the line, merchants joined newly formed Sons of Liberty chapters to organize the colonial resistance. For their part, British government officials defended the new taxes in their official capacities. The Newport Junto provided a rare defense for the Sugar and Stamp Acts from British civilians. The group's individual members viewed the taxes from different perspectives, but their writings about the taxes presented a united front. Attorneys Martin Howard and Augustus Johnston, physicians Thomas Moffat and William Hunter, and architect Peter Harrison were part of Newport's professional classes. They had the luxury of debating the new taxes on a purely intellectual level, whether in Howard's *Letter from a Gentleman at Halifax* or their columns in the *Newport Mercury*. By contrast, John Robinson was Newport's customs collector, while George Rome was the colonial agent for the London firm of Hopkins and Haley.[13] For them, the Sugar and Stamp Acts were necessary, if dangerous, tools for expanding greater control over Newport's thriving community of merchants. Sheila Skemp also notes that a letter from Moffat to the customs commissioners in 1766 demonstrates that he too saw links between agitation over the Sugar and Stamp Acts and the growing colonial attacks on British customs vessels.[14]

Spring 1765 saw Robinson struggling to prosecute the captain of the trading vessel *Polly* on charges that he had underdeclared the amounts of sugar and molasses he had brought into New England waters.[15] Robinson seized the *Polly* in Massachusetts and left it behind while he returned to Newport for reinforcements. During his absence, a mob of men broke into

Rhode Island and North Carolina: New Battles 131

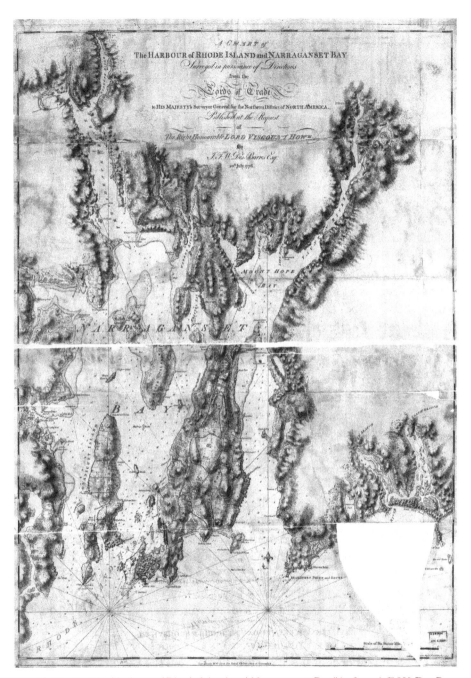

"A Chart of the Harbour of Rhode Island and Narragansett Bay," by Joseph F. W. Des Barres, London, 1776. (*Library of Congress*)

the *Polly* to steal its cargo and equipment before leaving it stranded at low tide. Massachusetts surveyor general John Temple managed to get the *Polly* afloat with the assistance of HMS *Maidstone*. The *Polly* was then returned to Newport, where it was placed under the control of HMS *Cygnet* in Newport Harbor with plans to deliver it to Halifax for prosecution before the vice admiralty court.

Newport was roiled by a new controversy in early June when the *Maidstone* returned to Rhode Island waters under the command of Captain Charles Antrobus. Naval ships were always undermanned, and impressing sailors in local ports was a common practice.[16] Governor Samuel Ward brokered an agreement with Antrobus that he would not impress men from ships in Newport Harbor. Desperate for new crew, Antrobus began patrolling Narraganset Bay just outside the harbor. The threat of impressment further destabilized the Newport economy, as ships refused to come near Acquidneck Island, and wages for sailors in the region soared.[17] In addition, the men who were most apt to be impressed were the ones who were suffering the most from the dismal post–French and Indian War economy. Finally, Antrobus "impressed all the Men out of a Brigantine from Africa, last from Jamaica" in early June.[18] In retaliation, a group of men described by Ward in an apologetic letter to Antrobus as "consisting altogether of the dregs of the people" destroyed the *Maidstone's* longboat later that same day.[19] These events added to the challenges posed by John Robinson's work as a customs collector, particularly since the *Maidstone* had helped to get the *Polly* afloat again.

Confrontations between colonists and customs agents were collateral damage for both sides in the march to revolution, but they posed real challenges for the customs agents who had to enforce the new taxes. Martin Howard, Thomas Moffat, and John Robinson all boarded the *Cygnet* on August 27 in Newport Harbor in order to escape the mob pursuing them. The dangers posed by the Newport Stamp Act riots were soon over for Howard and Moffat, both of whom were considered civilians by the British Empire. They boarded a second ship on August 31, which took them to London and safety. By contrast, as a customs collector, Robinson was an official representative of the British Empire who would face a disciplinary hearing if he abandoned his post. Consequently, the Stamp Act riots were a multiday standoff for Robinson. Newport resident Samuel Crandall threatened him in person shortly before he boarded the *Cygnet*. A message from Crandall delivered to Robinson the next day warned him that he would not be able to return safely to his home in Newport unless he delivered "the Sloop *Polly* and her Cargo, now under Prosecution before Doctor

Spry at Halifax."[20] Until Robinson returned to his work at the customs house, no ship could legally leave or enter Newport Harbor bound for waters outside Rhode Island. Trade slumped to a standstill, but Robinson remained obdurate, telling Governor Ward that he would not "attend to the Exercise of our Respective Functions, whatever Inconveniency it may be to the Trade, until you have appointed a proper Guard." The following week, a disgusted Ward assured Robinson that he was unlikely "to suffer the least insult or injury from any riotous Assembly," so, "the expense and trouble of a guard [is] entirely unnecessary."[21] Robinson eventually agreed to return to shore, and the customs house reopened in mid-September. Later that fall, he was forced to agree not to use stamped papers when clearing vessels after the Stamp Act took effect on November 1.[22] Shortly afterward, Robinson took up residence in Boston, where he enjoyed the protections of the royalist government, if not much in the way of tranquility.

Tensions between customs collectors and local merchants escalated in the coming years, particularly after the Townshend Acts were passed in 1767. The 1768 capture of Boston merchant John Hancock's sloop *Liberty* by HMS *Romney* and its recommission as a British naval vessel began in Massachusetts waters but ended in Rhode Island. The *Liberty* had seized two vessels from Connecticut for customs violations in summer 1769 and was towing them back to port when it was captured by New London merchant William Packard and a group of Rhode Island men.[23] Shortly afterward, the *Liberty* was burned to the waterline in Newport Harbor. Two years later, John Robinson's replacement, Charles Dudley, was beaten on a wharf in Newport. Congregationalist minister Ezra Stiles believed the attack stemmed from Dudley's willingness to take advantage of his position as customs collector. Dudley was reputed to have publicly stated "that he was obliged to refuse all Gratuities and dare not take any Thing," but a local ship captain claimed that "his people had wheeled home to the Collector Wines, Fruits &c. and they were not rejected."[24] By the time the *Gaspee* arrived in Narragansett Bay under the command of Lieutenant William Dudingston in February 1772, tensions between colonists and customs officials were already at fever pitch.[25]

Within days of arriving, the *Gaspee* seized twelve barrels of undeclared rum from the trading vessel *Fortune* and sent ship and rum to Boston for trial in the newly organized vice admiralty court. The Greene family, who owned the *Fortune*, appealed to Governor Joseph Wanton for redress.[26] The Rhode Island Charter of 1663 stated that "that no freeman [could] be . . . outlaw'd, or exil'd, or otherwise destroy'd, nor shall be oppressed, judged or condemned, but by the Law of this Colony.[27] Wanton ordered Lieutenant

Dudingston to "produce me your commission and instructions . . . which was your duty to have done when you first came within the jurisdiction of this Colony" in hope of brokering an agreement.[28] Dudingston summarily refused on the grounds that admiralty courts were allowed to supersede local laws in Britain and the colonies when prosecuting charges that fell under their jurisdiction, which this did. Nevertheless, Wanton and the Rhode Islanders continued to believe the presence of the *Gaspee* was a direct threat to their sovereignty.

The standoff between Dudingston and Rhode Island continued into summer 1772. Early in June, Captain Benjamin Lindsay saw the packet ship *Hannah* through customs inspection in Newport and headed up Narragansett Bay to his home port of Providence. When Dudingston and the *Gaspee* chased after the *Hannah* on June 9, Lindsey reportedly lured the *Gaspee* onto a sandbar during an outgoing tide.[29] Lindsey and the *Hannah* returned to Providence, where he told merchant John Brown about the *Gaspee's* plight. Brown and sea captain Abraham Whipple began making plans for an attack on the *Gaspee* before high tide lifted it from the sandbar. Eight longboats loaded with armed men rowed out to the *Gaspee* using muffled oars between midnight and one in the morning.[30] Dudingston ordered his men to shoot the attackers, but he was wounded almost immediately. He then agreed to surrender the *Gaspee* as long as he and his men were not further harmed. A ballad composed about the attack later reported that "Some Narragansett Indian men/Being sixty-four, if I remember/Which made the stout coxcomb surrender/And what was best of all their tricks/They in his breech a ball did fix."[31] Dudingston and the *Gaspee's* crew were bound and taken ashore, while the attack's leaders removed most of the documents from the ship before setting it on fire. A spark reached its powder magazine early in the morning of June 10, 1772, and it sank a few hours later.

Once again, the question of whether men arrested in Rhode Island were entitled to the protections provided by Rhode Island law erupted into a fierce debate. Admiral John Montagu, commander in chief of the North American Squadron, noted in his journal on June 14 that he had "received a letter from Lieut. Dudingston with the particulars of the Piratical People of Providence relative to his schooner."[32] Dudingston's use of the word "piratical" opened myriad possible charges for the perpetrators of the attack on the *Gaspee*. This was further reinforced when King George III signed the "Commission of Inquiry into Burning of the Gaspee" on September 2, authorizing the use of treason charges.[33] William Legge, the Earl of Dartmouth, was known for his support for the concerns expressed by British

North American colonists. Now, however, he was required by his new position as secretary of state for the colonies to fully enforce the terms laid out by George III's "Commission of Inquiry."[34] Furthermore, both Dudingston and Montagu were eager for revenge on the colonists of Rhode Island.

Rhode Island officials acknowledged that the attack needed to be investigated and punished, but they wanted to handle the matter as a purely local affair. Peter Messer notes that their process "followed a clearly identifiable script that sheds light upon the colonists' sense of both the legitimate boundaries of imperial authority and their right to correct imperial officials who transgressed those boundaries."[35] Deputy Governor Darius Sessions interviewed three of the *Gaspee's* crew on June 10 in an effort to identify the attack's leaders.[36] Governor Wanton assured Admiral Montagu in a June 12 letter that he could "rely upon the utmost & continued Exertions of the Officers of this Colony to detect & bring to Justice the Perpetrators of this Violent Outrage."[37] He also offered a reward of 100 pounds sterling to anyone who could provide information about the "perpetrators" as further evidence of his commitment to seeing the investigation through to its conclusion in a courtroom.[38]

In the end, none of the men involved with the attack on the *Gaspee* were extradited to London for trial. The matter was eventually dropped by George III and Parliament in favor of investigating and punishing the Boston Tea Party on December 16, 1773.[39] Burning a naval vessel was a serious crime, but the destruction of hundreds of pounds of tea was far more injurious to the British Empire. Nevertheless, the *Gaspee* Affair, as it came to be known, lingered in the memories of many Rhode Island residents. Dating back to Massachusetts's and Connecticut's first efforts to absorb Rhode Island in the 1630s and 1640s, the colony's commitment to its sovereignty had been challenged before. The actions of Rhode Island residents during and after the American Revolution demonstrate that they would long remain eager to protect that sovereignty.

Some colonial ministers did their best to avoid politics in their pulpits and their private lives in the 1770s. Others, like Ezra Stiles, became fierce proponents of the incipient Revolutionary movement. Boston minister John Allen delivered a sermon on December 3, 1772, intended to highlight the challenges to Rhode Island's sovereignty posed by the investigation into the attack on the *Gaspee*: "Are not the Rhode Islanders subjects to the King of Great Britain? Has not the King his attorney, his courts of judicatory to decide matters between the King and the subjects? Why then must there be New Courts of admiralty erected to appoint and order the inhabitants to be confin'd, and drag'd away?"[40] Allen's sermon was then printed as a pamphlet in a number of colonial communities, and it would become part of the arguments in favor of revolution in the coming years, even as the attack on the *Gaspee* was forgotten.

Interestingly, Allen also incorporated the Regulator Rebellion into his arguments for why Rhode Island possessed the right to investigate the attack on the *Gaspee*. Edmund Fanning and William Tryon were, in Allen's eyes, "like cruel blood-thirsty savages, who murdered mankind for thinking they had a right to oppose any power that attempted to destroy their LIBERTIES." Therefore, if the Regulators were rebels for breaking the law in North Carolina, then "the King's Ministry and Parliament must be REBELS, to God and mankind, in attempting to overthrow (by guns, swords, by the power of war) the laws, and government of Rhode Island."[41] Allen's portrayal of Edmund Fanning and William Tryon as "cruel blood-thirsty savages" was both an indictment of Britain's imperial abuse of its North American colonies and a demonstration of his support for the Regulators' efforts to defend their "liberties." It also demonstrates that Herman Husband had an eager audience in Massachusetts for his reporting on the Regulator Rebellion.

But the problem with John Allen's use of the Regulator Rebellion in this context was that like many of his counterparts, he had cast the movement's players in roles that many of them would find unrecognizable. On hearing the news of the Battle of Alamance on June 18, 1771, Ezra Stiles wondered "what shall an injured & oppressed people do, when their Petitions, Remonstrances, & Supplications are unheard & rejected" when they have been "insulted by the Crown Officers, and Oppression & Tyranny (under the name of Government)!"[42] The knowledge that Martin Howard was now North Carolina's chief justice and responsible for sentencing the men charged with treason after the battle reinforced Stiles's belief that the political motivations for the Regulator Rebellion corresponded to the political motivations for the Stamp Act crisis.[43] He later added on August 31 that "in Truth all the Province except the Crown officers & Connexions, are in heart Regulators," a statement that would have horrified North Carolina's colonial government.[44]

Nevertheless, residents in other colonies remained eager to cast the Regulators' challenges as part of a larger pattern of British imperial oppression. In the years after the war, popular mythology would continue to cast the Battle of Alamance as the first battle of the American Revolution. Jeremiah DeGennaro notes that "visual depictions of the battle—from sketches in the late 19th century to last year's season of *Outlander*—put Governor

Tryon's army in the redcoats of British Regulars, a simple shorthand to frame the battle as a forerunner to the revolution."[45] The reality, however, was that the Regulators had revolted against their own colonial government.

Furthermore, the Regulators had always acknowledged the possibility that they might meet with more resistance from their locally elected government officials than from their government officials whose appointments came from the British monarchy. An advertisement publicizing their intentions in 1766 noted that "Those Sons of Liberty . . . would soon corrupt again and oppress if they were not called upon to give an account of their Stewardship."[46] The Regulators acknowledged and appreciated the efforts of Sons of Liberty members throughout the colonies to protest parliamentary taxation. The Regulators were also aware that the men from eastern North Carolina who joined the Sons of of Liberty were the same locally elected members of the General Assembly who resisted the Regulators' pleas for reform in North Carolina. Governor William Tryon had orchestrated the battle that brought the Regulator Rebellion to a close on the banks of Alamance Creek in 1771, but he and his predecessor, Governor Arthur Dobbs, had attempted to address corruption in North Carolina in the mid-1760s.[47] After Governor Josiah Martin began his investigations in the Piedmont, an exultant James Hunter proclaimed on November 6, 1772, that "our new governor has been up with us and given us every satisfaction we could expect of him . . . and I think our officers hate him as bad as we hated Tryon only they don't speak so free."[48] By the end of the Regulator Rebellion, the Regulators had, indeed, "hated Tryon" but they still viewed locally elected government officials as the greater threat to their interests than the royal government.

Governor Martin's actions provide a window onto the complexities of relations between royal governors and British North American colonists. William Powell notes that Martin possessed "a more exalted idea of the royal prerogative than any of his predecessors . . . [insisting] that his instructions from the Crown took precedence over acts of the Assembly."[49] Tryon, by contrast, openly courted the loyalty of his eastern colonists throughout his time in North Carolina. The defeat of the Regulators at Alamance Creek in 1771 was the direct result of the alliance between Tryon and the assembly, as was the creation of Johnston's Riot Act earlier that year. While supportive of efforts to control unruly colonists, George III cautioned the North Carolina General Assembly in 1772 that its riot act was "unfit for any part of the British Empire."[50] Martin viewed these instructions as a directive to investigate the Regulator activities, which had prompted the creation of the Johnston act. When he realized that the Regulators' concerns were rooted in corruption at the local level, he swept into action. But as William Saunders observes, Martin was also "ill calculated generally to conduct an administration successfully ... his soldier life had perhaps dwarfed his mind and unfitted him for civil service. He knew nothing of duplicity or of diplomacy."[51] Where Tryon negotiated, Martin simply ordered. Like Rhode Island's governor and legislature during the *Gaspee* Affair, the assembly believed internal issues in North Carolina fell solely under its purview. Consequently, it was all too easy for its members to cast Martin's efforts to establish redress for the Regulators' concerns as further evidence of imperial overreach. Once again, the Regulator movement had run headlong into the imperial crisis, which, by that time, was rapidly evolving into a revolution.

Each event in the British North American colonies ran rapidly into the next one in the mid-1770s. On December 8, 1773, North Carolina authorized the creation of a Standing Committee of Correspondence to "obtain the most early and authentic intelligence of all such Acts and resolutions of the British Parliament" and to "maintain a correspondence and communication with our Sister Colonies."[52] The first task assigned to the committee was to research the justifications used by Parliament for holding the investigation into the attack on the *Gaspee* in London, which, again, suggests a sense of kinship between the two colonies.[53] An attack on the sovereignty of one historically vulnerable colony was an attack on them both, and they needed to support one another.

The correspondence committees were further outraged in late spring 1774 by the Intolerable Acts, as the Coercive Acts came to be known in the British North American colonies. The first three were specifically designed to punish the inhabitants of Massachusetts for the destruction of the tea in Boston Harbor on December 16, 1773.[54] The final two were intended to reshape parliamentary government of the colonies and would probably have been passed even without the Boston Tea Party. The Quartering Act was intended to clarify practices related to housing British soldiers in North America, and the Quebec Act expanded British control in southern Ontario and the area around the Great Lakes.[55] It also restored some French civil laws in Quebec and protected the right of Catholics to worship freely, a particularly controversial ruling for the deeply Protestant colonies, which feared that all British subjects would eventually be forced to convert to Catholicism.[56]

North Carolina's Committee of Correspondence reported early in winter 1774 that efforts to organize a unified response to the Coercive Acts were underway in most British colonies. Like Governor Tryon when the Stamp Act Congress was organized in 1765, Governor Martin hoped to forestall any formal response from North Carolina by dissolving the assembly.[57] Instead, Colonel John Harvey, the speaker of the House, asked the General Assembly members to hold a meeting to elect "Deputies to attend the General Congress at Philadelphia."[58] The resulting three-day gathering in New Bern was preceded by a meeting on August 24, 1774, in Halifax for men in the interior counties who could not make the long journey to New Bern. They appear to have taken a cautious approach to the matter at hand, perhaps because they represented so few voices in North Carolina. Their first resolution promised to "bear true and faithful allegiance to His Majesty King George the third ... [even] at the expence of our lives and fortunes."[59] The final resolution concluded that an economic approach was the best course of action available to the colonists. Accordingly, they would boycott imported goods, increase their exports to Britain, and so "magnify our firmness, patriotic virtue and Public spirit," which, in turn, would persuade Parliament to change its policies toward the colonies.

The gathering in New Bern on August 25–27 was the first meeting of the Provincial Convention or Congress of North Carolina.[60] It was attended by seventy men who represented twenty-nine of North Carolina's thirty-five counties, although the eastern counties sent more men than the western.[61] The first resolution passed at the meeting in Halifax had acknowledged their loyalty to the king. By contrast, the first resolution passed in New Bern was to appoint three attendees for the next "General Congress in Philadelphia." This body eventually convened on September 5, 1774, and is known today as the First Continental Congress.[62] The three men chosen to represent North Carolina were Richard Caswell, Joseph Hewes, and William Hooper, two of whom had fought against the Regulators at Alamance.[63] The Provincial Congress swore an oath of loyalty to George III, but it was accompanied by the caveat that it was their duty "in the present alarming state of British America ... to declare our sentiments in the most public manner, lest silence should be construed as acquiescence." The men present at the Provincial Congress ultimately agreed that boycotting British goods was the best method available for them to express their concerns. The First Continental Congress would come to much the same conclusion in Philadelphia the following month.[64]

Governor Martin was running out of time in spring 1775. His efforts to thwart John Harvey and the other assembly members from sending representatives to the Continental Congress in Philadelphia had failed. By that time, agitators in the individual British North American colonies were forming groups collectively known as Committees of Safety that were intended to oversee any challenges to their interests, such as refusals to honor nonimportation agreements.[65] Martin's March 1 proclamation condemning the Committees of Safety organized in North Carolina as "cabals and illegal proceedings . . . which can only tend to introduce disorder and anarchy to the destruction of the real interest and happiness of the people" had been greeted with silence in public and worse in private.[66] Determined to regain some control over the colony, Martin ordered the assembly to meet on April 4. Harvey again outmaneuvered him by organizing a second meeting of the Provincial Congress on April 3, which took place all but within the governor's earshot, as it was held in the legislative chambers in the other half of the Governor's Palace in New Bern. The members of the Provincial Congress elected Harvey as their speaker, thereby further solidifying his position as the most powerful man in North Carolina in 1775. Martin dissolved the assembly on April 8, but this only served to isolate him further.[67]

News of the skirmishes between Massachusetts colonists and British troops in Lexington and Concord added to the challenges facing Martin in May. He was still supported by some wealthy families like the McCullohs and the majority of the Highland Scots living in the Cross Creek region, but this was not enough to sustain his powers as governor.[68] Martin arranged for his wife and children to travel home to her father's house in New York in May and took shelter in Fort Johnston at the mouth of the Cape Fear River on May 31. That same day, the Committee of Safety in Mecklenburg County created a statement later known as the Mecklenburg Resolves that declared "all Commissions, civil and military, heretofore granted by the Crown . . . null and void."[69] Once the other Committees of Safety signed this document, the royal government was effectively dissolved in North Carolina. Martin condemned "these evil minded persons . . . [and their] most wicked, vile, false, and inflammatory suggestions, and insinuations," but the statement was little more than a public opportunity to vent his frustrations.[70] Sometime in June, Martin fled to rejoin his family in New York, leaving behind the remnants of the royal government.[71]

Among the remaining royal officials was Chief Justice Martin Howard. Since his arrival in North Carolina in 1767, he had developed a friendship with James Iredell, whose brother-in-law Samuel Johnston became governor following Martin's departure.[72] These connections helped Howard negotiate a compromise with the North Carolina Provincial Congress allowing his family to enter self-imposed house arrest at their plantation outside New Bern. From here in May 1777, he sent the letter to Iredell reflecting on the meadow where he "had made two blades of grass grow

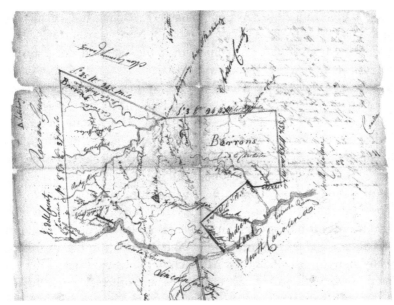

"Plann of the County of Mecklenburg," c. 1790, creator unknown. (*North Carolina Maps, State Archives of North Carolina*)

where only one grew before."[73] Later that year, Martin, Abigail, and Annie Howard traveled to New York and, eventually, to London, where they lived until Howard's death in 1781.[74]

On April 12, 1776, North Carolina's Halifax Resolves made the colony the first to instruct its delegates to the Second Continental Congress to vote in favor of independence from Britain.[75] On May 4, 1776, Rhode Island became the first colony to formally renounce its allegiance to the Crown.[76] These actions publicly claimed sovereignty for Rhode Island and North Carolina. They were also intended to demonstrate that Patriot leaders in both states were in the ascendency. Nevertheless, Loyalist communities in both states remained active to the point that prolonged occupations would be viable courses of action for the British army in the final years of the war.[77] Ultimately, the endless shifting between Patriot/American and Loyalist/British powers only deepened long-standing questions about political identities and loyalties in both states. John Shy notes that the British and Patriot occupations created a "triangularity of the struggle" in which two sides "contended less with each other than for the support and the control of the civilian population."[78] William Hooper, one of the three North Carolina men who signed the Declaration of Independence, wearily commented to Governor Abner Ash on June 7, 1779, "There is a lethargy about us in this place that to me is Unaccountable."[79] North Carolina had claimed independence from Britain early, but many in the state were uncertain about membership in the newly rising United States.

The years following the Treaty of Paris and the end of the American Revolution in 1783 were challenging ones. The United States was governed by the Articles of Confederation, which allowed each state to retain "its sovereignty, freedom, and independence, and every power, jurisdiction, and right, which is not by this Confederation expressly delegated to the United States."[80] Both the federal government and the individual states owed hundreds of thousands of dollars in debt to the European bankers who had supported them during the war, but the Articles of Confederation offered limited means for raising these funds via taxation.[81] Inequities in political representation and tax structures were roiling residents in the western parts of many states, most notably in Massachusetts, where Shays's Rebellion erupted in winter 1786.[82] These challenges, and others, brought fifty-five men from all the states, except Rhode Island, to Philadelphia in 1787 to decide how the United States should proceed as a nation. Despite the challenges facing the country, many Americans were hesitant to exchange the protections for individual states provided by the Articles of Confederation for the Constitution's vision of a newly empowered federal government.[83]

Once the debates on the Constitution had concluded, the fifty-five delegates returned to their home states to organize conventions at the state level. Some were determined to champion the Constitution, others wanted the country to continue with the Articles of Confederation. Article 7 of the Constitution states that "ratification of the conventions of nine states, shall be sufficient for the establishment of this constitution between the states so ratifying the same."[84] If nine or more states voted in favor of ratification, it would be used to govern these states, but the remaining states would be governed under the Articles of Confederation. The only path toward the Constitution becoming the law of the land throughout the United States was for all thirteen states to vote in favor of ratification. No states were more hesitant than North Carolina and Rhode Island to lose their positions as sovereign states under the Articles of Confederation.[85]

The Mecklenburg Resolves are best known for dissolving the royal government in North Carolina in 1775. They proclaim that "the Provincial Congress of each Province, under the Direction of the Great Continental Congress, is invested with all legislative and executive Powers within their respective Provinces."[86] This statement acknowledged the existence of the Continental Congress, but it emphasized preserving local control, which runs through North Carolina's and Rhode Island's colonial histories. Both were founded by colonists traveling overland from neighboring Massachusetts and Connecticut in the case of Rhode Island, and from Virginia and South Carolina in the case of North Carolina. Both prized the traditions of religious toleration, which distinguished them from many of their neighbors. Perhaps most importantly, both had residents who were all too accustomed to battling for their colony/state's political souls. Leaving Britain offered an independence that neither one was quite ready to relinquish.

As the state conventions dragged on through 1788 and into 1789, old battle lines from the colonial period rose up from the shadows. Pauline Maier notes that "many North Carolinians [were] acutely conscious of how much their welfare depended on being governed by officials who were accountable to the people, under laws written by legislators who knew the circumstances of their constituents."[87] Furthermore, the Constitution's primary advocate was Governor Samuel Johnston, who had created the infamous Johnston Riot Act in 1771. This time, Johnston recognized the need to incorporate the voices of farmers in western parts of North Carolina alongside the mercantile elites. He agreed to hold the ratifying convention in Hillsborough, once the epicenter of the Regulator Rebellion.[88] This first effort to ratify the Constitution failed in late summer 1788, but North Carolina eventually agreed to ratification in 1789 once the Constitution had been amended with the Bill of Rights.[89]

The political battles that tore Rhode Island apart in the 1750s had pitted Providence resident Stephen Hopkins against Samuel Ward from Acquidneck Island. Hopkins represented the rising mercantile classes while Ward represented the men who wanted Rhode Island to maintain its agrarian roots.[90] These alliances were reshaped during the imperial crisis as the Sons of Liberty championed the merchant class and the Newport Junto embraced Ward's emphasis on the older, landed families. Hopkins and Ward would resolve their differences in time to "walk arm in arm into Carpenter's Hall and the First Continental Congress" in 1774, but the older divisions remained.[91] The men who supported the Constitution were largely based in Providence and Newport, while the "Country Party," which dominated the General Assembly in 1788, represented the large farming families from southern Rhode Island.[92] As in North Carolina, these tensions would have to be resolved for Rhode Island to vote in favor of ratification.

News of Rhode Island's refusal to ratify the Constitution soon reached Federalist colonists in neighboring Massachusetts and Connecticut who "condemned the wickedness and folly of 'Rogue Island.'" However, as Pauline Maier adds, this only "hardened [Rhode Island's] determination to go their own way. Why should Rhode Islanders link arms with people who habitually denigrated them?"[93] In the end, like North Carolina, the promise of a Bill of Rights finally persuaded Rhode Island's delegates to ratify the Constitution on May 29, 1790, but tensions between rural and urban residents would continue into the nineteenth century.[94]

Read together, Rhode Island and North Carolina's interlocking experiences during the Stamp Act crisis and the Regulator Rebellion support a deeper study of the political and ideological shifts that underscored the turn from imperial crisis in the 1760s to the Revolutionary era in the 1770s, and, eventually to the ratification debates of the 1780s. Rhode Island and North Carolina embraced the American Revolution before many of their counterparts, but they were also reluctant participants in the rising union envisioned by the US Constitution in 1787. American history cannot be told without dissent and union alike, for these elements remain two halves of the same coin, perhaps more than ever in the twenty-first century.

Notes

PREFACE

1. Martin Howard to James Iredell, May 15, 1777, in James Iredell, *Life and Correspondence of James Iredell: One of the Associate Justices of the Supreme Court of the United States*, vol. 1, ed. John Griffith McRee (New York: Peter Smith, 1857), 363-364.

INTRODUCTION

1. Martin Howard's house is in the collection of the Newport Historical Society and is currently known as the Wanton-Lyman-Hazard House. See Joshua Fogarty Beatty, "Thinking Globally, Acting Locally: The Struggle for Community in Revolutionary Newport" (master's thesis, College of William and Mary, 2002), 57-60, for a more detailed description of the changes the Howards made to this house in the 1750s.

2. Ann Howard died in October 1764. Martin Howard wrote shortly afterward to Benjamin Franklin "that I have lost a Valuable and affectionate Wife, she is gone to 'that undiscovered Country, from whose Bourn, No Traveller returns.'" See Martin Howard to Benjamin Franklin, November 16, 1764, *The Papers of Benjamin Franklin, Founders Online*, National Archives, accessed March 21, 2023, https://founders.archives.gov/documents/Franklin/01/11-02-0137. The 1746 probate record for John Conklin, Ann Howard's first husband, indicates that she inherited three enslaved people identified as Castan, Briston, and Jenny. See Jonathon Conklin Probate Inventory, Newport Town Records, vol. 9, 131-132. Briston and Jenny were described as children in 1746 and so would have been in their mid-to-late twenties at the time of the Stamp Act crisis, though it is unknown whether they were members of the Howard household. Excavations beneath the attic floorboards of the Howard family home in 2005 uncovered a bundle of cloth holding a cowrie shell, nails, beads, pins, and corncobs. Katherine Garland writes that these objects were "a nkisi . . . a religious object associated with Bakongo spirituality. Minkisi were composite objects made of various objects which were designed to bridge the gap between the physical world and the spiritual realm, providing protection and healing." They were often hidden in domestic spaces, and this par-

ticular nkisi "shows that at least one of them had access to the attic; perhaps the attic was used as a living space. By placing a nkisi under the floorboards in the attic, the slave was seeking protection for the house, and holding on to his or her religious beliefs from home." Garland, "African Spirituality in Newport," *Spectacle of Toleration,* accessed March 21, 2023, https://web.archive.org/web/20170622121228/http://www.spectacleoftoleration.org/african-spirituality-in-newport/.

3. "Extract of a Letter from Boston," *Newport Mercury,* no. 363, August 19, 1765.

4. See Edmund S. Morgan and Helen M. Morgan, *The Stamp Act Crisis: Prologue to the Revolution* (Chapel Hill: University of North Carolina Press, 1995), 129-130. The Olivers and Howards gained a family connection in 1787 when Annie Howard married Andrew Spooner, Oliver's grandson. See Henry Edes, "Memoir of Martin Howard, Chief Justice of the Supreme Court of North Carolina," in *Publications of the Colonial Society of Massachusetts* (Boston: Colonial Society of Massachusetts, 1904), 395.

5. "The Author of the Halifax Letter," *Newport Mercury,* no. 364, August 26, 1765.

6. See Martin Howard, *Letter from a Gentleman at Halifax to his Friend in Rhode Island, Containing Remarks upon a Pamphlet, Entitled, The Rights of the Colonies Examined,* in *Pamphlets of the American Revolution, 1750-1776,* vol. 1., ed. Bernard Bailyn (Cambridge, MA: Harvard University Press, 1965), 523-544.

7. The August 26, 1765, edition of the *Newport Mercury* also included accounts of further protests against the Stamp Act in Boston and Connecticut from the previous week, which may have further instigated actions taken against the Stamp Act's supporters in Newport. See "Watchmen of the town of Boston" and "Reported last week from Connecticut," *Newport Mercury,* no. 364, August 26, 1765.

8. It is unknown where the other inhabitants of the Howard household spent the night of August 27. Annie may have joined her father on board the *Cygnet* since she had no other immediate family members in Newport. If there were enslaved members of the Howard household at that time, Howard may have arranged for them to go to the homes of other Newport Junto members on the outskirts of Newport, or they may have fled to shelter with other members of Newport's African American community.

9. Henry Conway, the secretary of state for the Southern Department, described their testimony as being "without passion or prejudice." Henry Conway to Samuel Ward, March 31, 1766, *Records of the Colony of Rhode Island and Providence Plantations,* ed. John Russell Bartlett (Providence, RI: Knowles, Anthony, 1861), 6:486.

10. See "Commission of William Tryon to Martin Howard," January 23, 1767, in *The Correspondence of William Tryon and Other Selected Papers,* vol. 1: 1758-1767, ed. William S. Powell (Raleigh: North Carolina Department of Cultural Resources, Division of Archives and History, 1980), 408. Fellow Rhode Island colonist John Whiting observed in 1767 that "perhaps the sons of liberty may claim some acknowledgment for his present honorary & lucrative situation, with which they have riggled him." John Whiting to Ezra Stiles, April 8, 1767, in Ezra Stiles, *The Literary Diary of Ezra Stiles,* ed. Franklin Bowditch Dexter (New York: Charles Scribner's Sons, 1901), 1:112.

11. See Robert Demond, *The Loyalists in North Carolina during the Revolution* (Durham, NC: Duke University Press, 1940), 183.

12. Most scholarship on the years prior to the American Revolution focuses on the period between 1770 and 1776. Examples include Richard Archer, *As If an Enemy's Country: The*

British Occupation of Boston and the Origins of Revolution (New York: Oxford University Press, 2012); Benjamin Carp, *Defiance of the Patriots: The Boston Tea Party and the Making of America* (New Haven, CT: Yale University Press, 2011); and Eric Hinderaker, *Boston's Massacre* (Cambridge, MA: Harvard University Press, 2017). Likewise, rhetoric used by modern-day political movements such as the Tea Party in 2009 has explicitly referenced events from the 1770s rather than events from the 1760s. See Jill Lepore, *The Whites of Their Eyes: The Tea Party's Revolution and the Battle over American History* (Princeton, NJ: Princeton University Press, 2011), 3-10, and Andrew Schocket, *Fighting over the Founders: How We Remember the American Revolution* (New York: New York University Press, 2015), 184-188, for a discussion of the Tea Party movement in 2009–2010.

13. This point should not be confused with the argument from the nineteenth and early twentieth centuries, which has continued in popular culture today, that the Regulator Rebellion was the first battle of the American Revolution, and this discrepancy will be addressed at later points. See William Fitch, *Some Neglected History of North Carolina, Being an Account of the Revolution of the Regulators and of the Battle of Alamance, the First Battle of the Revolution* (New York: Neale Publishing, 1906), 269, and Carole Watterson Troxler, *Farming Dissenters: The Regulator Movement in Piedmont North Carolina* (Raleigh: North Carolina Office of Archives and History, 2011), 167–170.

14. For more about the Duties in American Colonies Act, 5 George III, c. 12, see "Proceedings on the American Stamp Act," *Cobbett's Parliamentary History of England from the Earliest Period to the Year 1803*, vol. 16 (London: T.C. Hansard, 1813), 35.

15. Edmund Morgan, "Preface to the Third Edition," in Morgan and Morgan, *Stamp Act Crisis*, vii.

16. See Beatty, "Thinking Globally," and Zachary McLeod Hutchins, *Community without Consent: New Perspectives on the Stamp Act* (Hanover, NH: Dartmouth College Press, 2016). By contrast, Beatty's dissertation linked the Stamp Act crisis with the incipient abolition movement. See Beatty, "'The Fatal Year': Slavery, Violence, and the Stamp Act of 1765" (PhD diss., College of William and Mary, 2014).

17. Ken Shumate, *1764: The First Year of the American Revolution* (Yardley, PA: Westholme, 2021), ix.

18. A. Roger Ekirch, *"Poor Carolina": Politics and Society in Colonial North Carolina, 1729–1776* (Chapel Hill: University of North Carolina Press, 1981); Wayne E. Lee, *Crowds and Soldiers in Revolutionary North Carolina: The Culture of Violence in Riot and War* (Gainesville: University Press of Florida, 2001); Marjoleine Kars, *Breaking Loose Together: The Regulator Rebellion in Pre-Revolutionary America* (Chapel Hill: University of North Carolina Press, 2002); and Troxler, *Farming Dissenters*.

19. Bernard Bailyn described Rhode Island as "one of the most faction-ridden colonies in America" before introducing the "polemical explosions" created by the pamphlets composed by Rhode Island colonists Martin Howard and Stephen Hopkins. Bailyn, "Introduction to Hopkins, Rights of Colonies," in Bailyn, *Pamphlets of the American Revolution*, 500.

20. See Craig Yirush, "The Imperial Crisis," in *The Oxford Handbook of the American Revolution*, ed. Edward Gray and Jane Kamensky (New York: Oxford University Press, 2015), 85-102, for more on the period known as the imperial crisis.

21. See Lester Langley, *The Americas in the Age of Revolution, 1750–1850* (New Haven, CT: Yale University Press, 1996); Andrew Jackson O'Shaughnessy, *An Empire Divided: The*

American Revolution and the British Caribbean (New York: University of Pennsylvania Press, 2000); Mark Anderson, *Battle for the Fourteenth Colony: America's War of Liberation in Canada, 1774–1776* (Lebanon, NH: University Press of New England, 2013); and Kathleen Duval, *Independence Lost: Lives on the Edge of the American Revolution* (New York: Random House, 2015).

22. Pauline Maier, *From Resistance to Revolution: Colonial Radicals and the Development of American Opposition to Britain, 1765–1776* (New York: Vintage Books, 1972), 53.

23. See ibid.; Alfred Young, "Ebenezer Mackintosh: Boston's Captain General of the Liberty Tree," in *Revolutionary Founders: Rebels, Radicals, and Reformers in the Making of the Nation*, ed. Gary Nash Young and Ray Raphael (New York: Vintage Books, 2012), 17-24, and Lee, *Crowds and Soldiers*, 57–58.

24. See James Whittenberg, "Planters, Merchants, and Lawyers: Social Change and the Origins of the North Carolina Regulation," *William and Mary Quarterly* 34, no. 2 (1997): 215-17.

25. Pauline Maier, *Ratification: The People Debate the Constitution, 1787–1788* (New York: Simon and Schuster, 2010), 30-31.

26. See Sean Condon, *Shay's Rebellion: Authority and Distress in Post-Revolutionary America* (Baltimore: Johns Hopkins University Press, 2015), and William Hogeland, *The Whiskey Rebellion: George Washington, Alexander Hamilton, and the Frontier Rebels Who Challenged America's Newfound Sovereignty* (New York: Scribner, 2006).

27. "The Author of the Halifax Letter," *Newport Mercury*, no. 364, August 26, 1765.

28. See Don Higginbotham and William Price, "Was It Murder for a White Man to Kill a Slave? Chief Justice Martin Howard Condemns the Peculiar Institution in North Carolina," *William and Mary Quarterly* 54, no. 4 (1979): 593-601.

29. Anna Pavord, *The Naming of Names: The Search for Order in the World of Plants* (New York: Bloomsbury, 2005), 17.

30. Henry Lee Jr. to Nathanael Greene, April 2, 1781, in *Papers of Nathanael Greene*, vol. 8, ed. Dennis Conrad (Chapel Hill: University of North Carolina Press, 2015), 29.

31. Nathanael Greene to Thomas Walters, July 10, 1781, in ibid., 514. See John Maas, "North Carolina and Public Spirit in the American Revolution, 1775–1783," *Journal of the American Revolution*, May 4, 2021, accessed March 21, 2023, https://allthingsliberty.com/2021/05/north-carolina-and-public-spirit-in-the-american-revolution-1775-1783/.

32. See Lawrence C. Wroth, *The Colonial Printer* (Portland, ME: Southworth-Anthoensen Press, 1938), 224, and George Emery Littlefield, *Early Boston Booksellers, 1642–1711* (New York: Burt Franklin, 1969), 14.

33. See Hugh Amory, "Printing and Bookselling in New England, 1638–1713," in *The Colonial Book in the Atlantic World*, ed. Hugh Amory and David Hall (Chapel Hill: University of North Carolina Press, 2007), 111.

34. Lawrence Wroth notes that the printing of such documents was "by no means a hardship to the printer; on the contrary, there is evidence that he regarded the profits from the sale of this staple as the 'velvet' of his business." Wroth, *Colonial Printer*, 224.

35. See Louis Arthur Norton, "Print Media and Isaiah Thomas," *Journal of the American Revolution*, April 13, 2021, accessed March 21, 2023, https://allthingsliberty.com/2021/04/print-media-and-isaiah-thomas/.

36. See Arthur Schlesinger, *Prelude to Independence: The Newspaper War on Britain, 1764–1776* (Boston: Northeastern University Press, 1980), 303-304; Kathleen Wilson, *The Island*

Race: Englishness, Empire and Gender in the Eighteenth Century (New York: Routledge, 2003), 32-33; and Carol Sue Humphrey, *The American Revolution and the Press* (Evanston, IL: Northwestern University Press, 2013), 6-9.

37. Benjamin Carp, *Rebels Rising: Cities and the American Revolution* (New York: Oxford University Press, 2007), 12.

38. See Barbara Clark Smith, *The Freedoms We Lost: Consent and Resistance in Revolutionary America* (New York: New Press, 2010), 40-46, for a discussion on the early modern English belief that political and legal actions should be rooted in social contracts between leaders and the communities they governed, which included space for vocal commentary.

39. See Stephen Hopkins, *The Rights of Colonies, Examined*, in Bailyn, *Pamphlets of the American Revolution*, 499-522, and Howard, *Letter from a Gentleman at Halifax*, in ibid., 523-544. Bailyn notes that the title of the Howard pamphlet was "effectively allusive (every reader recognized Halifax as the seat of the new superior vice-admiralty court that had been created by the Sugar Act." Bailyn, "Introduction to Howard's Halifax Letter," in ibid., 527.

40. See Isaiah Thomas, *The History of Printing in America, with a Biography of Printers & an Account of Newspapers* (New York: Weathervane Books, 1970), 315.

41. See Wroth, *Colonial Printer*, 22.

42. Carol Sue Humphrey documents an equally short-lived experiment in bipartisan newspaper reporting when bookseller John Mein "establish[ed] the *Boston Chronicle* in 1767 in partnership with John Fleeming. Mein and Fleeming originally stated that their newspaper would be impartial, in the tradition long held in the colonies, to 'throw some light on the complexion of the times.' . . . [B]ut the goal of impartiality proved impossible to achieve in the wake of the Stamp Act crisis [when] Mein found himself irresistibly drawn into the debate over the Stamp Act, and insisted on expressing his opposition to the trade boycotts." A mob assaulted Mein and Fleeming in 1769, and the paper was shut down in 1770. Humphrey, *American Revolution*, 57.

43. Correspondence between Samuel Hall and the Vernon family suggests his 1769 departure from Newport was for both political and financial reasons. The Vernons were a wealthy family of Newport merchants who opposed the Stamp Act and the Townshend Acts. See Samuel Hall Correspondence, box 49, folder 2, vault A, Newport Historical Society, Newport, Rhode Island.

44. See Schlesinger, *Prelude to Independence*, 289.

45. See ibid., 56, 75-83.

46. See Leona Hudack, *Early American Women Printers and Publishers, 1639–1820* (Metuchen, NJ: Scarecrow Press, 1978).

47. Maurice Moore, *The Justice and Policy of Taxing The American Colonies, in Great Britain, considered*, in *Not a Conquered People: Two North Carolinians View Parliamentary Taxation*, ed. William Price (Raleigh: North Carolina Department of Cultural Resources, Division of Archives and History, 1975), 35-48.

48. See Herman Husband, *An Impartial Relation of the First Rise and Cause of the Recent Differences in Publick Affairs* (1770), and *A Fan for Fanning, and A Touchstone to Tryon* (1771), in *Some Eighteenth Century Tracts Concerning North Carolina*, ed. William K. Boyd (Raleigh, NC: Edwards and Broughton, 1927), 247–392. Boyd notes that the title page for *A Fan for Fanning* stated that it was issued at "the Printing-office . . . at the head of Queen Street" in Boston. Boyd adds that "tradition has held that Isaiah Thomas published *A Fan for Fan-*

ning," which was advertised in Thomas's *Massachusetts Spy*. Boyd, "Introduction," in *Some Eighteenth Century Tracts*, 337-338.

49. Minutes of the Lower House of the North Carolina General Assembly, October 17, 1749, in *Colonial and State Records of North Carolina*, ed. William Laurence Saunders (Raleigh, NC: P.M. Hale, 1886), 4:976-994.

50. William Powell, *North Carolina through Four Centuries* (Chapel Hill: University of North Carolina Press, 1989), 129.

51. See Isaiah Thomas, *The History of Printing in America: With a Biography of Printers & an Account of Newpapers* (New York: Weathervane Books, 1970), 376-377.

52. See Liam Riordan, "A Loyalist Who Loved His Country Too Much: Thomas Hutchinson, Historian of Colonial Massachusetts." *New England Quarterly* 90, no. 3 (2017): 346-347.

53. Jane Kamensky, *A Revolution in Color: The World of John Singleton Copley* (New York: W. W. Norton, 2016), 179-180.

54. Edmund Morgan, *The Gentle Puritan: A Life of Ezra Stiles, 1727–1795* (New York: W. W. Norton, 1962), vii.

55. For a longer discussion of Stiles's research on the Stamp Act crisis, see Abby Chandler, "'The Basis of Alienation will never be healed': The Historicity of Protest in Ezra Stiles' Stamp Act Notebook," in *Protest in the Long Eighteenth Century*, ed. Yvonne Fuentes and Mark Malin (New York: Routledge, 2021), 159-173.

56. I imposed these sections on the "Stamp Act Notebook" when I was transcribing it, as the original document is unpaginated, to aid with examining and citing its different components. See Ezra Stiles, "Stamp Act Notebook," MS vault film 1523, reel 16, Beineke Rare Book and Manuscript Library, Yale University, New Haven, CT. The original "Stamp Act Notebook" is on file in the Ezra Stiles Papers, Beineke Rare Book and Manuscript Library.

57. See Schlesinger, *Prelude to Independence*, and Humphrey, *American Revolution*.

58. See William Smith, *The history of the province of New-York: from the first discovery to the year MDCC. XXXII, to which is annexed a description of the country, with a short account of the inhabitants, their trade, religious and political state, and the constitution of the courts of justice in that colony* (London: T. Wilcox, 1757). Smith was also a contemporary of Ezra Stiles's at Yale University. Smith graduated in 1745, and Stiles graduated in 1746, but it is unknown whether they discussed their mutual interest in history as undergraduates.

59. See Lorenzo Sabine, *Biographical Sketches of Loyalists of the American Revolution, with an Historical Essay*, vol. 2 (Boston: Little Brown, 1864), 312-313, and Cho-Chien Feng, "The Revolutionary Memories of New York Loyalists Thomas Jones and William Smith, Jr.," *Journal of the American Revolution*, January 31, 2019, accessed March 21, 2023, https://allthingsliberty.com/2019/01/the-revolutionary-memories-of-new-york-loyalists-thomas-jones-and-william-smith-jr/.

60. See "Notes and Extracts from Papers of Governor William Tryon," Manuscripts and Archives Division, New York Public Library, accessed March 21, 2023, https://digitalcollections.nypl.org/items/b7d32740-48a3-0135-8950-15544719209b.

61. See William Smith, "Introduction to the History of Governor Tryon's Administration from 1764 to 1768," https://digitalcollections.nypl.org/items/e70e8490-48a3-0135-653a-61e475fb942a, and William Smith, "Introduction to the History of Governor Tryon's Administration from 1769 to 1771," both in the Manuscripts and Archives Division, New

York Public Library, both accessed March 21, 2023, https://digitalcollections.nypl.org/items/52c761f0-48a5-0135-82a37331ca554750.

62. William Smith, *Historical Memoirs 1763 to 1778*, vol. 1, ed. William Sabine (New York: Colburn and Tegg, 1971), 107.

63. See "The Rhode Island Resolves," in *Prologue to Revolution: Sources and Documents on the Stamp Act Crisis, 1764-1766*, ed. Edmund Morgan (Chapel Hill: University of North Carolina Press, 1959), 50-51.

64. See "On Saturday the 19th of Last Month," *North-Carolina Gazette*, and "Monday the 18th instant," *North- Carolina Gazette*, both no. 58, November 20, 1765.

65. David Zaret, *Origins of Democratic Culture: Printing, Petitions, and the Public Sphere in Early-Modern England* (Princeton, NJ: Princeton University Press, 2000), 75.

66. Ibid., 82.

67. For a discussion on the uses of family histories when studying the Early American period, see Karin Wulf, "Situating Self, Seeking Lineage: Family Histories in 17th and 18th Century British North America," in *The Uses of First Person Writings: Les Usages des ecrits du for prive*, ed. Francois-Joseph Ruggiu (New York: Peter Lang, 2013), 203-205.

68. Lucius to Solomon Southwick, date unknown, box 121, folder 13, Newport Historical Society, Newport, RI. My thanks to Ingrid Peters at the Newport Historical Society for verifying the citation to this letter.

69. The Rogers's Rangers regiment was organized in 1755 by Major Robert Rogers as a company within New Hampshire's provincial forces. See Fred Anderson, *Crucible of War: The Seven Years' War and the Fate of Empire in British North America, 1754–1766* (New York: Alfred A. Knopf, 2000), 181-189.

70. Another such example noted that "The Temper of the Times called for conciliatory measures, and your L_d_p *wisely* met this temper, by irritating resolves." See "From a London Paper, Oct. 12," *Newport Mercury*, no. 597, February 12, 1770. The essay is addressed to the "E_ of H_h," who was probably Wills Hill, the Earl of Hillsborough, who served as secretary of state for the colonies from 1768 to 1772. See George Fisher Russell Baker, "Wills Hill (1718–1793)," in *Dictionary of National Biography*, accessed March 23, 2023, https://en.wikisource.org/wiki/Dictionary_of_National_Biography,_1885-1900/Hill,_Wills.

71. The Coercive Acts were Parliament's response to the Boston Tea Party in 1773. See *Cobbett's Parliamentary History*, vol. 17, 1159-1210.

72. Daniel Morgan served in the Virginia Rangers company during the French and Indian War before organizing equivalent companies for the Continental army. See Don Higginbotham, *Daniel Morgan: Revolutionary Rifleman* (Chapel Hill: University of North Carolina Press, 1979), 6-7.

73. *OED Online*, s.v. "Temper, v.," accessed March 21, 2023, www.oed.com/view/Entry/198875.

CHAPTER 1: FOUNDING RHODE ISLAND AND NORTH CAROLINA

1. Milton Klein and Jacob Cooke add that if "the history of the tiny colony of Rhode Island has been dwarfed by that of its better-known neighbors," it is only because "its pioneering accomplishments have 'been taken for granted.'" Milton Klein and Jacob Cooke, eds., *Colonial Rhode Island: A History* (New York: Scribner, 1975), xiii.

2. Patrick Conley, *Democracy in Decline: Rhode Island's Constitutional Development, 1776–1841* (Providence: Rhode Island Historical Society, 1977), 111.

3. John Barry, *Roger Williams and the Creation of the American Soul: Church, State, and the Birth of Liberty* (New York: Penguin, 2012), 3-4.

4. For more about Rhode Island's early founding period, see Sydney James, *Colonial Rhode Island: A History* (New York: Scribner, 1975), 1-32, and Bruce Daniels, *Dissent and Conformity on Narragansett Bay, The Colonial Rhode Island Town* (Middletown, CT: Wesleyan University Press, 1983).

5. The phrase "livelie experiment" was used by Charles II to describe Rhode Island in the charter granted to its colonists in 1663. See "The Charter Granted by His Majesty, King Charles the Second to the Colony of Rhode-Island and Providence Plantations in America," in *The Earliest Acts and Laws of the Colony of Rhode Island and Providence Plantations, 1647–1719*, ed. John D. Cushing (Wilmington, DE: M. Glazier Press, 1977).

6. See James, *Colonial Rhode Island*, 57.

7. See Carp, *Rebels Rising*, 99-113.

8. G. B. Worden, "Rhode Island Civil Code of 1647," in *Saints and Revolutionaries: Essays on Early American History*, ed. David D. Hall, John M. Murrin, and Thad W. Tate (New York: W. W. Norton, 1984), 141.

9. For more on Rhode Island's legal structures, see Worden, "Rhode Island Civil Code," and Mary Sarah Bilder, *The Transatlantic Constitution: Colonial Legal Culture and the Empire* (Cambridge, MA: Harvard University Press, 2004), 51-72.

10. For more about John Clarke's negotiations for Rhode Island's charter, see Sydney James, *John Clarke and His Legacies: Religion and Law in Colonial Rhode Island, 1638–1750* (University Park: Pennsylvania State University Press, 1999), 59-84.

11. See James, *Colonial Rhode Island*, 69-72.

12. Bilder, *Transatlantic Constitution*, 30.

13. See Alan Taylor, *American Colonies: The Settling of North America* (New York: Penguin, 2002), 137.

14. The men who received proprietorships in Carolina Colony were Edward Hyde, the Earl of Clarendon; George Monck, the Duke of Albemarle; John Berkely, the Baron Berkeley of Stratton; William Craven, the Earl of Craven; Sir George Carteret; Sir William Berkeley; Anthony Cooper, the Earl of Shaftesbury; and Sir John Colleton. All eight had supported the Stuart family and the Crown during the English Civil War. See William Powell, *North Carolina through Four Centuries* (Chapel Hill: University of North Carolina Press, 1989), 53-54.

15. See Viviana Díaz Balsera and Rachel May, eds., *La Florida: Five Hundred Years of Hispanic Presence* (Gainesville: University of Florida Press, 2016), 69-82.

16. Powell, *North Carolina*, 55.

17. David Leroy Corbitt, *The Formation of the North Carolina Colonies, 1663–1943* (Raleigh: North Carolina Department of Cultural Resources, Division of Archives and History, 1975), xiii.

18. "The Fundamental Constitutions of Carolina: March 1, 1669," Avalon Project: Documents in Law, History and Diplomacy, accessed March 21, 2023, https://avalon.law.yale.edu/17th_century/nc05.asp.

19. See Taylor, *American Colonies*, 282-285.

20. See Steven Oatis, *A Colonial Complex: South Carolina's Frontiers in the Era of the Yamasee War, 1680–1730* (Lincoln: University of Nebraska Press, 2008), and William Ramsey, *The*

Yamasee War: A Study of Culture, Economy, and Conflict in the Colonial South (Lincoln: University of Nebraska Press, 2010).
21. See Powell, *North Carolina*, 86.
22. See Daniel Vickers, *Farmers & Fishermen: Two Centuries of Work in Essex County, Massachusetts, 1630–1850* (Chapel Hill: University of North Carolina Press, 1994), 31-99.
23. The Narragansett remained the largest tribal group in southern New England until they were defeated by an allied group of English colonists and Mohegan peoples during King Philip's War in 1676. See Christoph Strobel, *Native Americans of New England* (Santa Barbara, CA: Praeger, 2020), 104-105.
24. Cotton Mather, *Magnalia Christi Americana or the Ecclesiastical History of New England* (Hartford, CT: Silas Andrus and Son, 1853), 521.
25. James, *Colonial Rhode Island*, 50.
26. See Jay Coughtry, *The Notorious Triangle: Rhode Island and the African Slave Trade 1700–1807* (Philadelphia: Temple University Press, 1981), and Sarah Deutsch, "Those Elusive Guineamen: Newport Slavers, 1735–1774," *New England Quarterly* 55, no. 2 (1982): 229-253.
27. See Christy Clark-Pujara, *Dark Work: The Business of Slavery in Rhode Island* (New York: New York University Press, 2016), 25-29.
28. Matthew Mulcahy, *Hubs of Empire: The Southeastern Low Country and British Caribbean* (Baltimore: Johns Hopkins University Press, 2014), 84-111.
29. See Ekirch, *"Poor Carolina,"* 18.
30. Smith, "Introduction to the History of Governor Tryon's Administration from 1764 to 1768," 14. Also see Bradford Wood, *This Remote Part of the World: Regional Formation in Lower Cape Fear, North Carolina, 1725–1775* (Columbia: University of South Carolina Press, 2004), 178-179, and Kimberly Sherman, "A Spirit of Industry: The Colonial Origins of Rice Culture in the Lower Cape Fear," *North Carolina Historical Review* 91, no. 3 (2014): 255-287.
31. Wood, *This Remote Part*, 180-181.
32. See Theda Purdue and Christopher Oakley, *Native Carolinians: The Indians of North Carolina* (Raleigh: North Carolina Department of Natural and Cultural Resources, Division of Archives and History, 2010).
33. See Abraham Wood to John Richards, August 22, 1674, in "The Travels of James Needham and Gabriel Arthur through Virginia, North Carolina, and Beyond, 1673–1674," ed. R. P. Stephen Davis Jr., *Southern Indian Studies* 39 (1990): 46.
34. John Lawson, *A New Voyage to Carolina; Containing the Exact Description of that Country: Together with the Present State thereof*, ed. Hugh Talmadge Lefler (Chapel Hill: University of North Carolina Press, 1967), 61.
35. Ibid., 132.
36. See Powell, *North Carolina*, 69-74, and Harry Roy Merrens, *Colonial North Carolina in the Eighteenth Century: A Study in Historic Geography* (Chapel Hill: University of North Carolina Press, 1964), 113-114.
37. See James Merrell, *The Indians' New World: Catawbas and Their Neighbors from European Contact through the Era of Removal* (Chapel Hill: University of North Carolina Press, 2009), 136, and Tom Hatley, *The Dividing Paths: Cherokees and South Carolinians through the Era of Revolution* (New York: Oxford University Press, 1993), 5-8, 22-23.
38. See Kars, *Breaking Loose*, 15.

39. Merrell, *Indians' New World*, 195.
40. Powell, *North Carolina*, 101. Also see Minutes of the Southern Congress at Augusta, Georgia; North Carolina; Cherokee Indian Nation; Catawba Indian Nation; Et Al. October 01, 1763–November 21, 1763, in Walter Clark, ed., *Colonial and State Records of North Carolina*, vol. 11 (Raleigh: P. M. Hale, 1895), 156-207.
41. Merrens, *Colonial North Carolina*, 164-165.
42. Ekirch, *"Poor Carolina,"* 68-71, and William Price, "'Men of Good Estates': Wealth among North Carolina's Royal Councilors," *North Carolina Historical Review* 49, no. 1 (1972): 72-82.
43. Kars, *Breaking Loose*, 9-26.
44. Ekirch, *"Poor Carolina,"* 110.
45. See Condon, *Shay's Rebellion*.
46. See Hogeland, *Whiskey Rebellion*.
47. Ekirch, *"Poor Carolina,"* 110.
48. See Joseph Conforti, *Saints and Strangers: New England in British North America* (Baltimore: Johns Hopkins University Press, 2006), 170.
49. Conley, *Democracy in Decline*, 223.
50. See Erik Chaput, *The People's Martyr: Thomas Wilson Dorr and his 1842 Rebellion* (Lawrence: University Press of Kansas, 2013), 12-47.
51. Ibid., 78.
52. Chaput, *People's Martyr*, 59-64.
53. Robert Coakely, *The Role of Federal Military Forces in Domestic Disorders, 1789–1878* (Washington, DC: Center of Military History, 1988), 120.
54. Chaput, *People's Martyr*, 136.
55. See Powell, *North Carolina*, 61-63.
56. Culpeper's Rebellion is described in ibid., 63-67.
57. Ibid., 63, 67.
58. Ibid., 75-77.
59. "Fundamental Constitutions of Carolina," Avalon Project.
60. Powell, *North Carolina*, 69-74.
61. See Rosemary Moore, "Seventeenth-Century Context and Quaker Beginnings," in *The Oxford Handbook of Quaker Studies*, ed. Stephen Angell and Pink Dandelion (New York: University of Oxford Press, 2015), 22.
62. Powell, *North Carolina*, 150.
63. John Carteret received his title as the Earl of Granville in 1742. While he became known as Granville after this point, I have chosen to continue referring to him as Carteret for clarity's sake.
64. The British government divided the management of its diplomatic relations into the Southern Department and the Northern Department in 1660. Each department had its own secretary of state who conveyed information between Parliament and the political bodies they represented. The British North American colonies were represented by the secretary of state for the Southern Department until 1768, when they were provided with a separate secretary of state. See "Lists of Appointments," in University of London Institute of Historical Research, *Office-Holders in Modern Britain*, vol. 2 (London: J. C. Sainty, 1973), 22-58.

65. Ekirch, *"Poor Carolina,"* 129; see William Bennet, ed., *Orange County Records*, vol. 1, *Granville Proprietary Land Office, Abstracts of Loose Papers* (Raleigh, NC: privately published, 1987), held at the North Carolina Government and Heritage Library, Raleigh.
66. Ekirch, *"Poor Carolina,"* 135-137.
67. Ibid., 141.
68. See Lee, *Crowds and Soldiers*, 28-35.
69. Lewis Hampton Jones, *Captain Roger Jones of London and Virginia, Some of his antecedents and descendants* (Albany, NY: Joel Munsell's Sons, 1891), 4.
70. Frederick Jones to Elizabeth Cocke Jones, December 10, 1756, in ibid., 399-401.
71. Claude Nash, *Some Nashes of Virginia: Two Hundred Years of an American Family, 1774–1974* (self-pub., 1975), 131.
72. John Whiting to Ezra Stiles, April 8, 1767, in Stiles, *Literary Diary*, 112.
73. Lee, *Crowds and Soldiers*, 27.

CHAPTER 2: BEFORE THE STAMP ACT

1. See Elaine Forman Crane, *A Dependent People: Newport, Rhode Island in the Revolutionary Era* (New York: Fordham University Press, 1985), 49-52.
2. See Carp, *Rebels Rising*, 100-114.
3. Z.Y., "Mr. Printer," *Newport Mercury*, no. 294, April 23, 1764.
4. Joshua Fogarty Beatty notes that "the members of the Newport Junto were disturbed by the corrupt, faction-ridden government of Rhode Island and saw a forceful Parliament as a far more legitimate authority." Beatty, "Thinking Globally," 5.
5. See Sheila Skemp, "Newport's Stamp Act Rioters: Another Look," *Newport History* 47, no. 2 (1989): 51-52, for a discussion on the economic challenges facing Rhode Island colonists after the French and Indian War. See Crane, *Dependent People*, 5, for a discussion of the "political revolving door known as the Hopkins-Ward controversy."
6. Beatty, "Thinking Globally," vi.
7. Most writings connected with the Loyalist position on the American Revolution were not composed until the 1770s and so the Newport Junto also provided an early look at the evolution of Loyalist ideas. For more on the emergence of Loyalist political rhetoric, see Philip Gould, *Writing the Rebellion: Loyalists and the Literature of Politics in British America* (New York: Oxford University Press, 2013).
8. James Otis, "Brief Remarks on the Defence of the Halifax Libel on the British American Colonies," in Bailyn, *Pamphlets of the American Revolution*, 549.
9. "The Author of the Halifax Letter," *Newport Mercury*, no. 364, August 26, 1765. Martin Howard's parents, Martin and Ann Howard, were both Anabaptists, and Howard was almost certainly brought up within one of Newport's Baptist communities. He did not formally convert to the Anglican faith until summer 1770, when he joined the Anglican church in New Bern, North Carolina. See Edes, "Memoir of Martin Howard," 386-387.
10. For more about Ann Brenton Conklin Howard's family, see Elisha Reynolds Potter, *The Early History of Narragansett: with an appendix of original documents, many of which are now for the first time published* (Providence, RI: Marshall, Brown, 1835), 295.
11. See Timothy Shannon, *Indians and Colonists at the Crossroads of Empire: The Albany Congress of 1754* (Ithaca, NY: Cornell University Press, 2000), 133. Like James Otis before him, David Lovejoy's description of Martin Howard and the Newport Junto as a "cabal" borders

on hyperbolic slander. Lovejoy, *Rhode Island Politics and the American Revolution, 1760–1776* (Providence, RI: Brown University Press, 1958), 49.

12. See Daniel Snydacker, "The Remarkable Career of Martin Howard," *Newport History* 61, no. 1 (1988): 2-17, and Abby Chandler, "Reexamining the Remarkable Career of Martin Howard," *Newport History* 90, no. 2 (2019): 1-30. Overseers of the poor were town officials who were responsible for guaranteeing housing for indigent residents, whether in "individual household[s] under a town-approved caretaker, or in a poorhouse or workhouse." Ruth Wallis Herndon, *Unwelcome Americans: Living on the Margin in Early America* (Philadelphia: University of Pennsylvania Press, 2001), 7.

13. See Albert J. Wright, *History of the State of Rhode Island with Illustrations* (Philadelphia: Hong, Wade, 1878), 154–158.

14. See Carl Bridenbaugh, *Peter Harrison, American Architect* (Chapel Hill: University of North Carolina Press, 1949), 76.

15. See George Champlin Mason, *Annals of the Redwood Library and Athenaeum* (Newport, RI: Redwood Library, 1891), 20.

16. Bridenbaugh, *Peter Harrison*, 7-20, 68-73, 76; Lovejoy, *Rhode Island Politics*, 174-175.

17. Bridenbaugh, *Peter Harrison*, 125.

18. See Lovejoy, *Rhode Island Politics*, 42.

19. Edes, "Memoir of Martin Howard," 386-387.

20. Abraham Van Honeyman, *The Honeyman Family in Scotland and America, 1504–1598* (Plainfield, NJ: Honeyman's Publishing House, 1909), 82-83.

21. Bridenbaugh, *Peter Harrison*, 76.

22. Mary and Margaret Sanford were the daughters of Peleg Sanford, Ann Brenton Conklin Howard's uncle by marriage. Andrew Oliver became the first Stamp Tax master in Boston, while Thomas Hutchinson was the last royal governor in Massachusetts. See Potter, *Early History*, 299. The Olivers sold their share in the Sanford farm on Narragansett Bay to the Hutchinsons in 1737. See Historic New England, "History of the Watson Farm," accessed March 21, 2023, https://www.historicnewengland.org/property/watson-farm/. Martin Howard's daughter, Annie Howard, married Andrew Spooner, Mary and Andrew Oliver's grandson and Margaret and Thomas Hutchinson's great nephew, on June 16, 1787, at Trinity Church in Newport, Rhode Island. See Edes, "Memoir of Martin Howard," 395.

23. Honeyman, *Honeyman Family*, 86.

24. See Bridenbaugh, *Peter Harrison*, 182.

25. The Redwood Library was the third library constructed in the British North American colonies, following the Library Company of Philadelphia in 1731 and the Library Company of Darby, Pennsylvania, in 1743. Wilmarth Lewis, "Preface," *The 1764 Catalogue of the Redwood Library Company at Newport, Rhode Island* (Hartford: Connecticut Printers, 1965), ix.

26. The Redwood Library believes that Peter Harrison's plan for the library "was probably derived from the headpiece of Book IV of Edward Hoppus' 1735 edition of Andrea Palladio's architecture." Redwood Library, "Our Building," accessed March 21, 2023, https://redwoodlibrary.org/our-building#overlay-context=user.

27. Abraham Redwood, quoted in Lewis, "Preface," *1764 Catalogue*, ix.

28. The Redwood Library directors made John Tomlinson and Stephen Greenleaf honorary members of the library to thank them for their efforts. See Bridenbaugh, *Peter Harrison*, 53. Greenleaf, who was the last royally appointed sheriff for Suffolk County, Massachusetts,

later became Martin Howard's second father-in-law. Ann Brenton Conklin Howard died in fall 1764, and Howard married Abigail Greenleaf in summer 1767 at the Portsmouth home of John Wentworth, the last royally appointed governor of New Hampshire. For the wedding announcement, see "Portsmouth: Last Saturday morning was Married here, by the Rev. Arthur Brown, at the Seat of His Excellency JOHN WENTWORTH, Esq; the Honorable MARTIN HOWARD, Esq; Chief JUDGE OF NORTH CAROLINA, to Miss ABIGAL GREENLEAF, Daughter of STEPHEN GREENLEAF Esq; of Boston," *New-Hampshire Gazette*, no., 561, August 28, 1767.

29. See Mason, *Annals of the Redwood Library*, 11-12.

30. Lewis, "Preface," *1764 Catalogue*, xiii.

31. Mason, *Annals of the Redwood Library*, 40-42.

32. Benjamin Carp writes, "Newport had developed an attitude of latitudinarianism, or the toleration of other beliefs, yet the variety of religious groups also led to disagreements about various issues, doctrinal or otherwise. The crowded urban landscape forced these groups to articulate their differences in close quarters, often with acrimonious results." Carp, *Rebels Rising*, 99.

33. All quotations from this document are from Z.Y., "Mr. Printer," *Newport Mercury*, no. 294, April 23, 1764. This passage suggests that the Newport Junto were familiar with Cotton Mather's *Magnalia Christi Americana or the Ecclesiastical History of New England*, which had decried the "lewd things which have been done or said by the giddy sectaries of [Rhode] Island" in 1702. See Mather, *Magnalia Christi Americana*, 521.

34. See Margaret Ezell, "John Locke's Images of Childhood: Early Eighteenth Century Response to Some Thoughts Concerning Education," *Eighteenth-Century Studies* 17, no. 2 (1984): 140.

35. Zaret, *Origins of Democratic Culture*, 82.

36. Benjamin Franklin to Richard Jackson, May 1, 1764, *Papers of Benjamin Franklin*, Founders Online, National Archives, accessed March 21, 2023, https://founders.archives.gov/documents/Franklin/01-11-02-0046. Richard Jackson often assisted British colonists by conveying letters and petitions to their recipients in London and regularly corresponded with Franklin on a variety of issues.

37. Martin Howard to Benjamin Franklin, November 16, 1764, *Papers of Benjamin Franklin*, Founders Online, National Archives, accessed March 21, 2023, https://founders.archives.gov/documents/Franklin/01/11-02-0137.

38. "Proceedings of the General Assembly, held for the Colony of Rhode Island and Providence Plantations, at Providence, on the last Wednesday in October, 1764," in Bartlett, *Records of the Colony of Rhode Island*, 6:411; "Position of the Governor and Company of Rhode Island to the King, November 4, 1764," in ibid., 6:415.

39. Mack Thompson, "The Ward-Hopkins Controversy and the American Revolution in Rhode Island: An Interpretation," *William and Mary Quarterly* 16, no. 3 (1959): 366.

40. See John Austin, *Genealogical Dictionary of Rhode Island* (Albany, NY: J. Munsell's Sons, 1887), 325-326.

41. See ibid., 202, 370, 406.

42. See Thomas Williams Bicknell, *The History of the State of Rhode Island and Providence Plantations*, vol. 3 (New York: American Historical Society, 1920), 1074. Bicknell writes that "it is of interest to note that the farmer class of Narragansett country was made of many

of the most intelligent, most cultivated and wealthy people of Rhode Island . . . the farmer barons of the Colony." Ibid., 1073.

43. David Lovejoy writes that Samuel Ward "spent as much time worrying about cattle, hogs, and crops as he did about politics. Hopkins, on the other hand, was involved with politics most of his life and was familiar with the business life of the colony. Lovejoy, *Rhode Island Politics*, 13-14.

44. Ibid., 11-12.

45. Crane, *Dependent People*, 5.

46. See Lovejoy, *Rhode Island Politics*, 81.

47. Carl Bridenbaugh writes that "the basic explanation of Peter Harrison is that having won a place in the colonial gentry he sought to emulate in Rhode Island the life of the eighteenth-century aristocrats he had known in Yorkshire and Nottinghamshire." Bridenbaugh, *Peter Harrison*, 74.

48. See Abby Chandler, "'Let us unanimously lay aside foreign Superfluities': Textile Production and British Colonial Identity in the 1760s," *Early American Studies: An Interdisciplinary Journal* 19, no. 1 (Winter 2021): 138-165, for a longer discussion of the textile debate in the *Newport Mercury*.

49. Lovejoy, *Rhode Island Politics*, 50.

50. Morgan and Morgan, *Stamp Act Crisis*, 50; Bailyn, "Introduction," in Bailyn, *Pamphlets of the American Revolution*, 1: 526.

51. Beatty, "Thinking Globally," 24-25.

52. For the primary scholarship linking arguments for home textile production with the Patriot cause, see these works by T. H. Breen: "An Empire of Goods: The Anglicization of Colonial America, 1690–1776," *Journal of British Studies* 25, no. 4 (1986): 467-499; "'Baubles of Britain': The American and Consumer Revolutions of the Eighteenth Century," *Past & Present* 119 (1988): 73-104; "Narrative of Commercial Life: Consumption, Ideology, and Community on the Eve of the American Revolution," *William and Mary Quarterly* 50, no. 3 (1993): 471-501; "Ideology and Nationalism on the Eve of the American Revolution: Revisions Once More in Need of Revising," *Journal of American History* 84, no. 1 (1997): 13-39; and *The Marketplace of Revolution: How Consumer Politics Shaped American Independence* (New York: Oxford University Press, 2004). Other studies include Laurel Thatcher Ulrich, *The Age of Homespun: Objects and Stories in the Creation of an American Myth* (New York: Alfred A. Knopf, 2001); Kate Haulman, *The Politics of Fashion in Eighteenth-Century America* (Chapel Hill: University of North Carolina Press, 2011); and Jennifer Van Horn, *The Power of Objects in Eighteenth-Century British North America* (Chapel Hill: University of North Carolina Press, 2017).

53. See *Newport Mercury*, issues 312–341, August 27, 1764–March 18, 1765. It is unclear why the Newport Junto used the pseudonym O.Z. during this period. Philip Gould examined many of their writings in relation to British literature in the mid-eighteenth century and was unable to find any literary origins for the name. See Gould, *Writing the Rebellion*, 30-57.

54. See A Lover of Pennsylvania, "Industry *exalteth a nation* and *the hand of the diligent maketh rich*," *Newport Mercury*, no. 306, July 16, 1764; "Extract from a late PUBLICATION," *Newport Mercury*, no. 307, July 23, 1764; and "The Method of Raising HEMP in Pennsylvania," *Newport Mercury*, no. 347, April 29, 1765. Benjamin Franklin's testimony

before Parliament opposing the Stamp Act in 1765 included a discussion of textile production in Pennsylvania. See "Examination of Dr. Benjamin Franklin," *Cobbett's Parliamentary History*, 16:137-160, for Franklin's testimony before Parliament. Franklin was probably the primary source for much of the Newport Junto's information on the topic inasmuch as he and Howard had corresponded on topics of mutual interest since the Albany Congress in 1754.

55. See O.Z., "Letter to Mr. Hall," *Newport Mercury*, no. 315, September 17, 1764, and "Letter to Mr. Hall," *Newport Mercury*, no. 317, October 1, 1764.

56. "Resolutions of the Committee of Ways and Means for the Year 1764," *Cobbett's Parliamentary History*, vol. 15, 1426. See Shumate, *1764*, 44-50, for a longer discussion of the Sugar Act.

57. O.Z., "Letter to Mr. Hall," *Newport Mercury*, no. 340, March 11, 1765.

58. See Hopkins, *Rights of the Colonies Examined*, and Howard, *Letter from a Gentleman at Halifax*, in Bailyn, *Pamphlets of the American Revolution*, 1: 499-544. See Gould, *Writing the Rebellion*, 30-57, for further discussion on the Hopkins and Howard pamphlets.

59. "Hemp Premium," *Newport Mercury*, no. 306, July 14, 1764.

60. "Letter to Mr. Hall," *Newport Mercury*, no. 313, September 3, 1764, and "Letter to Mr. Hall," *Newport Mercury*, no. 314, September 10, 1764; O.Z., "Letter to Mr. Hall," *Newport Mercury*, no. 315, September 17, 1764.

61. "The following Piece is inserted in this Paper at the Request of a constant Reader," *Providence Gazette*, no. 100, September 15, 1764.

62. The source of the enmity between the two men is unknown, but Howard was firmly in Ward's political camp in the 1750s, and the seeds of discord may have been sown in that initial period. Hopkins and Howard also served as Rhode Island's representatives to the Albany Congress in 1754, and it seems likely that they disagreed over imperial policies in the British North American colonies while in Albany, though there is no written record of their discussions. See Shannon, *Indians and Colonists*, 133.

63. O.Z., "Letter to Mr. Hall," *Newport Mercury*, no. 320, October 22, 1764; O.Z., "Letter to Mr. Hall," *Newport Mercury*, no. 321, October 29, 1764.

64. O.Z., "Letter to Mr. Hall," *Newport Mercury*, no. 311, August 20, 1764.

65. Chester Brenton, "Descendants of William Brenton, Governor of Rhode Island" (unpublished manuscript), Newport Historical Society.

66. Crane, *Dependent People*, 138.

67. Advertisement from the first page of the *Newport Mercury*, no. 311, August 20, 1764. See Harrison Ellery, "The Vernon Family and Arms," *New England Historical and Genealogical Register* 33 (1879): 316, for more about Samuel and William Vernon.

68. See S. D. Smith, "The Market for Manufactures in the Thirteen Continental Colonies, 1698–1776, *Economic History Review* 51, no. 4 (1998): 676-708, for statistics on the amounts of goods imported into individual colonies, which greatly increased immediately after the close of the Seven Years' War in 1763.

69. See Elaine Forman Crane, *Ebb Tide in New England: Women, Seaports, and Social Change, 1630–1800* (Boston: Northeastern University Press, 1985), and Gary Nash, "The Failure of Female Factory Labor in Colonial Boston," *Labor History* 20 (1979): 165-188, for discussions on women's struggles to support themselves as spinners. See Robert Allen, "The Industrial Revolution in Miniature: The Spinning Jenny in Britain, France, and India," *Jour-*

nal of Economic History 69, no. 4 (2009): 901-927, for discussion of efforts to industrialize the labor of spinning.

70. Laurel Thatcher Ulrich, "'Daughters of Liberty': Religious Women in Revolutionary New England," in *Women of the Age of Revolution*, ed. Ronald Hoffman and Peter Albert (Charlottesville: University of Virginia Press, 1989), 215-218. Ulrich's primary sources for these events were announcements in newspapers like the ones in the *Newport Mercury*, and as she notes, many of these events took place at ministers' homes. Newport minister Ezra Stiles hosted at least one such event at his home in spring 1770 that does not appear to have been reported in the *Newport Mercury*.

71. "News," *Newport Mercury*, no. 392, March 10, 1766.

72. The nine announcements in the *Newport Mercury* were "News," no. 392, March 10, 1766; "To Mr. Printer," no. 401, May 12, 1766; "The following is an Account," no. 403, May 26, 1766; "A Number of Young Ladies," no. 489, January 18, 1768; "To Mr. Southwick," no. 554, April 17, 1769; "To Mr. Southwick," no. 557, May 8, 1769; "To Mr. Southwick," no. 558, May 15, 1769); "We hear from Brooklyn," no. 559, May 22, 1769; and "In Newport," no. 559, May 22, 1769.

73. "In Newport," *Newport Mercury*, no. 491, February 1, 1768.

74. The Townshend Acts were named for the British chancellor of the exchequer, Charles Townshend. "Resolutions of the Committee of Ways and Means for the Year 1767," *Cobbett's Parliamentary History*, 16:331-343, 359-361, 369-375.

75. Christopher Berry, *The Idea of Luxury: A Conceptual and Historical Investigation* (New York: Cambridge University Press, 1994), 173.

76. The three Newport Junto members who were educated in Scotland were Thomas Moffat, William Hunter, and James Keith. See Bridenbaugh, *Peter Harrison*, 76.

77. See Maxine Berg, "In Pursuit of Luxury: Global History and British Consumer Goods in the Eighteenth Century," *Past & Present* 182 (2004): 85-142, and Jan de Vries, *The Industrious Revolution: Consumer Behavior and the Household Economy, 1650 to the Present* (New York: Cambridge University Press, 2008), 41-72.

78. Berry, *Idea of* Luxury, 62.

79. O.Z., "Letter to Mr. Hall," *Newport Mercury* no. 311, August 20, 1764.

80. "American Watchman to the Fair-Sex in North-America," *Newport Mercury*, no. 557, May 8, 1769.

81. "Letter to Mr. Southwick," *Newport Mercury*, no. 557, May 8, 1769.

82. See Carole Shammas, "How Self-Sufficient Was Early America?", *Journal of Interdisciplinary History* 13, no. 2 (1982): 247-272.

83. Ibid., 252. Laurel Thatcher Ulrich makes similar arguments in both "Of Pens and Needles: Sources in Early American Women's History," *Journal of American History* 77, no. 1 (1990): 200-207, and "Wheels, Looms, and the Gender Division of Labor in Eighteenth-Century New England," *William and Mary Quarterly* 55, no. 1 (1998): 3-38, as does Kate Haulman in *Politics of Fashion*, 52.

84. Shammas, "How Self-Sufficient?," 247.

85. See Linda Kerber, *Women of the Republic: Intellect and Ideology in Revolutionary America* (Chapel Hill, NC: Omohundro Institute of Early American History and Culture, 1997).

CHAPTER 3: THE STAMP ACT IN RHODE ISLAND

1. See Anderson, *Crucible of War*, 503-506.
2. Ibid., 312, 583-584.
3. See Reed Browning, *The Duke of Newcastle* (New Haven, CT: Yale University Press, 1975), 271-274.
4. The full text of the debate on the "Cyder Tax" and the resulting protests is available in "Second Session of the Twelfth Parliament of Great Britain," *Cobbett's Parliamentary*, 15:1307-1315.
5. See Justin Du Rivage, *Revolution against Empire: Taxes, Politics, and the Origins of American Independence* (New Haven, CT: Yale University Press, 2017), 91-100.
6. See Philip Lawson, *George Grenville: A Political Life* (Oxford: Clarendon Press, 1984), 154.
7. The full text of the debate on the repeal of the "Cyder Tax" is available in "Summary of the Debates in Both Houses on the Right of Taxing America," *Cobbett's Parliamentary History*, 16:206-207.
8. The full text of the Molasses Act, or the Act for the better securing and encouraging the trade of his Majesty's sugar colonies in America, can be found in *Cobbett's Parliamentary History*, vol. 8, 856-857.
9. See Ken Shumate, "The Molasses Act: A Brief History," *Journal of the American Revolution*, January 24, 2019, accessed March 21, 2023, https://allthingsliberty.com/2019/01/the-molasses-act-a-brief-history/.
10. See Ken Shumate, "The Sugar Act: A Brief History," *Journal of the American Revolution*, September 17, 2018, accessed March 21, 2023, https://allthingsliberty.com/2018/09/the-sugar-act-a-brief-history/.
11. The full text of the Sugar Act, or the American Duties Act, is available in "Resolutions of the Committee of Ways and Means for the Year 1764," *Cobbett's Parliamentary History*, 15:1426.
12. Stephen Hopkins, "An Essay on the Trade of the Northern Colonies, Part One," *Newport Mercury*, no. 283, February 6, 1764, and "An Essay on the Trade of the Northern Colonies, Part Two," *Newport Mercury*, no. 284, February 13, 1764.
13. Sugar Act, *Cobbett's Parliamentary History*, 15:1426.
14. "Proceedings on the American Stamp Act," ibid., 15:35.
15. Gauthram Rao, *National Duties: Customs Houses and the Making of the American State* (Chicago: University of Chicago Press, 2016), 39.
16. See John Phillip Reid, *Constitutional History of the American Revolution: The Authority of Rights* (University of Wisconsin Press, 1995), 179. Also see Jerry Bannister, *The Rule of the Admirals: Law, Custom, and Naval Government in Newfoundland, 1699–1832* (Toronto: University of Toronto Press, 2014), for a broader history of British admiralty courts in the Maritimes.
17. Connecticut Governor Thomas Fitch helped compose Connecticut's response to the Stamp Act. But his belief that his oath of office as governor bound him to uphold the Stamp Act when it took effect on November 1, 1765, led directly to his gubernatorial defeat by William Pitkin in 1766. See Albert Carlos Bates, "Sketch of William Pitkin," in *The Pitkin Papers: Correspondence and Documents during William Pitkin's Governorship of the Colony of Connecticut, 1766–1769* (Hartford: Connecticut Historical Society, 1921), xxiv.

18. Allen Mansfield Thomas, "'*Circumstances* not Principles': Elite Control of the Newport Stamp Act Riots," *Newport History* 67, no. 2 (1996): 129.
19. See Bicknell, *History of the State of Rhode Island*, 1086.
20. See Shannon, *Indians and Colonists*, 214-215.
21. See Ron M. Potvin, "Washington Slept Here? Reinterpreting the Stephen Hopkins House," *History News* 66, no. 2 (2011): 17-20; Snydacker, "Remarkable Career of Martin Howard"; and Chandler, "Reexamining the Remarkable Career of Martin Howard."
22. See Hopkins, *Rights of Colonies, Examined*, in Bailyn, *Pamphlets of the American Revolution*, 1: 499-522, and Howard, *Letter from a Gentleman at Halifax*, in ibid., 523-544. Bernard Bailyn notes that the title of the Howard pamphlet was "effectively allusive (every reader recognized Halifax as the seat of the new superior vice-admiralty court that had been created by the Sugar Act)." Bailyn, "Introduction to Howard's Halifax Letter," in Bailyn, *Pamphlets of the American* Revolution, 1: 527.
23. See Edmund Morgan and Helen Morgan, *The Stamp Act Crisis: Prologue to Revolution* (Chapel Hill: University of North Carolina Press, 1995), 59-65, and Morgan, *Prologue to Revolution*, 27-28.
24. Hopkins, *Rights of the Colonies*, in Bailyn, *Pamphlets of the American Revolution*, 1:511.
25. Howard, *Letter from a Gentleman at Halifax*, in Bailyn, *Pamphlets of the American Revolution*, 535. Howard's definition of rights was, like Thomas Jefferson's Declaration of Independence in 1776, modeled on John Locke's political philosophies. See Locke, *The Two Treatises of Civil Government*, ed. Thomas Hollis (London: J. M. Dent, 1924).
26. See Otis, *The Rights of the British Colonies Asserted and Proved*, in Bailyn, *Pamphlets of the American Revolution*, 1: 408-483.
27. Bailyn, "Introduction to Hopkins, Rights of Colonies," in Bailyn, *Pamphlets of the American Revolution*, 1: 500.
28. Stephen Hopkins noted that "the importation of foreign molasses ... puts an end to all the costly distilleries in these colonies, and to the rum trade to the coast of Africa, and throws it in the hands of the French. With the loss of the foreign molasses trade, the cod fishery of the English in America must also be lost thrown also into the hands of the French." Hopkins, *Rights of the Colonies Examined*, in Bailyn, *Pamphlets of the American Revolution*, 1: 514.
29. Joshua Fogarty Beatty also examines Stephen Hopkins's implicit willingness to condone smuggling and Martin Howard's frustration with this same willingness. He notes "that piece of wishful thinking was one of many exploded by Martin Howard." Beatty, "Thinking Globally," 30.
30. Also Gould, *Writing the Rebellion*, 30-57.
31. Howard, "Letter from a Gentleman at Halifax," in Bailyn, *Pamphlets of the American Revolution*, 535.
32. Ibid., 537. Other restrictions on suffrage, including gender and race, would not be addressed until much later in British history.
33. See Mark Kishlansky, *Parliamentary Selection: Social and Political Choice in Early Modern England* (New York: Cambridge University Press, 1986), for more about early modern parliamentary districts in the United Kingdom. This system was eventually abolished in the nineteenth century, and suffrage was gradually expanded into the twentieth century. See Sean Lang, *Parliamentary Reform, 1785-1928* (New York: Routledge, 1999).

34. Howard, *Letter from a Gentleman at Halifax*, in Bailyn, *Pamphlets of the American Revolution*, 538.
35. Stephen Hopkins and Martin Howard reported on their experiences in Albany at the Rhode Island assembly on August 20, 1754. See Bartlett, *Records of the Colony of Rhode Island*, 5:393-394. Hopkins repudiated the Albany Plan of Union in 1755. See Stephen Hopkins, *A True Representation of the Plan Formed at Albany for Uniting All the British Colonies*, in *Rhode Island Historical Tracts* (Providence, RI: S. S. Rider, 1877), 3-46.
36. The opening paragraphs of the Otis pamphlet describe finding "inaccuracies in abundance, declamation and false logic without end; *verse* is retailed in the shape of *prose*, solecisms are attempted to be passed off for good grammar, and the most indelicate fustian for the fine taste." Otis, *A Vindication of the British Colonies, against the Aspersions of the Halifax Gentleman*, in Bailyn, *Pamphlets of the American* Revolution, 554. "Fustian" is defined in the Oxford English Dictionary as "formerly, a kind of coarse cloth made of cotton and flax. Now, a thick, twilled, cotton cloth with a short pile or nap, usually dyed of an olive, leaden, or other dark colour." *OED Online*, s.v. "Fustian, n.," accessed March 21, 2023, www.oed.com/view/Entry/75820. This may have been a direct reference to the Newport Junto's campaign for domestic textile production in Rhode Island.
37. Hopkins, *Postcript* in *A Vindication of the British Colonies*, in Bailyn, *Pamphlets of the American Revolution*, 578. Joshua Fogarty Beatty also discusses Stephen Hopkins's efforts to portray Martin Howard as an outsider in Rhode Island. See Beatty, "Thinking Globally," 41-44.
38. Brendan McConville, *The King's Three Faces: The Rise and Fall of Royal America, 1688–1776* (Chapel Hill: University of North Carolina Press, 2006), 249.
39. Howard, *Letter from a Gentleman at Halifax*, in Bailyn, *Pamphlets of the American Revolution*.
40. Michael Laird, *A Natural History of English Gardening* (New Haven, CT: Yale University Press, 2015), 3.
41. Ezra Stiles noted that the first ship carrying news of the Stamp Act's official passage into law "arrived from London to Boston first week of April. News reached Newport 10 April." This information informed the actions of colonial agitators throughout New England in spring 1765. Stiles, "Stamp Act Notebook," sect. 3.
42. See Christopher Minty, "Mobilization and Voluntarism: The Political Origins of Loyalism in New York, c. 1768–1778 (PhD diss., University of Stirling, 2014), for a further look at early Loyalist political movements in New York.
43. See Young, "Ebenezer Mackintosh," 17-24.
44. Morgan and Morgan, *Stamp Act Crisis*, 128.
45. Edmund and Helen Morgan add that "perhaps this division of labor was deliberate, in order to keep the radical leaders of the Assembly, who were always conspicuously in the public eye, from bringing too much attention to the group. Or perhaps the effectiveness of the radical leaders in the Assembly might have been impaired if they were openly associated with an organization engaged in the treasonable activities which the Loyal Nine envisaged." Morgan and Morgan, *Stamp Act Crisis*, 128.
46. See Morgan, *Gentle Puritan*, 166-196.
47. Elaine Forman Crane notes that "Stiles listed 55 people who supported the Stamp Act. Fifty-three would remain loyal to the Crown throughout the next decade. At the same time, 36 of the 40 men committed to 'liberty' in 1765 constituted the nucleus of the Revolutionary movement and would support the cause of independence in 1776. Crane, *Dependent People*, 128.

48. Stiles, "Stamp Act Notebook," sect. 3.
49. Samuel Vernon's daughter, Mary Vernon, married William Ellery's brother, Christopher Ellery, on November 26, 1760, and so the families were connected by marriage as well as economic and political interests. See Ellery, "Vernon Family," 316. Samuel and William Vernon's younger brother, Thomas, remained loyal to Britain throughout the American Revolution and was eventually imprisoned in Newport for eight months for his beliefs. See Thomas Vernon, "Journal while in the Custody of the Whigs," box 44, folder 2, Newport Historical Society, Newport, RI.
50. Ellery, "Vernon Family," 315-317.
51. Advertisement from the first page of *Newport Mercury*, no. 311, August 20, 1764.
52. Crane, *Dependent People*, 113.
53. See ibid., 54-55.
54. Bicknell, *History of the State of Rhode Island*, 1085.
55. Thomas Bicknell notes that "the term of service of the father, Richard, and his two sons, Thomas and Henry as Secretary of State extended over a period of seventy-five years." Ibid., 1067.
56. The Coggeshalls were among the first settlers in Portsmouth, Rhode Island, in the 1630s. See Charles Pierce Coggeshall, *The Coggeshalls in America: Genealogy of the Descendants of John Coggeshall of Newport, with a brief notice of their English antecedents* (Boston: C. E. Godspeed, 1930), 22.
57. Stiles, "Stamp Act Notebook," sect. 3.
58. Morgan and Morgan, *Stamp Act Crisis*, 188.
59. Pauline Maier adds that "the officers and committee members of the Sons of Liberty were largely drawn from the middle and upper ranks of colonial Society." Maier, *From Resistance to Revolution*, 86. Alfred Young argues that shoemaker Ebenezer Mackintosh's relationship with Boston's Sons of Liberty chapter evolved over time. See Young, "Ebenezer Mackintosh," 15-34. T. H. Breen argues, however, that the Revolutionary movements stemmed from populist roots rather than elite. See Breen, *American Insurgents, American Patriots: The Revolution of the People* (New York: Farrar, Straus and Giroux, 2010).
60. See Skemp, "Newport's Stamp Act Rioters," 41-60, and Ruth Kennedy Myers and Bradford A. Becken, "Who Was John Webber?", *Newport History* 70, no. 2 (2000): 1-21.
61. Advertisement for *Letter from a Gentleman at Halifax*, *Newport Mercury*, no. 336, February 11, 1765.
62. The Wanton family's political interests were highly fluid during this period. Joseph Wanton Jr. and his father, Joseph Wanton Sr., are listed in Ezra Stiles's "Stamp Act Notebook" as supporting the Crown, and both men were accused of being Tories during the outbreak of the American Revolution, in part owing to Joseph Wanton Jr.'s agreement to drop the investigation into Martin Howard's *Letter from a Gentleman at Halifax* pamphlet in February 1765. Joseph Wanton Sr. was able to fend off these charges, in part owing to his efforts to shield the Rhode Island colonists responsible for burning the HMS *Gaspee* in 1772, and was allowed to remain in Rhode Island. Joseph Wanton Jr. married Sarah Brenton, one of Abigail Brenton Howard's cousins in 1775, and they fled with the British army in 1780 when the United States retook Newport. See Wilkins Updike, *A History of the Episcopal Church in Narragansett, Rhode Island: Including a History of Other Episcopal Churches in the State* (Boston: Merry Mount Press, 1907), 278-279. One of Joseph Wanton Sr.'s nephews,

John G. Wanton, purchased Martin Howard's house in Newport after the Stamp Act riots. An advertisement in the *Newport Mercury* on November 18, 1765, noted that "John G. Wanton is removed from the Point to the House formerly occupied by Martin Howard, jun. Esq; in Broad Street, where he keeps the Naval Office; and likewise the Store of Goods, lately kept by Gideon & John Wanton, at the Point, is removed to the back Part of said House." John Wanton, "Advertisement," *Newport Mercury*, no. 376, November 18, 1765.

63. O.Z., "Letter to Mr. Hall," *Newport Mercury*, no. 341, March 18, 1765. See Lovejoy, *Rhode Island Politics*, 228. Samuel Hall would continue to publish columns written by the members of the Newport Junto until the eve of the Newport Stamp Act riots in August, but their days were clearly numbered in Rhode Island.

64. Morgan and Morgan, *Stamp Act Crisis*, 195.

65. "From the South-Carolina Gazette," *Newport Mercury*, no. 341, March 18, 1765.

66. "To the King's Most Excellent Majesty," "To the Right Honorable the Lords Spiritual and Temporal in Parliament assembled," and "To the Honorable Knights, Citizens and Burgesses of Great Britain," *Newport Mercury*, no. 343, April 1, 1765. These appeals would later be reformulated as the Virginia Resolves, which will be discussed in chapter 4.

67. "A pamphlet has lately been published in London," *Newport Mercury*, no. 346, April 22, 1765.

68. "Advertisement," *Newport Mercury*, no. 342, March 25, 1765, and "Advertisement," *Newport Mercury*, no. 343, April 1, 1765.

69. "Method of Raising Hemp in Pennsylvania," *Newport Mercury*, no. 347, April 29, 1765.

70. "The Speech of His Excellency Governor Bernard," *Newport Mercury*, no. 353, June 10, 1765.

71. See Stiles, "Stamp Act Notebook," sect. 3.

72. The opening line of the instructions read, "As a full and free Enjoyment of *British* Liberty, and our particular Rights as Colonists, long since precisely known and ascertained, By uninterrupted Practice and Usage from the first Settlement of this Country down to this time." "At a Town-Meeting of the Town of Providence," *Newport Mercury*, no. 363, August 19, 1765).

73. Henry Seymour Conway was the secretary of state for the Southern Department in 1765, the parliamentary body responsible for southern England, Wales, Ireland, and the British North American colonies. See "Lists of Appointments," in *Office-Holders*, 2:22-58. Isaac Barré was familiar with North America owing to his service in the British army during the French and Indian War. See Morgan and Morgan, *Stamp Act Crisis*, 69. Both Conway and Barré are listed in Ezra Stiles's "The Stamp Act Notebook" as parliamentary members who opposed the Stamp Act. See Stiles, "Stamp Act Notebook," sect. 4.

74. See "Proceedings of the General Assembly [on] the second Monday in September, 1765," in Bartlett, *Records of the Colony of Rhode Island*, 6:447-452.

75. Lovejoy, *Rhode Island Politics*, 72.

76. See Joseph Sherwood to Stephen Hopkins, April 11, 1765, in *The Correspondence of the Colonial Governors of Rhode Island, 1723–1775*, vol. 2, ed. Gertrude Selwyn Kimball (Freeport, NY: Books for Libraries Press, 1969), 361.

77. "Proceedings of the Massachusetts House of Representatives, respecting sending a Committee to New York, to consult with Committees from other colonies, on the state of the country, June 6, 1765," in *Speeches of the Governors of Massachusetts, 1765–1775; the answers of the*

House of Representatives thereto; with their resolutions and addresses for that period. And other public papers relating to the dispute between this country and Great Britain which led to the independence of the United States, ed. Allen Bradford (New York: Da Capo Press, 1971), 35-36.

78. Samuel White, "The Speaker of the House of Representatives of Massachusetts to the Speaker of the House of Representatives of Rhode Island," in Bartlett, *Records of the Colony of Rhode Island*, 6:441.

79. Morgan and Morgan, *Stamp Act Crisis*, 108.

80. See "An Act for dividing the town of Providence," in Bartlett, *Records of the Colony of Rhode Island*, 6:435-44, and "The Governor of Rhode Island to Joseph Sherwood, the colony's agent in London," in ibid., 6:434.

81. See "Secretary Sharpe to the Governor and Company of Rhode Island, with accompanying documents concerning certain disorderly proceedings in Newport," in ibid., 6:427-430.

82. See "The Governor of Rhode Island to Capt. Charles Antrobus," in ibid., 6:444-447.

83. See Steven Park, *The Burning of His Majesty's Schooner Gaspee* (Yardley, PA: Westholme, 2016).

CHAPTER 4: THE STAMP ACT RIOTS

1. See Morgan, *Prologue to Revolution*, 47-61, for the full texts of all the colonial resolves against the Stamp Act.

2. For a summary of these events in colonies other than Massachusetts, North Carolina, and Rhode Island, see Maier, *From Resistance to Revolution*, and Morgan and Morgan, *Stamp Act Crisis*.

3. See Stiles, "Stamp Act Notebook," sect. 3.

4. Maier, *From Resistance to Revolution*, 53.

5. Edmund and Helen Morgan note that portions of the Virginia Resolves were first published by the *Newport Mercury* in Rhode Island, and it appears likely that "instead of obtaining a relatively reliable text from a publication in the colony itself, [other colonies] got news of Virginia's action from the more ardent supporters of the resolutions." Morgan and Morgan, *Stamp Act Crisis*, 102.

6. See Morgan, *Prologue to Revolution*, 27-28.

7. Morgan and Morgan, *Stamp Act Crisis*, 104.

8. This invitation is the only discussion related to the Stamp Act in the Rhode Island records prior to the Newport Stamp Act riots late in August 1765. See Samuel White, "The Speaker of the House of Representatives of Massachusetts to the Speaker of the House of Representatives of Rhode Island," in Bartlett, *Records of the Colony of Rhode Island*, 6:441.

9. "To the Printers," *Boston Gazette*, no. 536, July 8, 1765.

10. Morgan and Morgan, *Stamp Act Crisis*, 108-110.

11. Ibid., 128.

12. See McConville, *King's Three Faces*, 56-63; Owen Stanwood, *The Empire Reformed: English America in the Age of the Glorious Revolution* (Philadelphia: University of Pennsylvania Press, 2011), 1-21; and Richard Archer, *As If an Enemy's Country: The British Occupation of Boston and the Origins of Revolution* (New York: Oxford University Press, 2010), 34-46.

13. See Young, "Ebenezer Mackintosh, 17-24.

14. "Early on Wednesday morning," *Boston Gazette*, no. 542, August 19, 1765.

15. See Potter, *Early History*, 299. See Maier, *From Resistance to Revolution*, 56, for references to the Earl of Bute in other demonstrations throughout the British colonies.
16. Hinderaker, *Boston's Massacre*, 32.
17. Francis S. Drake, *The town of Roxbury: its memorable persons and places, its history and antiquities, with numerous illustrations of its old landmarks and noted personages* (Roxbury, MA: self-published, 1878), 77.
18. Maier, *From Resistance to Revolution*, 58.
19. Morgan and Morgan, *Stamp Act Crisis*, 133.
20. See Breen, "'Baubles of Britain,'" 73-104, "Narrative of Commercial Life," and *Marketplace of Revolution*. Further discussion of these connections in Newport can be found in chapters 3 and 4.
21. See Robert Blair St. George, *Conversing by Signs: Poetics of Implication in Colonial New England Culture* (Chapel Hill: University of North Carolina Press, 1998), 263-268.
22. See Thomas Hutchinson to Richard Jackson, August 30, 1765, in *The Stamp Act of 1765*, ed. Jonathan Mercantini (Peterborough, ON: Broadview Press, 2018), 96-98. Jackson often assisted British colonists on political matters and corresponded with multiple colonists during this period.
23. St. George, *Conversing by Signs*, 266.
24. See Riordan, "Loyalist," 346-347.
25. Stiles, "Stamp Act Notebook," sect. 1.
26. Morgan and Morgan, *Stamp Act Crisis*, 134.
27. "The Massachusetts Resolves," in Morgan, *Prologue to Revolution*, 56.
28. Morgan and Morgan, *Stamp Act Crisis*, 138.
29. Thomas Moffat to Joseph Harrison, October 16, 1765, in Morgan, *Prologue to Revolution*, 109-113.
30. "The Author of the Halifax Letter," *Newport Mercury*, no. 364, August 26, 1765. This statement became even more important in the days following the Newport Stamp Act riots when Ezra Stiles described Howard as one of the members of the Newport Junto who had "went home" following the riots and the near destruction of Howard's house. See Stiles, "Stamp Act Notebook," sect. 2.
31. None of the surviving records indicate whether Martin Howard's ten-year-old daughter, Annie, joined them that night, but it seems likely she was present since Howard had few other relatives close at hand.
32. See William Almy to Elisha Story, August 29, 1765, in *Collections of the Massachusetts Historical Society* 55 (1923): 36; Thomas Moffat to Joseph Harrison, October 16, 1765, in Morgan, *Prologue to Revolution*, 109-113; and "Last Tuesday Morning," *Newport Mercury*, no. 365, September 2, 1765.
33. Skemp, "Newport's Stamp Act Rioters," 44.
34. "Last Tuesday Morning," *Newport Mercury*, no. 365, September 2, 1765.
35. St. George, *Conversing by Signs*, 251.
36. William Almy to Elisha Story, August 29, 1765, 36.
37. See Gould, *Writing the Rebellion*, 52.
38. See chapter 3 for more on the Newport Junto's advocacy for textile production, including hemp, in Rhode Island and the process by which home textile production became part of the Revolutionary movement after 1766.

39. Thomas Moffat to Joseph Harrison, October 16, 1765, in Morgan, *Prologue to Revolution*, 109-113.
40. A complete list of the damaged items can be found in Bartlett, *Records of the Colony of Rhode Island*, 7:217.
41. Augustus Johnston later published a letter in the *Newport Mercury* on October 21, 1765, announcing his resignation as Stamp Tax distributor and asking forgiveness for his earlier support for the Stamp Act. See A. Johnston, "Letter to Mr. Hall," *Newport Mercury*, no. 372, October 21, 1765. Johnston and his family remained in Rhode Island until his death in 1779, though their decision to remain after the war began may have resulted from protections afforded by the British occupation of Newport in the early years of the war. Johnston's widow, Patience Johnston, wrote to Newport Junto member Peter Harrison describing her husband's death and asking for financial support for herself and her family. See Johnston, January 20, 1779, letter to Peter Harrison, box 173, series 4 folder, Newport Historical Society, Newport, Rhode Island.
42. Martin Howard placed his remaining business affairs in the hands of Newport Junto member George Rome, who arranged for the first notice of the sale of the Howard family home to be posted in the *Newport Mercury* on September 9. See "To Be Sold," *Newport Mercury*, no. 366, September 9, 1765.
43. See Myers and Becken, "Who Was John Webber?," 1-21.
44. Stiles, "Stamp Act Notebook," sect. 3.
45. Henry Conway to Samuel Ward, March 31, 1766, in Bartlett, *Records of the Colony of Rhode Island*, 6:486. The Southern Department was responsible for governing southern England, Wales, Ireland, and the British North American colonies, while the Northern Department was abolished in 1782 with the creation of the secretary of state for the home department and the secretary of state for foreign affairs. See "Lists of Appointments," in *Office-Holders*, 2:22-58.
46. Samuel Ward to Joseph Sherwood, November 6, 1766, in Bartlett, *Records of the Colony of Rhode Island*, 6:513.
47. Charles Lennox to Samuel Ward, May 23, 1766, in ibid., 6:513.
48. See "Warrant to Appoint Martin Howard as Chief Justice of North Carolina, July 29, 1766," in Clark, *Colonial and State Records of North Carolina*, 11:209.
49. Bridenbaugh, *Peter Harrison*, 53.
50. Abigail Greenleaf Howard was also one of the founding members of the Boston Library Society in 1796. See Phebe Goodman, *The Garden Squares of Boston* (Hanover, NH: University Press of New England, 2003), 33. Her will left most of the books that she and Martin Howard had jointly collected to this institution in 1801. See Abby Chandler, "Loyalists and the Birth of Libraries in New England: The Marriage of Martin and Abigail Howard," Selected Papers of the Consortium of the Revolutionary Era, 2020, *Age of Revolutions*, accessed March 21, 2023, https://ageofrevolutions.com/2021/01/13/loyalists-and-the-birth-of-libraries-in-new-england-the-marriage-of-martin-and-abigail-howard/.
51. This portrait of Martin Howard is held by the Museo Nacional Thyssen-Bornemisza in Spain. It is unclear when it became part of the museum's collection.
52. See "Portsmouth: Last Saturday morning was Married here, by the Rev. Arthur Brown, at the Seat of His Excellency JOHN WENTWORTH, Esq; the Honorable MARTIN HOWARD, Esq; Chief JUDGE OF NORTH CAROLINA, to Miss ABIGAL GREEN-

LEAF, Daughter of STEPHEN GREENLEAF Esq; of Boston," *New-Hampshire Gazette*, no. 561, August 28, 1767.

53. See "Introduction to the History of Governor Tryon's Administration from 1764 to 1768," 1-4, 8-12.

54. See Paul David Nelson, *William Tryon and the Course of Empire: A Life in British Imperial Service* (Chapel Hill: University of North Carolina Press, 1990), 8.

55. Morgan and Morgan, *Stamp Act Crisis*, 40.

56. The *Viper* was captained by Jacob Lobb and was assigned to patrol the Carolina coast in search of pirates during this period. Lobb moved his family to Brunswick since his assignment lasted for several years. Governor Dobbs's refusal to retire left the Tryon family without an official residence, and Tryon eventually purchased the Lobb family home in Brunswick for his wife and daughter. See Nelson, *William Tryon*, 12.

57. "To his Excellency Arthur Dobbs Esquire Captain General, Governor and Commander in Chief in and over his Majestys Province of North Carolina, October 31, 1764," in Saunders, *Colonial and State Records of North Carolina*, 6:1257-1318.

58. Scott M. Smith notes that "to his credit, Tryon recognized that Parliament could not arbitrarily levy taxes on the colonies. He tried to steer a middle course, but common ground became increasingly hard to find." Smith, "William Tryon and the Park That Still Bears His Name," *Journal of the American Revolution*, May 17, 2021, accessed March 21, 2023, https://allthingsliberty.com/2021/05/william-tryon-and-the-park-that-still-bears-his-name.

59. See Morgan and Morgan, *Stamp Act Crisis*, 91-102, 161-162.

60. Ibid., 162.

61. See Moore, *Justice and Policy*, in Price, *Not a Conquered People*, 35-48.

62. Ibid., 45.

63. James Conniff, *The Useful Cobbler: Edmund Burke and the Politics of Progress* (Albany: State University of New York Press, 1994), 158.

64. Bilder, *Transatlantic Constitution*, 3.

65. William Price, "Introductory Essay," in Price, *Not a Conquered People*, 10.

66. "William Tryon to the Board of Trade," April 30, 1765, in Saunders, *Colonial and State Records of North Carolina*, 7:200-2002.

67. Edmund Fanning would become one of the Regulators' primary targets during the Regulator Rebellion. See chapters 6 and 7 for more on interactions between Fanning and the Regulators.

68. See Morgan and Morgan, *Stamp Act Crisis*, 162.

69. "On Saturday the 19th of Last Month," *North Carolina-Gazette* 58, November 20, 1765.

70. See Stephen Beauregard Weeks, *The Press of North Carolina in the Eighteenth Century* (Brooklyn: Historical Printing Club, 1891), 26-30, for more on Andrew Steuart's press.

71. "Monday the 18th instant," *North-Carolina Gazette* 58, November 20, 1765.

72. Nelson, *William Tryon*, 41.

73. Ibid.

74. These items consisted of "Warrants and Patents for Land; Testimonials; Injunctions in Chancery; Licences for Marriages; Letters of Administration and Testamentary with four Wine Licences for each of the Towns of Edenton, Newbern, Wilmington, Salisbury, and Halifax; two for Brunswick and Cross-Creek; and for Bath and Tarborough, one Licence each." Nelson, *William Tryon*, 41.

75. "Monday the 18th instant," *North Carolina-Gazette* 58, November 20, 1765.

76. These remarks are similar to the conclusion of Maurice Moore's pamphlet, *The Justice and Policy of Taxing The American Colonies, in Great Britain, considered*, which reads, "If the British Parliament will insist on taxing the Colonists, as their virtual representatives, then they are stripped of that constitutional right on which their liberty and property depends, and reduced to the most abject state of slavery." Moore, *Justice and Policy*, 48. It seems likely that even if Moore was not present at this meeting, the colonists present drew on his pamphlet when composing their response.

77. "Notwithstanding what passed," *North-Carolina Gazette* 72, February 26, 1766. Ezra Stiles's "Stamp Act Notebook" describes the Newport chapter of the Sons of Liberty as the "most respectable Committee of the Sons of Liberty on this Continent." Stiles, "Stamp Act Notebook," sect. 3.

78. The Stamp Act crisis healed other divisions in Rhode Island, as former opponents Stephen Hopkins and Samuel Ward formed an alliance cemented by their mutual support for independence from Britain in the 1770s. Elaine Forman Crane notes that "in 1774 Samuel Ward and Stephen Hopkins walked arm in arm into Carpenter's Hall and the First Continental Congress." Crane, *Dependent People*, 126.

CHAPTER 5: THE REGULATOR REBELLION BEGINS

1. See Wood to Richards, August 22, 1674, in Wood, "Travels of James Needham," 46. The English traders who traveled to the Piedmont in the 1670s were following in the footsteps of Spanish explorers who traveled in this region in the sixteenth century. See Michael Leroy Oberg and David Moore, "Voyages to Carolina: Europeans in the Indians' Old World," in *New Voyages to Carolina: Reinterpreting North Carolina History*, ed. Larry Tise and Jeffrey Crow (Chapel Hill: University of North Carolina Press, 2017), 41-59.

2. Scholars are uncertain about the cultural identity of the Tomahattan tribe, who may have been ethnically Cherokee. See Wayne Lee, "Fortify, Fight, or Flee: Tuscarora and Cherokee Defensive Warfare and Military Culture Adaptation," *Journal of Military History* 68, no. 3 (2004), 749, and H. Warwick Ward and R. P. Stephen Davis, *Time before History: The Archaeology of North Carolina* (Chapel Hill: University of North Carolina Press, 1999, 256-260.

3. See Powell, *North Carolina*, 69-74; Merrens, *Colonial North Carolina*, 113-114.

4. See Minutes of the Southern Congress at Augusta, Georgia; North Carolina; Cherokee Indian Nation; Catawba Indian Nation; Et Al. October 1, 1763–November 21, 1763, Clark, *Colonial and State Records of North Carolina*, 11:156-207.

5. See Corbitt, *Formation of the North Carolina Counties*, 167-169; Merrens, *Colonial North Carolina*, 162-163; and Whittenberg, "Planters, Merchants," 221.

6. James Whittenberg notes that "concentration of power in a few hands is not the issue here ... what is significant is the revised cast of characters. Whereas in the 1750s planters had dominated local government, in the 1760s and 1770s lawyers and merchants held the upper hand." Whittenberg, "Planters, Merchants," 234.

7. Z.Y., "Mr. Printer," *Newport Mercury*, no. 294, April 23, 1764.

8. See Smith, *Freedoms We Lost*, 40–46.

9. Kathleen Wilson, *The Sense of the People: Politics, Culture and Imperialism in England, 1715–1785* (New York: Cambridge University Press, 1998), 3.

10. See Abby Chandler, "'Unawed by the Laws of their Country': Finding Local and Imperial Legitimacy in North Carolina's Regulator Rebellion," *North Carolina Historical Review* 93, no. 2 (April 2016): 1-28.

11. See Joseph Ernst, *Money and Politics in America, 1755–1775: A Study in the Currency Act of 1764 and the Political Economy of Revolution* (Chapel Hill: University of North Carolina Press, 1973), 200, and Alan Watson, *Money and Monetary Problems in Early North Carolina* (Raleigh: North Carolina Department of Cultural Resources, Division of Archives and History, 1980), 2-3.

12. The Currency Act was an extension of an earlier law passed in 1751 that had prohibited the use of paper money in New England. Charles Townshend did briefly consider allowing colonists to print paper money that would carry interest as a further means of raising funds, but nothing came of this. See Patrick Griffins, *The Townshend Moment: The Making of Empire and Revolution in the Eighteenth Century* (New Haven, CT: Yale University Press, 2017), 127. This particular plan was suggested by Benjamin Franklin and by North Carolina colonist Henry McCulloh during the Stamp Act crisis. See John Bullion, *A Great and Necessary Measure: George Grenville and the Genesis of the Stamp Act, 1763–1765* (Columbia: University of Missouri Press, 1982), 2, 108-109.

13. Lord Hillsborough to William Tryon, April 16, 1768, in Tryon, *Correspondence*, vol. 2, 1768–1818, 74. Lord Hillsborough was the president of the Board of Trade and Plantations from 1763 to 1769 and secretary of state for the colonies between 1768 and 1772. See Nelson, *William Tryon*, 8.

14. See Alonzo Thomas Dill, *Governor Tryon and His Palace* (Chapel Hill: University of North Carolina Press, 1955), 130; Marvin Michael Kay, "Provincial Taxes in North Carolina during the Administrations of Dobbs and Tryon," *North Carolina Historical Review* 42, no. 4 (1965): 441–443; and William S. Powell, *The War of the Regulation and the Battle of Alamance, May 16, 1771* (Raleigh: North Carolina Department of Cultural Resources, Division of Archives and History, 1975), 5–6.

15. Kay, "Provincial Taxes," 442.

16. Kars, *Breaking Loose*, 168.

17. See William Smith, "Introduction to the History of Governor Tryon's Administration from 1764 to 1768," 15, 22, 27-28. Smith further noted that in order to "remov[e] the complains of the Populace," Tryon agreed to "regulate the fees." Smith, "Introduction to the History of Governor Tryon's Administration from 1769 to 1771," 15.

18. William Tryon to the Earl of Shelburne, July 4, 1767, in Tryon, *Correspondence*, 1:531. William Petty, the Second Earl of Shelburne, was appointed secretary of state for the Southern Department in 1766. See Edmond George Petty-Fitzmaurice, *Life of William, Earl of Shelburne* (London: Macmillan, 1912), 284.

19. Kay, "Provincial Taxes," 447–449.

20. The Anglican Church had been the only recognized church in Virginia since 1619. See Edward Bond, *Damned Souls in the Tobacco Colony: Religion in Seventeenth-Century Virginia* (Macon, GA: Mercer University Press, 2000). It became the only recognized church in Maryland when the Act of Establishment was passed in 1692. See Debra Meyers, *Common Whores, Vertuous Women, and Loveing Wives: Free Will Christian Women in Colonial Maryland* (Bloomington: Indiana University Press, 2003), 85-90.

21. "Fundamental Constitutions of Carolina," Avalon Project.

22. See Smith, "Introduction to the History of Governor Tryon's Administration from 1764 to 1768," 5-7, 13, 20. Smith was a devout Presbyterian, another of the eighteenth-century dissenter faiths. He told Tryon in summer 1771 that Baptists in New York "were full of fears on Account of a Letter written by [Tryon] from Carolina to the Society for propagating the Gospel" that had noted that "the peculiarities of the sects [were] in his Opinion, repugnant to Common Sense." Tryon claimed to only be opposed to Baptists in North Carolina since they were "the People who opposed Govt. in Carolina" and he was happy to support religious toleration in New York. Smith's later memoir noted that these efforts helped Tryon "over a Stumbling Block in his way." Smith, *Historical Memoirs*, 107.

23. "Acts for the North Carolina General Assembly, 1760," in Clark, *Colonial and State Records of North* Carolina, 25:430-432.

24. Dill, *Governor Tryon*, 27–28. Tryon also unsuccessfully petitioned King George III for furniture to fill his new home on the grounds that it would reflect well on the British Empire.

25. Dill, *Governor Tryon*, 110–115. William Smith initially described this building as "a Palace . . . suitable to the Dignity of his station." Smith, "Introduction to the History of Governor Tryon's Administration from 1764 to 1768," 12. Smith later added that it was "the most magnificent of any Governor's House in the Provinces." Smith, "Introduction to the History of Governor Tryon's Administration from 1769 to 1771," 8.

26. Marvin L. Michael Kay notes that the poll tax was charged for all "white males, freemen or servants, sixteen years of age and over; Negroes, mulattoes, and 'Persons of Mixt Blood to the Fourth Generation,' slave or free, male or female, twelve years and over; and all individuals who married persons of color and their progeny, twelve years and over." Kay, "Provincial Taxes," 442n5.

27. Dill, *Governor Tryon*, 128.

28. Smith, "Introduction to the History of Governor Tryon's Administration from 1769 to 1771," 8.

29. Zaret, *Origins of Democratic Culture*, 82.

30. Carole Watterson Troxler notes that "the following set of names is not a list of 'the Regulators.' It is a compilation of names on petitions and depositions backing issues advocated by Regulators during 1766–1771; in letters or statements indicating sympathy with Regulator individuals or causes, in indictments or other official actions against individuals as Regulators; or in descriptions by contemporaries." Troxler, *Farming Dissenters*, 159.

31. The Trading Path is marked by North Carolina Historical Highway Marker E-30. Additional information for the marker notes that "the Trading Path was the central highway, the most fabled route, the interstate of its day."
See "NCHHM E-30," North Carolina Historical Highway Marker Program, accessed March 21, 2023, http://www.ncmarkers.com/Markers.aspx?MarkerId=E-30.

32. The Alamance site is marked by North Carolina Historical Highway Marker G-24. See "NCHHM G-24," North Carolina Historical Highway Marker Program, accessed March 21, 2023, http://www.ncmarkers.com/Markers.aspx?MarkerId=G-24.

33. The Hunter house site is marked by North Carolina Historical Highway Marker K-61. See "NCHHM K-61," North Carolina Historical Highway Marker Program, accessed March 21, 2023, http://www.ncmarkers.com/Markers.aspx?MarkerId=K-61.

34. See "The Humble Petition of us the Subscribers Inhabitants of the County of Roan and Orange," October 4, 1768, and "The Humble Petition of Us the Inhabitants of Orange

Notes to Pages 80–81   173

County Bordering on Cumberland," November 11, 1768, in North Carolina General Assembly Session Records, Colonial (Upper and Lower Houses), box 3, November–December 1768 Lower House Papers Petitions Rejected or Not Acted on, Bills Folder, and "The humble Petition of us Inhabitants of Orange and Rowan countys," October 27, 1769, North Carolina General Assembly Session Records, Colonial (Upper and Lower Houses), box 4, October–November 1769 Lower House Papers Petitions Rejected or not acted on, Bills Folder. The North Carolina General Assembly Session Records are held by the State Archives of North Carolina, Raleigh. The fourth petition, "Petition of the Inhabitants of Orange County," September 25, 1770, was not at the State Archives in Raleigh in spring 2015. The copy of the petition reprinted in 1886 did not include the names of the petitioners. See "Petition of the Inhabitants of Orange County," September 25, 1770, in *The Colonial Records of North Carolina*, vol. 8, ed. William Laurence Saunders (Raleigh: State of North Carolina, 1886–1890), 231–234.

35. John Lowe, James Hunter, Rednap Howell, Harmon Cox, John Marshel, William Cox, William Moffit, and George Hendry, "Regulators' Advertisement No. 11," 1768, in *The Colonial Records of North Carolina*, vol. 7, ed. William Laurence Saunders (Raleigh: State of North Carolina, 1886), 759-766.

36. May 21, 1771, entry in "Order Book: Orders Given out by His Excellency Governor Tryon to the Provincials of North Carolina Raised to March against the Insurgents," State Archives of North Carolina, Raleigh. William Smith further noted that "being an Outlaw, his [unclear] with the barn were burned and three hours were spent taking fresh supplies." Smith, "Introduction to the History of Governor Tryon's Administration from 1769 to 1771," 36.

37. Herman Husband published a pamphlet reflecting on his religious evolution in 1761 "for the consideration of all PEOPLE." See Husband, *Some Remarks on Religion with the Author's Experience in Pursuit Thereof*, in Boyd, *Some Eighteenth Century Tracts*, 201-246. Perhaps similar to his relationship with the Regulator movement, Husband's relationship with the Quaker Church proved equally tenuous over time.

38. The site for Herman Husband's house is marked by North Carolina Historical Highway Marker K-62. Additional information for the marker notes that "at the time of the War of the Regulation, Husband resided and operated a mill on Sandy Creek in what is now Randolph County. See "NCHHM K-62," North Carolina Historical Highway Marker Program, accessed March 21, 2023, http://www.ncmarkers.com/Markers.aspx?MarkerId=K-62.

39. Herman Husband's land grants can be found in *Orange County Records*, Granville Proprietary Land Office, Abstracts of Loose Papers, vol. 1, ed. William Bennet (Raleigh, NC: privately published, 1987), 1, 8; *Orange County Records, Granville Proprietary Land Office, Deeds and Surveys, 1752–1760*, vol. 5, ed. William Bennet (Raleigh, NC: privately published, 1989), 41, 128; *Orange County Records, Granville Proprietary Land Office, Deeds and Surveys, 1761–1763*, vol. 6, ed. William Bennet (Raleigh, NC: privately published, 1989), 91, 98, 101; and *Orange County Records, Granville Proprietary Land Office, Miscellaneous Records*, vol. 7, ed. William Bennet (Raleigh, NC: privately published, 1991), 33-34. These publications are held by the North Carolina State Government and Genealogy Library, Raleigh. Also see Whittenberg, "Planters, Merchants," 215-216, for a discussion of Husband's activities as a planter and small-scale land speculator.

40. See Thomas P. Slaughter, *The Whiskey Rebellion: Frontier Epilogue to the American Revolution* (New York: Oxford University Press, 1986), 276.
41. The Howell house site is marked by North Carolina Historical Highway Marker K-64. See "NCHHM K-64," North Carolina Historical Highway Marker Program, accessed March 21, 2023, http://www.ncmarkers.com/Markers.aspx?MarkerId=K-64.
42. The text of the Howell letter can be found in the minutes for this meeting of the Governor's Council. See Minutes of the North Carolina Governor's Council, March 18–19, 1771, in Saunders, *Colonial and State Records of North Carolina*, 8:537-538.
43. Arthur Palmer Hudson, "Songs of the North Carolina Regulators," *William and Mary Quarterly* 4, no. 4 (1947): 476.
44. See Troxler, *Farming Dissenters*, 24.
45. William Tryon, "Proclamation of Governor William Tryon," June 11, 1771, in William Tryon, 1765–1771, box 6, Colonial Governors Papers, State Archives of North Carolina, Raleigh.
46. Henry Eustace McCulloh to John Harvey, March 30, 1770, in Saunders, *Colonial and State Records of North Carolina*, 8:183.
47. The Hamilton family's land grants can be found in *Orange County Records*, vol. 1, 20, 48; *Orange County Records, Granville Proprietary Land Office, Abstracts of Loose Papers*, vol. 3, ed. William Bennet (Raleigh, NC: privately published, 1990), 70; and *Orange County Records*, vol. 6, 102.
48. "Advertisements, August 1766," in *The Regulators in North Carolina: A Documentary History, 1759–1776*, ed. William S. Powell, James K. Huhta, and Thomas J. Farnham (Raleigh, NC: State Department of Archives and History, 1971), 35.
49. Hudson, "Songs of the North Carolina Regulators," 476.
50. Minutes of Regulator Meeting on April 4, 1768, in Powell, Huhta, and Farnham, *Regulators in North Carolina*, 80.
51. This sequence of events was described in a letter from John Gray to Edmund Fanning that noted that the "Mob who stand in opposition to paying their Levies and who have so long threatened us appeared yesterday in Town to the number of about 100. In order to take from the Sheriff a horse which he had distrained for a Levy [during which time they] treated sundry of the Inhabitants of the Town very ill." John Gray to Edmund Fanning, April 9, 1768, in Powell, Huhta, and Farnham, *Regulators in North Carolina*, 80.
52. Hudson, "Songs of the North Carolina Regulators," 480.
53. William Tryon, "Proclamation of Governor William Tryon," April 27, 1768; "Proclamation of Governor William Tryon," May 17, 1768, both in William Tryon, 1765–1771, box 6, Colonial Governors Papers, State Archives of North Carolina.
54. Smith, "Introduction to the History of Governor Tryon's Administration from 1764 to 1768," 35-36.
55. Powell, *War of the Regulation*, 15.
56. William Tryon, "Proclamation of Governor William Tryon," October 4, 1768, in William Tryon, 1765–1771, box 6, Colonial Governors Papers, State Archives of North Carolina.
57. "The Humble Petition of us the Subscribers Inhabitants of the County of Roan and Orange," October 4, 1768, North Carolina General Assembly Session Records, Colonial (Upper and Lower Houses), box 3, November–December 1768 Lower House Papers Petitions Rejected or Not Acted on, Bills Folder, State Archives of North Carolina.

58. Kars, *Breaking Loose*, 143. Wayne Lee also notes the absence of women in North Carolina political activities in the 1750s and 1760s and asks whether early modern women largely confined their political activities to protesting food shortages. See Lee, *Crowds and Soldiers*, 43–44.
59. Zaret, *Origins of Democratic Culture*, 90. The italics are his.
60. Hunter et al., "Regulators' Advertisement No. 11," 759.
61. "The Humble Petition of Us the Inhabitants of Orange County Bordering on Cumberland," November 11, 1768, North Carolina General Assembly Session Records, Colonial (Upper and Lower Houses), box 3, November–December 1768 Lower House Papers Petitions Rejected or Not Acted on, Bills Folder, State Archives of North Carolina.
62. "The humble Petition of us Inhabitants of Orange and Rowan countys," October 27, 1769, North Carolina General Assembly Session Records, Colonial (Upper and Lower Houses), box 4, October–November 1769 Lower House Papers Petitions Rejected or not acted on, Bills Folder, State Archives of North Carolina.
63. Pot ash, pot-ash, or potash, as it was alternately known in the eighteenth century, was derived from concentrated wood ashes, preferably from hardwood trees, which, in turn, could be made into potassium carbonate. Mary Tolford Wilson notes that the "annual amount leaving United States harbors had reached 8,000 pounds by 1790." See Wilson, "Amelia Simmons Fills a Need: American Cookery, 1796," *William and Mary Quarterly* 14, no. 1 (January 1957): 23.
64. Howard, *Letter from a Gentleman at Halifax*, in Bailyn, *Pamphlets of the American Revolution*, 538.
65. Zaret, *Origins of Democratic Culture*, 9.
66. "The Petition of the Inhabitants of Granville County, December 10, 1770," North Carolina General Assembly Session Records, Colonial (Upper and Lower Houses), box 4, December 1770–January 1771, Lower House Committee Public Bills Propositions and Grievances, State Archives of North Carolina.
67. See Serena Zabin, *The Boston Massacre: A Family History* (New York: Houghton Mifflin Harcourt, 2020), 47-59, for more on the sociopolitical impact created by the arrival of the British regiments in Boston in October 1768.
68. See Griffin, *Townshend Moment*, 142-151, for more on responses to the Townshend Acts in the other British North American colonies.
69. Bernard Bailyn, "The Pamphlets of the Revolution," in Bailyn, *Pamphlets of the American Revolution*, 1: 3-5.
70. See Hopkins, *Rights of the Colonies Examined*, and Howard, *Letter from a Gentleman at Halifax*, in Bailyn, *Pamphlets of the American Revolution*, 1: 499-544.
71. See Husband, *Impartial Relation* and *Fan for Fanning*, in Boyd, *Some Eighteenth Century Tracts*, 247–392.
72. Husband, *Fan for Fanning*, in ibid., 341.
73. William Boyd notes that "Husband was a man of ideas, never satisfied with the political and social conditions of his environment, an agitator of that radical type which characterizes the later eighteenth century. Yet he was not of the stuff which makes martyrs or great leaders; he never quite found himself." Boyd, "Introduction to Herman Husband," in Boyd, *Some Eighteenth Century Tracts*, 196.

CHAPTER 6: THE REGULATOR REBELLION AND THE IMPERIAL CRISIS

1. See Carole Watterson Troxler, "Land Tenure as Regulator Grievance and Revolutionary Tool," in *New Voyages to Carolina: Reinterpreting North Carolina History*, ed. Larry Tise and Jeffrey Crow (Chapel Hill: University of North Carolina Pres, 2017), 111. Similar tensions appeared throughout the United States before and after the American Revolution. See Paul Douglas Newman, *Fries's Rebellion: The Enduring Struggle for the American Revolution* (Philadelphia: University of Pennsylvania Press, 2004); Hogeland, *Whiskey Rebellion*; Condon, *Shay's Rebellion*; Dana Nelson, *Commons Democracy: Reading the Politics of Participation in the Early United States* (New York: Fordham University Press, 2015); and Eric Morser, *The Fires of New England: A Story of Protest and Rebellion in Antebellum America* (Amherst: University of Massachusetts Press, 2018).

2. William Tryon's marriage to Margaret Wake Tryon on December 26, 1757, brought him wealth and a family connection to Wills Hill, the first Earl of Hillsborough, who was "the president of the Board of Trade and Plantations from 1763 to 1769 and secretary of state for the colonies between 1768 and 1772." Nelson, *William Tryon*, 8.

3. See Archibald Henderson, *The Star of Empire: Phases of the Westward Movement in the Old Southwest* (Durham, NC: Seeman Printery, 1919), 8-9.

4. The connection between Henderson and Williams was further reinforced when Henderson married Williams' stepdaughter, Elizabeth Keeling, in 1763. See Henderson, *Star of Empire*, 10-14.

5. Governor Tryon described Richard Henderson "as a gentleman of candor and ability, born in Virginia and about thirty three years of age. He lives near Hillsborough in the back country, among a people whom I am persuaded will be happy at having such a distinction paid to one, who resides among them." Letter from William Tryon to William Petty, Marquis of Lansdowne, March 14, 1768, in Saunders, *Colonial and State Records of North Carolina*, 7:697-698.

6. See John Cannon, "Henry McCulloch and Henry McCulloh," *William and Mary Quarterly* 15, no. 1 (1958): 71-73, and Price, "'Men of Good Estates,'" 72-82. For more about failed efforts to collect quitrents in North Carolina, see Edwin Wexler Kennedy, "Quitrents and currency in North Carolina 1663–1776" (PhD diss., Johns Hopkins University, 1897), 8-15. Patrick Spero's *Frontier Country: The Politics of War in Early Pennsylvania* (Philadelphia: University of Pennsylvania Press, 2016) explores similar issues in central Pennsylvania in the 1760s.

7. Charles Sellers, "Private Profits and British Colonial Policy: The Speculations of Henry McCulloh, *William and Mary Quarterly* 8, no. 4 (1951): 538.

8. See DeMond, *Loyalists in North Carolina*, 158-160.

9. See Troxler, "Land Tenure as Regulator Grievance," 119-120. The four Inns of Court consist of Middle Temple, Inner Temple, Gray's Inn, and Lincoln Court. These institutions provide professional associations and legal training for barristers in England and Wales. See Margaret McGlynn, *The Royal Prerogative and the Learning of the Inns of Court* (New York: Cambridge University Press, 2003).

10. William David Nelson notes that while the lower house of the General Assembly supported Henry McCulloh Jr.'s appointment as North Carolina's colonial agent, the Governor's Council initially rejected him for the position. Similar to the other British royal colonies,

the members of the lower house were North Carolina colonists who had been elected by their peers, but a position in the Governor's Council required a royal appointment. It is unclear why the council initially rejected Tryon's nomination of McCulloh as colonial agent, but it seems likely that the lower house's support was based on his family's connections to members of the assembly. See Nelson, *William Tryon*, 17-22.

11. Powell, *North Carolina*, 151.

12. For more about Associate Justice Maurice Moore's suspension, see "William Tryon to the Board of Trade," April 30, 1765, in Saunders, *Colonial and State Records of North Carolina*, 7:200. Both William Tryon and Edmund Fanning continued to support the interests of the British Empire through the 1770s and 1780s. When Tryon left North Carolina in 1771 to become the royal governor of New York, Fanning followed as his secretary. See Nelson, *William Tryon*, 90-91.

13. "Writ-at-Large for the Arrest of the Regulators," May 1, 1768, in "Military Collection War of the Regulation, 1768–1771," box 1, North Carolina State Archives, Raleigh.

14. Hudson, "Songs of the North Carolina Regulators," 480.

15. See Edmund Fanning to Simon Dixon, May 1768, Edmund Fanning to Jacob Fudge, May 1, 1768, and Edmund Fanning to William Tryon, May 3, 1768, in Powell, Huhta, and Farnham, *Regulators in North Carolina*, 104-110.

16. Governor Tryon to the "Inhabitants on the South Side Haw River in Orange County," June 21, 1768, in Tryon, *Correspondence*, 2:137-139.

17. Sellers, "Private Profits," 538.

18. John Carteret, the Earl of Granville, was a descendent of Sir George Carteret, one of the eight lords proprietor who received the first land grants in Carolina Colony. The other seven lords proprietor had sold their lands outright to the Crown in 1729, but Granville agreed in 1744 to exchange his right to a political voice in North Carolina for the Granville Tract or Granville District which made up approximately one-eighth of the original Carolina Colony. See Powell, *North Carolina*, 86.

19. Troxler, "Land Tenure as Regulator Grievance," 119.

20. See Marvin Michael Kay, "The Payment of Provincial and Local Taxes in North Carolina, 1748–1771, *William and Mary Quarterly* 26, no. 2 (1969): 442, and Kars, *Breaking Loose*, 168.

21. The members of the Brantley family who signed the petition submitted on November 11, 1768, were James Brantley, Jos. Brantley, Joshua Brantley, John Brantley Sr., Philip Brantley, and William Brantley. See "The Humble Petition of Us the Inhabitants of Orange County Bordering on Cumberland," November 11, 1768, North Carolina General Assembly Session Records, Colonial (Upper and Lower Houses), box 3, November–December 1768 Lower House Papers Petitions Rejected or Not Acted on, Bills Folder, State Archives of North Carolina.

22. This transaction can be found in *Orange County Records*, vol. 2, *Deed Books 1 and 2*, Abstracts, ed. William Bennet (Raleigh, NC: privately published, 1989), 129. This volume is held at the North Carolina State Government and Genealogy Library, Raleigh.

23. All quotes from the Edmund Fanning Extortion Trial Document, March 22, 1769, Military Collection: War of the Regulation 1768–1771, box 1, State Archives of North Carolina, Raleigh.

24. See J. R. Pole, *Contract and Consent: Representation and the Jury in Anglo-American Legal History* (Charlottesville: University of Virginia Press, 2010).

25. William Lawrence Saunders, "Preface," in Saunders, *Colonial and State Records of North Carolina*, 7:xv.

26. "The humble Petition of us Inhabitants of Orange and Rowan countys," October 27, 1769, North Carolina General Assembly Session Records, Colonial (Upper and Lower Houses), box 4, October–November 1769 Lower House Papers Petitions Rejected or not acted on, Bills Folder, State Archives of North Carolina.

27. All quotations from Henry Eustace McCulloh to Edmund Fanning, August 4, 1770, Fanning-McCulloh Papers, 1752–1806, Private Collection 57.1, State Archives of North Carolina, Raleigh.

28. Sir William de Grey was first called to the British bar in 1742 and went on to serve as solicitor general to Queen Charlotte, queen consort of King George III, and then King George III in the 1760s. He became attorney general for Great Britain in 1766 and later served as the lord chief justice of the Common Pleas between 1771 and 1780. He also served in the British Parliament in the late 1760s and early 1770s. See Gordin Godwin, "Grey, William de (1719-1781)," *Dictionary of National Biography*, accessed March 21, 2023, https://en.wikisource.org/wiki/Dictionary_of_National_Biography,_1885-1900/Grey,_William_de.

29. John Morgan was a barrister at the Inner Temple, one of the four Inns of Court, in the late eighteenth century. His publications include *Essays: Upon I. The Law Of Evidence. II. New Trials. III. Special Verdicts. IV. Trials at Bar. And V. Repleaders* (Dublin: printed for Messrs. E. Lynch, H. Chamberlaine, L. White, P. Byrne, A. Gruebier, C. Lewis, J. Jones, and J. Moore, 1789).

30. All quotations from the de Grey letter are from "Memorandum from William De Grey to John Morgan concerning the regulation of fees for public officials in North Carolina," Military Collection: War of the Regulation 1768–1771, box 1, State Archives of North Carolina, Raleigh. The location of the de Grey letter and the ensuing Morgan letter with the trial documents initially puzzled me in spring 2015, as neither one explains how de Grey or Morgan became involved with the Fanning trial. Later research in the Fanning-McCulloh correspondence answered this question, but since this correspondence is housed in a different collection at the State Archives of North Carolina in Raleigh, the connection is not immediately apparent.

31. All John Morgan quotes taken from "Report by John Morgan concerning the regulation of fees for public officials in North Carolina and the indictment against Edmund Fanning," Military Collection: War of the Regulation 1768–1771, box 1, State Archives of North Carolina, Raleigh.

32. See S. Max Edelson, *The New Map of Empire: How Britain Imagined America before Independence* (Cambridge, MA: Harvard University Press, 2017), 22-26.

33. See Julie Flavel, *When London Was Capital of America* (New Haven, CT: Yale University Press, 2010), and Alison Olson, "The London Mercantile Lobby and the Coming of the American Revolution," *Journal of American History* 69, no. 1 (1982): 21-41.

34. William Smith approvingly noted Governor Tryon's willingness to investigate extortion charges but did not comment on the final outcome of the Fanning trial, though this may also have been because there was no record of it in Tryon's letter book. See Smith, "Introduction to the History of Governor Tryon's Administration from 1764 to 1768," 37.

35. See "The Humble Petition of us the Subscribers Inhabitants of the County of Roan and Orange," October 4, 1768, North Carolina General Assembly Session Records, Colonial (Upper and Lower Houses), box 3, November–December 1768 Lower House Papers Petitions Rejected or Not Acted on, Bills Folder, State Archives of North Carolina.

36. The fourth Regulator petition was signed by 174 men whose names are unknown. The original petition with the signatures was not at the state archives in Raleigh in spring 2015, and the copy of the petition reprinted in 1886 did not include the names of the petitioners. See "Petition of the Inhabitants of Orange County," September 25, 1770, in Saunders, *Colonial and State Records of North Carolina*, 8:533.

37. Henderson, *Star of Empire*, 33.

38. See Hudson, "Songs of the North Carolina Regulators," 480.

39. All quotations from "March 18, 1771 letter from John Frohock and Alexander Martin to William Tryon" are from Saunders, *Colonial and State Records of North Carolina*, 8:533.

40. Higginbotham and Price, "Was It Murder," 594-601. The incident discussed by Higginbotham and Price took place the following year, but it offers further evidence of Howard's commitment to following his own conscience.

41. John Murrin, "The Legal Transformation: The Bench and Bar of Eighteenth-Century Massachusetts," in *Colonial America: Essays in Politics and Social Development*, ed. Stanley N. Katz and John M. Murrin (New York: Alfred A. Knopf, 1983), 95. Also see Christopher Brooks, *Pettyfoggers and Vipers of the Commonwealth: The "Lower Branch" of the Legal Profession in Early Modern England* (New York: Cambridge University Press, 1986), for a wider discussion on tensions between justices and attorneys in the eighteenth century.

42. All quotations from Richard Henderson to William Tryon, September 29, 1770, in Powell, Huhta, and Farnham, *Regulators in North Carolina*, 244-248. Henderson's letter is the only full account of the Hillsborough riots, but it is impossible to determine how accurate it is.

43. This was probably Jeremiah Fields, who was later identified by Ralph McNair as one of the eleven men who "assaulted and beat John Williams, Esquire," "attempted to strike Richard Henderson, Esq.," and "beat and pursu[ed] Col Edmund Fanning till He took Shelter" in Hillsborough on September 24, 1770. See Ralph McNair, "October 9, 1770, Deposition," in Powell, Huhta, and Farnham, *Regulators in North Carolina*, 261.

44. "Extraordinary Conduct of the Regulators," *New York Gazette*, October 5, 1770, in Powell, Huhta, and Farnham, *Regulators in North Carolina*, 257; "Notice from the Public Press," *Virginia Gazette*, Williamsburg, October 25, 1770, in ibid., 250; "An Account of the Regulators," *Evening Post*, Boston, November 12, 1770, in *Virginia Gazette*, October 25, 1770, in ibid., 253.

45. Dill, *Governor Tryon*, 146; Troxler, *Farming Dissenters*, 88; Lee, *Crowds and Soldiers*, 66.

46. William Tryon to Wills Hill, Lord Hillsborough, October 7, 1770, in Tryon, *Correspondence*, 2:512; William Tryon, "Proclamation of Governor William Tryon," October 18, 1770, William Tryon, 1765–1771, box 6, Colonial Governors Papers, State Archives of North Carolina.

47. William Tryon, "Proclamation of Governor William Tryon," October 18, 1770, William Tryon, 1765–1771, box 6, This was not the first time Tryon had engaged in such tactics. Two years earlier, he had authorized the colony's justices of the peace to rule on all "Treasons, Felonies, Poysenings, Enchangments, Sorceries Art Magick Trespasses and Extortions," though there is little evidence of such activities in the colonial North Carolina court records.

Colonial Governors Papers, State Archives of North Carolina. Governor William Tryon to the Council, April 29, 1768, in Tryon, *Correspondence*, 2:95.

48. Kathleen Wilson's research documents the growing use of varying "readings of national history that gave legitimacy to current constellations of power" in the eighteenth century. Linking the Regulators to the Jacobites, who had supported overthrowing the Hanoverian monarchs in 1715 and 1745, provided Tryon with a historically rooted argument for rejecting their demands in the name of maintaining order and legitimacy. See Wilson, *Sense of the People*, 107. For more information on lingering concerns about Jacobite rebellions, see Paul Kléber Monod, *Jacobitism and the English People* (New York: Cambridge University Press, 1993), 343-350.

49. Lee, *Crowds and Soldiers*, 69.

50. Thomas Hutchinson to Lord Hillsborough, November 30, 1770, in Powell, Huhta, and Farnham, *Regulators in North Carolina*, 281. It is also likely Governor Hutchinson saw similarities between the Regulators and the Boston colonists.

51. Thomas Hutchinson to William Tryon, January 25, 1771, in Powell, Huhta, and Farnham, *Regulators in North Carolina*, 334.

52. "Extract of a Letter from Mecklenburg," *Boston Chronicle*, vol. 1, issue 47, November 7, 1768.

53. See Husband, *Impartial Relation*, and *Fan for Fanning*, in Boyd, *Some Eighteenth Century Tracts*, 247–392. Boyd notes that the title page for *A Fan for Fanning* stated it was issued at "the Printing-office ... at the head of Queen Street" and that this print shop was run by Daniel Kneeland. Boyd adds that "tradition has held that Isiah Thomas published *A Fan for Fanning*," which was advertised in Thomas's *Massachusetts Spy*, and this did lead to a copy of the *Massachusetts Spy* being burned in New Bern alongside an effigy of Thomas. Boyd, "Introduction," in Boyd, *Some Eighteenth Century Tracts*, 337-338.

54. See Hiller B. Zobel, *The Boston Massacre* (New York: W. W. Norton, 1970), 294, and Archer, *As If an Enemy's Country*, 221. John Adams was defense attorney for Thomas Preston and the accused soldiers. Preston and six of the soldiers were acquitted on murder charges, while the remaining two soldiers were convicted on manslaughter charges and were punished by having their thumbs branded.

55. Thomas McGuire to William Tryon, October 18, 1770, William Tryon, 1765–1771, and 1783–1786, box 6, Colonial Governors Papers, State Archives of North Carolina. William Smith further noted that the Regulators' actions "did not amount to treason" and could only be classified as "Crimes and Misdemeanors." Smith, "Introduction to the History of Governor Tryon's Administration from 1769 to 1771," 10.

56. All quotations from "The Humble Address of the House of Assembly of North Carolina to his Excellency &c," December 10, 1770, Colonial Governors Papers William Tryon 1765-1771, State Archives of North Carolina, Raleigh.

57. All quotations from "Bill for preventing tumultuous & riotous Assemblies, etc.," December 15, 1770, North Carolina General Assembly Session Records, Colonial (Upper and Lower Houses), box 4, December 1770–January 1771, Lower House Committee Public Bills Propositions and Grievances, State Archives of North Carolina.

58. Ibid.

59. Ibid. The phrase "oyer and terminer" is a partial transition of a French phrase that literally means "to hear and determine." Courts of oyer and terminer were called to investigate trea-

son, felony, or misdemeanors and could also be used when political and judicial leaders did not want to wait for the quarterly courts. See "oyer and terminer," n., William Stewart and Robert Burgess, *Collins Dictionary of Law* (New York: HarperCollins, 2001).

60. J. M. Beattie, *Crime and the Courts in England, 1660–1800* (Princeton, NJ: Princeton University Press, 1986), 452–473. This defense was used in the trial for the British soldiers after the Boston Massacre and is the reason why the two soldiers convicted on manslaughter charges were branded, rather than hanged. See Archer, *As If an Enemy's Country*, 225.

61. William Smith noted that the Johnston Riot Act included charges for colonists declared "guilty of high treason." Smith, "Introduction to the History of Governor Tryon's Administration from 1769 to 1771," 13-14.

CHAPTER 7: IMPERIAL CRISIS TO REVOLUTIONARY ERA

1. Fitch, *Some Neglected History*, 269.

2. Mary Sarah Bilder notes, "The Crown's requirement that colonies send laws to England for review and acceptance of assembly lawmaking authority combined to produce the laws of their 'Majesties' province." Bilder, "English Settlement and Local Governance," *The Cambridge History of Law in America*, vol. 1, ed. Michael Grossberg and Christopher Tomlins (New York: Cambridge University Press, 2008), 102.

3. Lee, *Crowds and Soldiers*, 71. Lee writes that "the apparent threat of a march on New Bern became a key, and recurring, component in the actions of the political elite from December through March." Ibid.

4. Smith, "Introduction to the History of Governor Tryon's Administration from 1769 to 1771," 8.

5. See Brent Tarter, "Botetourt, Norborne Berkeley, baron de," in *Dictionary of Virginia Biography*, vol. 2, ed. Sara B. Bearss et al. (Richmond: Library of Virginia, 2001), 108-109.

6. The Earl of Gower served as the lord privy seal from 1755 to 1757 and as the lord president of the council from 1767 to 1779. See George Fisher Russell Baker, "Leveson-Gower, Granville (1721-1803)," *Dictionary of National Biography*, accessed November 18, 2020, https://en.wikisource.org/wiki/Dictionary_of_National_Biography,_1885-1900/Leveson-Gower,_Granville_(1721-1803). He was also brother-in-law to Lord Dunmore's wife, Lady Charlotte Dunmore, and so had a vested interest in propelling Dunmore's political career. See Glenn Williams, *Dunmore's War: The Last Conflict of America's Colonial Era* (Yardley, PA: Westholme, 2018), 257.

7. See William Lowe, "John Murray fourth earl of Dunmore," *Encyclopedia Virginia*, accessed November 18, 2020, http://www.EncyclopediaVirginia.org/Dunmore_John_Murray_fourth _earl_of_c_1730-1809.

8. See Nelson, *William Tryon*, 88-89.

9. See Dill, *Governor Tryon*, 110–115, and Kay, "Provincial Taxes," 441–443.

10. Griffins, *Townshend Moment*, 142-143.

11. See Minutes of the North Carolina Governor's Council, December 20, 1770, in Saunders, *Colonial and State Records of North Carolina*, 8:268-270.

12. The State Archives of North Carolina digitized all surviving issues of the *North-Carolina Gazette* in 2009, but these issues did not include the December 14, 1770 issue. See "Early Newspapers from the State Archives of North Carolina," Digital NC, accessed March 21, 2023, https://www.digitalnc.org/newspapers/the-north-carolina-gazette-wilmington-n-c/.

The December 14 letter signed by James Hunter also appeared in the *Pennsylvania Journal* on July 11, 1771, along with six other articles that also supported the Regulator Rebellion. See "To the Honourable Maurice Moore," *Pennsylvania Journal and Weekly Advertiser*, issue 1492, July 11, 1771. Neither issue of the *North-Carolina Gazette* is extant.

13. See Minutes of the North Carolina Governor's Council, December 20, 1770, in Saunders, *Colonial and State Records of North Carolina*, 8:268-270.

14. See Moore, *Justice and Policy*, in Price, *Not a Conquered People*, 35-48.

15. William Tryon to Wills Hill, Lord Hillsborough, April 12, 1771, in Tryon, *Correspondence*, 2:657-660.

16. Lee, *Crowds and Soldiers*, 74. Tryon's frustration with the situation is further evident in his observation to Lord Hillsborough that he was "apprehensive while Husbands continued in Gaol without being brought to Tryal, and the Courts of Law open, no vigorous support could be relied upon from the Militia; but when He was found Guilty of the charge, there would be better Grounds to keep Him in prison until He had complied with the Penalties of the Law." William Tryon to Wills Hill, Lord Hillsborough, April 12, 1771, in Tryon, *Correspondence*, 2:657-660.

17. For an additional description of these activities, see William Tryon to Thomas McGuire, February 27, 1771, in Saunders, *Colonial and State Records of North Carolina*, 8:695-696.

18. William Smith noted dryly that "Mr. Tryon was disappointed by the Inefficacies of his legal court." Smith, "Introduction to the History of Governor Tryon's Administration from 1769 to 1771," 21.

19. William Tryon to Wills Hill, Lord Hillsborough, January 31, 1771, in Tryon, *Correspondence*, 2:599.

20. "Strange tales daily arrive," *South-Carolina Gazette*, issue unknown. This passage is quoted by Alonzo Dill, but he did not provide an additional citation for it. I could not find the passage in any of the South Carolina papers of the period, but the issue where it was published may no longer be extant. Dill, *Governor Tryon*, 149.

21. See Letter from William Tryon to John Hinton and Needham Bryan, February 27, 1771, in Tryon, *Correspondence*, 2:618.

22. See "Newbern, March 15," *Virginia Gazette*, issue 1026, March 28, 1771.

23. See Minutes of the New Bern District Court of Oyer and Terminer, March 11, 1771–March 16, 1771, in Saunders, *Colonial and State Records of North Carolina*, 8:528-532, for the full text of the indictment and the names of the sixty-two men charged on March 11.

24. See Minutes of the North Carolina Governor's Council, March 18-19, 1771, in Saunders, *Colonial and State Records of North Carolina*, 8:537-539.

25. See John Frohock and Alexander Martin to William Tryon, March 18, 1771, in *Colonial and State Records of North Carolina*, 8:533. This letter was also discussed in chapter 6.

26. William Tryon to John Frohock and Alexander Martin, April 5, 1771, Powell, Huhta, and Farnham, *Regulators in North Carolina*, 394-395.

27. Smith, "Introduction to the History of Governor Tryon's Administration from 1769 to 1771," 26.

28. Dill, *Governor Tryon*, 151.

29. Governor Tryon offered "forty shillings for an Encouragement to Serve in this Expedition, and to be intitled to receive two Shillings a Day while on Service." See William Tryon to the Commanding Officers of the Militia, March 19, 1771, in Tryon, *Correspondence*,

2:641-642. Wayne Lee notes that "the privates' pay was identical to that offered for a small expedition against the Cherokees in February 1771 . . . [and] 40 shillings was the same bounty as that offered to North Carolinians to enlist in the Continental troops in 1775–76." Lee, *Crowds and Soldiers*, 77.

30. The *General Orders of the Army* record book noted that on hearing that "the Army had committed outrages on the property of the Inhabitants settled on the Road," Governor Tryon did "once more strictly forbid every Person belonging to the Army from taking or disturbing the property of any person whatsoever." See *General Orders of the Army* record book, May 13, 1771, in Powell, Huhta, and Farnham, *Regulators in North Carolina*, 427.

31. See "Minutes of a meeting of officers of the North Carolina Militia, May 10, 1771," in Saunders, *Colonial and State Records of North Carolina*, 8:608, for a description of Waddell's retreat.

32. "Address by inhabitants of Orange County to William Tryon concerning the military campaign against the Regulators," 1771, in ibid., 544. This "Address" further noted that "since the legislature of this Province has not made the Constitution of Great Britain Prescribed by charter their Precedent—they paid very little regard to that Bullwark of life the *habeas Corpus* when they enacted for a law the Court of Oyer to be held at Newberne for the tryal of riots, where the accused Persons must attend tho' living in the most remote parts of the Province." This was not the only time that onlookers would question whether Governor Tryon and the General Assembly's efforts to end the Regulator Rebellion had broken with British law.

33. Lee, *Crowds and Soldiers*, 5.

34. Smith, "Introduction to the History of Governor Tryon's Administration from 1769 to 1771," 36.

35. E. W. Caruthers, *A Sketch of the Life and Character of the Rev. David Caldwell* (Greensborough, NC: Sherwood, 1842), 156-163.

36. Smith, "Introduction to the History of Governor Tryon's Administration from 1769 to 1771," 24.

37. "Petition of Inhabitants of Orange County," May 15, 1771, in Powell, Huhta, and Farnham, *Regulators in North Carolina*, 454. The wording in this petition resembles the wording in the third Regulator petition submitted October 27, 1769. While none of the five men who signed this petition signed the 1769 petition, the 1771 petition was signed by a John Williams, while the 1769 petition was signed by a Moses Williams and a Humphrey Williams, so it is possible that there was a connection between their authors. See "The humble Petition of us Inhabitants of Orange and Rowan countys," October 27, 1769, North Carolina General Assembly Session Records, Colonial (Upper and Lower Houses), box 4, October–November 1769 Lower House Papers Petitions Rejected or not acted on, Bills Folder, State Archives of North Carolina.

38. See Caruthers, *Sketch of the Life*, for more about David Caldwell.

39. William Tryon, "Proclamation of Governor William Tryon," May 16, 1771, in William Tryon, 1765–1771, box 6, Colonial Governors Papers, State Archives of North Carolina. Wayne Lee notes that this caveat allowed Tryon to continue functioning within the framework of Johnston's Riot Act, which gave men time to disband before shots were fired. See Lee, *Crowds and Soldiers*, 86. A letter by "Atticus" in the *Virginia Gazette* later that year suggested that Tryon personally shot Robert Thompson. See "Letter to his Excellency, William Tryon," *Virginia Gazette*, issue 1058, November 7, 1771.

40. Coverage of the Battle of Alamance appeared in multiple colonial newspapers. The *Virginia Gazette* praised "the cool, intrepid, and Soldier-like Behavior of his Excellency the Governor, who was in the Center of the Line during the whole Engagement." "New Bern, May 24," *Virginia Gazette*, issue 1037, May 28, 1771.
41. Fitch, *Some Neglected History*, 222.
42. See Lee, *Crowds and Soldiers*, 269-270n153, for a discussion of inconsistent casualty reports from the Battle of Alamance.
43. Ibid., 89.
44. "Proclamation by William Tryon concerning a pardon for rioters," May 17, 1771, in Saunders, *Colonial and State Records of North Carolina*, 8:608-609.
45. Atticus, "Letter to his Excellency," *Virginia Gazette*, issue 1058, November 7, 1771. This letter further added that "The sacrifice of Few, under its criminal circumstances, could neither atone for his crime nor abate your rage; this task was reserved for his unhappy parents. Your vengeance, Sir, in this instance, it seems, moved in a retrograde direction to that proposed in the second commandment against idolaters."
46. "Proclamation by William Tryon concerning a reward for the capture of Regulator leaders," June 9, 1771, in Saunders, *Colonial and State Records of North Carolina*, 8:617.
47. "A Proclamation," June 11, 1771, in Saunders, *Colonial and State Records of North Carolina*, 8:617-619.
48. Smith, "Introduction to the History of Governor Tryon's Administration from 1769 to 1771," 39.
49. Kars, *Breaking Loose*, 206.
50. William Tryon to Lord Hillsborough, December 14, 1771, in Tryon, *Correspondence*, 2:846. William Smith notes that Tryon pardoned "one half of [them] as the Perquisite of his Offices and afterwards recommended for a pardon, the rest suffered the Punishment of High Treason, in the Presence of the Army escorted by Col. Ashe." Smith, "Introduction to the History of Governor Tryon's Administration from 1769 to 1771," 39. The letter writer who used the pseudonym Atticus later condemned Tryon, stating that "the lives of six only were spared. Do you know, Sir, that your lenity on this occasion was less than that of the bloody Jeffries in 1685? He condemned five hundred persons, but saved the lives of two hundred and seventy." See "Letter to his Excellency," *Virginia Gazette*, issue 1058, November 7, 1771.
51. Robert Mateer was one of the two hostages taken by Governor Tryon on the eve of the Battle of Alamance. See Stephen C. Compton, "'James Pugh,' Regulator Sharpshooter: A Conundrum Unfolded," *North Carolina Historical Review* 90 (April 2013): 174. Compton also argues that James Pugh was not executed in Hillsborough but that the member of the Pugh family hanged that day was his brother, Enoch Pugh. Ibid., 173.
52. Josiah Martin's older half brother, Samuel Martin Jr., was the secretary of the Treasury in the 1750s and was closely allied with John Stuart, third Earl of Bute, who became Britain's prime minister in the early 1760s. Another brother, Henry Martin, was made a baronet in 1791 and was the comptroller for the British navy until he retired in 1794. For more about Martin's family, see Vernon Stumpf, "Josiah Martin and His Search for Success: The Road to North Carolina," *North Carolina Historical Review* 53, no. 1 (1976): 56-61. For more about Lord Bute, see Andrew Jackson O'Shaughnessy, *The Men Who Lost America: British Leadership, the American Revolution, and the Fate of the Empire* (New Haven, CT: Yale University Press, 2014), 50.

53. See Sir William Johnson to Lieutenant Governor James De Lancy, December 10, 1758, in *The Papers of Sir William Johnson*, ed. James Sullivan (Albany: University of the State of New York, 1921), 3:950, for the text of the warrant appointing Josiah Martin to this position.
54. See Stumpf, "Josiah Martin," 60-61.
55. See *Journal of the Commissioners for Trade and Plantations*, vol. 8 (London: His Majesty's Stationery Office, April 1704 to May 1782), 218.
56. Stumpf, "Josiah Martin," 55.
57. "Instructions to our Trusty and Well-beloved Josiah Martin Esquire, our Captain General and Governor in Chief in and over our Province of North Carolina in America, given at our Court at St. James's the 6th day of Febry 1771 in the eleventh year of our Reign," in *Colonial and State Records of North Carolina*, Vol. 8, 513-515.
58. "Additional Instructions to our Trusty and Wellbeloved Josiah Martin Esquire, our Captain General and Governor in Chief in and over our Province of North Carolina in America," undated in Saunders, *Colonial and State Records of North Carolina*, 8:515.
59. Bilder, *Transatlantic Constitution*, 3.
60. "Additional Instructions," in Saunders, *Colonial and State Records of North Carolina*, 8:516.
61. Ibid.
62. William Lawrence Saunders, "Preface to Volume 8 of the Colonial Records of North Carolina," in Saunders, *Colonial and State Records of North Carolina*, 8:iii. Saunders further notes that "Fresh from the Stamp Act rebellion, in which the leaders of the forces against the Regulators had been leaders against the Crown, they were rebels by habit and by descent. Rebels themselves, and the sons and grandsons of rebels, they hesitated not to use force when to them it seemed expedient. But neither the best nor the wisest people are always consistent." Ibid, iii.
63. "Advertisements, August 1766," in Powell, Huhta, and Farnham, *Regulators in North Carolina*, 35.
64. See Stumpf, "Josiah Martin," 63-65.
65. John Butler, "Petition from inhabitants of Guilford and Orange Counties concerning the pardon of Thomas Welborn, including related certification," August 25, 1771, in Saunders, *Colonial and State Records of North Carolina*, 9:25-27.
66. See Ninion Hamilton, "Petition from Niny Hamilton concerning his pardon," October 23, 1771, in Saunders, *Colonial and State Records of North Carolina*, 9:38.
67. Josiah Martin to Marquis of Downshire, August 30, 1772, in Saunders, *Colonial and State Records of North Carolina*, 9:330.
68. Martin Howard, "Memorandum by Martin Howard concerning the case against the Regulators," August 30, 1772, in Saunders, *Colonial and State Records of North Carolina*, 9: 333-334.
69. Ekirch, *"Poor Carolina,"* 205–206. Vernon Stumpf further notes that while Josiah Martin "was quick to suggest the use of coercive measures against the radicals in the stamp act and Quartering Crisis . . . when he thought he might be affected personally as governor in the Regulator troubles, he questioned the use of force." Stumpf, "Josiah Martin," 75.
70. Josiah Martin to William Legge, the 2nd Earl of Dartmouth, March 16, 1775, in Powell, Huhta, and Farnham, *Regulators in North Carolina*, 544-545.

71. See "Petition of the Inhabitants of Orange County," September 25, 1770, in *Colonial Records of North Carolina*, 8:231–234.
72. "To Governor Tryon," *Massachusetts Spy*, issue 17, June 27, 1771. "Saracen" is defined in the *Oxford English Dictionary* as "a name for the nomadic peoples of the Syro-Arabian desert which harassed the Syrian confines of the Empire; hence, an Arab; by extension, a Muslim, *esp.* with reference to the Crusades." *OED Online*, "Saracen, n.," accessed March 21, 2023, http://www.oed.com/view/Entry/170917. Herman Husband's pamphlet, *A Fan for Fanning, and A Touchstone to Tryon* was published around the same time as the Battle of Alamance. William Boyd notes that *A Fan for Fanning* was advertised in the *Massachusetts Spy*, and local tradition contends that it was published by Isaiah Thomas, the *Spy's* editor. This did lead to a copy of the *Massachusetts Spy* being burned in New Bern alongside an effigy of Thomas. Boyd, "Introduction," in Boyd, *Some Eighteenth Century Tracts*, 337-338.
73. "Letter to his Excellency, William Tryon," *Virginia Gazette*, issue 1058, November 7, 1771.
74. Husband, *Fan for Fanning*, in Boyd, *Some Eighteenth Century Tracts*, 247–392.
75. Fitch, *Some Neglected History*, 93.
76. Kay, "Provincial Taxes," 443.
77. Pauline Maier notes that "to North Carolinians, [such an] interpretation of events was dumfounding. Local radicals had supported the forceful suppression of the Regulators," not the other way around. Maier, *From Resistance to Revolution*, 197.
78. "From the Virginia Gazette," *Massachusetts Spy*, issue 33, October 17, 1771.

CHAPTER 8: RHODE ISLAND AND NORTH CAROLINA: NEW BATTLES

1. Park, *Burning*, vii-viii. This perception is probably rooted in the fact that Massachusetts was largely quiet between the Boston Massacre in 1770 and the Boston Tea Party in 1773. See Archer, *As If an Enemy's Country*; Carp, *Defiance*; and Hinderaker, *Boston's Massacre*.
2. See Maya Jasanoff, *Liberty's Exiles: American Loyalists in the Revolutionary World* (New York: Alfred A. Knopff, 2011).
3. Maier, *Ratification*, xi.
4. For more about the attack on the *Gaspee*, see Abby Chandler, "'But by the Law of this Colony': The *Gaspee* Affair in American History," in *The Bridge: The* Gaspee *Affair in Context*, a joint edition of the *Rhode Island History Journal* and the *Journal of Newport History* (2022): 1-3.
5. "London, July 18," republished in *Virginia Gazette*, issue 1107, October 15, 1772.
6. See John Reeves, *A History of the Law of Shipping and Navigation* (London: Thomas Burnside, 1792) for the histories and texts of these laws before 1792. For more about the history of the Navigation Acts in the British North American colonies, see Oliver Dickerson, *The Navigation Acts and the American Revolution* (Philadelphia: University of Pennsylvania Press, 1951), 7-10; Thomas Barrow, *Trade and Empire: The British Customs Service in Colonial America, 1660–1775* (Cambridge, MA: Harvard University Press, 1967), 177; and Rao, *National Duties*, 26-27.
7. See Jonathan Eacott, *Selling Empire: India in the Making of America and Britain, 1600–1830* (Chapel Hill: University of North Carolina Press, 2016), 45-48.
8. See Clark-Pujara, *Dark Work*, 25-29.

9. "An Essay on the Trade of the Northern Colonies," *Newport Mercury*, no. 284, February 14, 1764. Hopkins further commented in the same essay that "upon the Whole, how very unkind and ungenerous must it be, in the rich, proud and overbearing Planters of the West-Indies to make Use of all their Weight and Influence to limit and Distress the Trade and thereby to cramp and impoverish the poorer Northern Colonies." Ibid.
10. See "Resolutions of the Committee of Ways and Means for the Year 1764," *Cobbett's Parliamentary History*, 15:1426.
11. Rao, *National Duties*, 39.
12. For the complete text of the *Duties in American Colonies Act*, 5 George III, c. 12, see "Proceedings on the American Stamp Act," *Cobbett's Parliamentary History*, 16:35.
13. For more about John Robinson and George Rome, see Lovejoy, *Rhode Island Politics*, 42-49, and Bridenbaugh, *Peter Harrison*, 75-76.
14. Skemp, "Newport's Stamp Act Rioters," 56.
15. See Park, *Burning*, 45-46.
16. Denver Brunsman writes that "impressment was more than a stopgap measure to keep the British navy afloat: it was a fundamental component of Britain's early imperial success ... the purpose of impressment was not to target the idle, poor, and criminal elements within British society but rather the most skilled Atlantic seafarers." Brunsman, *The Evil Necessity: British Naval Impressment in the Eighteenth-Century Atlantic World* (Charlottesville: University of Virginia Press, 2013), 3.
17. See Beatty, "Thinking Globally," 42.
18. See "Dear Mr. Hall," *Newport Mercury*, no. 353, June 10, 1765, for a full account of the attack on the *Maidstone's* longboat. Captain Charles Antrobus was also identified by Ezra Stiles as having "gone home" after the Stamp Act riots. Stiles, "Stamp Act Notebook," sect. 3.
19. Governor Samuel Ward to Captain Charles Antrobus, July 12, 1765, in Bartlett, *Records of the Colony of Rhode Island*, 6:447.
20. John Robinson to Commissioners of Customs, September 5, 1765, in ibid., 6:413.
21. John Robinson to Governor Samuel Ward, August 31, 1765, On Board the Cygnet in Newport Harbour, in Ward Family Papers, Manuscript Collection 776, series 4, box 1, folder 26, Rhode Island Historical Society, Providence; Governor Samuel Ward to John Robinson, September 8, 1765, in ibid.
22. John Robinson's exchanges with Governor Ward and other Rhode Island officials during this period are summarized in Morgan and Morgan, *Stamp Act Crisis*, 154-158.
23. See Constance Sherman, "An Accounting of His Majesty's Armed Sloop *Liberty*," *American Neptune* 20 (1960): 243-249.
24. Stiles, *Literary Diary*, 271.
25. William Dudingston had served as the captain of the *Gaspee* for four years in 1772. Steven Park notes that "very little biographical or genealogical information is available about William Dudingston." Park, *Burning*, 119n52.
26. Captain Rufus Greene later sued Dudingston for damages for the loss of the rum. His trial deposition stated that Dudingston had "thrust him into the cabin, jammed the companion leaf upon his head, knocked him down upon a chest in said cabin, and confined him there for a considerable time" during his search of the *Fortune*. See "Rufus Greene deposition before Justice Hopkins Cook, January 14, 1773," in *The Documentary History of the Destruction of the Gaspee*, ed. William R. Staples (Providence: Rhode Island Publications, 1990), 67. The

Fortune was owned by Greene's cousin, Nathanael Greene, who would later command the Continental army in the southern states. See Terry Golway, *Washington's General: Nathanael Greene and the Triumph of the American Revolution* (New York: Holt Paperbacks, 2006), 33-38.

27. See "Charter of Rhode Island and Providence Plantations, July 15, 1663," Avalon Project, accessed May 5, 2021, https://avalon.law.yale.edu/17th_century/ri04.asp#1.

28. Captain Joseph Wanton to Lieutenant William Dudingston, March 22, 1772, in Gaspee Papers Collection, box 434, folder 1, Rhode Island Historical Society, Providence.

29. A later ballad would report that Dudingston "did chase the sloop, called the Hannah/Of whom one Lindsey was commander/they dogged her up Providence Sound/and there the rascal got aground." Anonymous, "Song on the Gaspee," in Staples, *Documentary History*, 109.

30. The group may have included Captain Rufus Greene from the *Fortune*. *Gaspee* crew member Peter May testified that he recognized Greene from the seizure of the *Fortune* four months earlier. See "Peter May deposition before Governor Joseph Wanton, January 19, 1773," in Staples, *Documentary History*, 76-77.

31. Anonymous, "Song on the Gaspee," in Staples, *Documentary History*, 109. See Benjamin Carp, "Resolute Men (Dressed as Mohawks)," in Carp, *Defiance*, 141-160, for more on the use of Native American disguises during colonial protests.

32. John Montagu, "Journal Entry for June 13, 1772," in "Copy of Admiral Montagu's Journal," Gaspee Papers Collection, box 434, folder 2, Rhode Island Historical Society, Providence. John Montagu was the naval commander in chief in North America between 1770 and 1774. See "Montagu, John (1719–1795)," Heritage, Newfoundland and Labrador, accessed March 21, 2023, https://www.heritage.nf.ca/articles/politics/naval-john-montagu.php.

33. See George III, "Instructions to our trusty and well beloved Joseph Wanton, Daniel Horsmanden, Frederick Smythe, Peter Oliver and Robert Auchmuty, Esquires," September 4, 1772," in Staples, *Documentary History*, 40-42.

34. William Legge, the second Earl of Dartmouth, succeeded Wills Hill, the Earl of Hillsborough, as the secretary of state for the colonies on August 27, 1772. He held the office for the next four years. See Franklin Wickwire, *British Subministers and Colonial America, 1763–1783* (Princeton, NJ: Princeton University Press, 1966), 139-142, and J. C. Sainty, *Office-Holders in Modern Britain*, vol. 3, *Officials of the Boards of Trade 1660–1870* (London: University of London and History of Parliament Trust, 1974), 28-37.

35. Peter Messer, "A Most Insulting Violation: The Burning of the HMS *Gaspee* and the Delaying of the American Revolution," *New England Quarterly* 88, no. 4 (2015): 585.

36. See statements from boatswain John Johnson and seamen William Caple and Bartholomew Cheevers in Staples, *Documentary History*, 17-19.

37. Governor Joseph Wanton to Admiral John Montagu, June 12, 1772, in "Copy of the Official Documents Relating to the Destruction of the *Gaspee*, June 10, 1772," Gaspee Papers Collection, box 434, folder 10, Rhode Island Historical Society, Providence.

38. Joseph Wanton, "Proclamation of Governor Joseph Wanton," June 12, 1772, in "Staples, *Documentary History*, 21.

39. See Park, *Burning*, 99-101, for more on the transition from investigating the attack on the *Gaspee* to the attack on the *Dartmouth*, *Eleanor*, and *Beaver* in Boston Harbor.

40. John Allen, *An Oration on the Beauties of Liberty, or The Essential Rights of the Americans*, in Bailyn, *Pamphlets of the American Revolution*, 2:240-241.
41. Ibid., *245*.
42. Stiles, *Literary Diary*, 112.
43. Edmund Morgan notes that Ezra Stiles believed that Martin Howard "was taking revenge on the people of North Carolina for the insults he had suffered in Newport." Morgan, *Gentle Puritan*, 259.
44. Stiles, *Literary Diary*, 149. In 1962, Edmund Morgan noted that this belief was incorrect. Morgan, *Gentle Puritan*, 259.
45. Jeremiah DeGennaro, "North Carolina's Regulators, the Battle of Alamance, and Public Memory," *Emerging Revolutionary War Era*, accessed May 24, 2021, https://emergingrevolutionarywar.org/2021/05/16/north-carolinas-regulators-the-battle-of-alamance-and-public-memory/. DeGennaro adds that "people certainly tried to make the connection. At the battle site there are two monuments . . . [which] claimed Alamance as the true Shot Heard Round the World. Local pride, misreading of primary sources, and a desire to get a leg up on haughty New Englanders may have all played a role in the push to remember the battle this way. Unfortunately, the facts do not support the claim."
46. "Advertisements, August 1766," in Powell, Huhta, and Farnham, *Regulators in North Carolina*, 35.
47. See Ekirch, *"Poor Carolina,"* 122-124, 162-163.
48. Letter from James Hunter to William Butler, November 6, 1772, in Powell, Huhta, and Farnham, *Regulators in North Carolina*, 537.
49. Powell, *North Carolina*, 168.
50. See "Additional Instructions to our Trusty and Wellbeloved Josiah Martin Esquire, our Captain General and Governor in Chief in and over our Province of North Carolina in America," in *Colonial and State Records of North Carolina*, Vol. 8, William Saunders, Ed. (Raleigh: P.M. Hale, 1886), 515-516.
51. Saunders, "Prefatory Notes to Ninth Volume," in *Colonial and State Records of North Carolina*, Vol. 9, (Raleigh: P.M. Hale, 1886), iii.
52. Minutes of the Lower House of the North Carolina General Assembly, December 8, 1773, in Saunders, *Colonial and State Records of North Carolina*, 9:740-741. Committees of Correspondence were organized in many British North American colonies in 1773 and 1774 to support the exchange of information from one colony to the next. See Yirush, "Imperial Crisis," 94.
53. This section of the minutes reads, "Resolved that it be an instruction to the said Committee that they do without delay inform themselves particularly of the principles and Authority on which was Constituted a Court of Enquiry said to have been lately held in Rhode Island with powers to transmit persons accused of offences committed in America to places beyond the seas to be tried."
54. See "The King's Message relating to the outrageous Proceedings at Boston in the Province of Massachusetts Bay," "The Boston Port Bill," "The regulating of the Government of Massachusett's Bay," and "The Administration of Justice Act," in *Cobbett's Parliamentary*, 17:1159-1210, for the debates on the laws intended to punish Massachusetts.
55. See Don Gerlach, "A Note on the Quartering Act of 1774," *New England Quarterly* 39, no. 1 (1966): 80-88.

56. See Vernon P. Creviston, "'No King unless it be a Constitutional King': Rethinking the Place of the Quebec Act in the Coming of the American Revolution," *Historian* 73, no. 3 (2011): 463-479.

57. William Saunders writes that "The regular way of appointing delegates to such bodies, being by election by the Assembly, he thought, having dissolved the existing Assembly on the 30th of March, that he had the matter in his own hands, and determined, in imitation of the course of Governor Tryon, in 1765, in reference to the New York Congress of that year, not to allow any Assembly to meet until matters were in better shape." Saunders, "Prefatory Notes to Ninth Volume," in Saunders, *Colonial and State Records of North Carolina*, 9:xxix.

58. John Harvey, "Memorandum concerning the election of delegates for the Provincial Congress of North Carolina," February 11, 1775, in ibid., 9:1125-1126.

59. John Webb et al., "Resolutions by inhabitants of Halifax (town) concerning resistance to Parliamentary taxation and the Provincial Congress of North Carolina," in Saunders, *Colonial and State Records of North Carolina*, 9:1038-1041.

60. William Saunders notes that this was the "first representative assemblage that ever met in North Carolina, or in America, save by royal authority. Instead of having royal authority it had popular authority, and met in open, flagrant defiance of the Crown, its Governor and his proclamations." Saunders, "Prefatory Notes to Ninth Volume," in *Colonial and State Records of North Carolina*, Vol. 9, xxxi.

61. Six of nine identified towns were also listed as sending representatives, with, again, the eastern towns better represented than the western towns. For the full list of delegates, see Minutes of the Provincial Congress of North Carolina, August 25, 1774, in *Colonial and State Records of North Carolina*, vol. 9, 1043-1044.

62. Powell, *North Carolina*, 172.

63. Richard Caswell was one of Governor Tryon's militia commanders during the Battle of Alamance. See Robert Connor, *Revolutionary Leaders of North Carolina* (High Point, NC: Petrie, 1916), 79-101. William Hooper was appointed deputy attorney general of North Carolina in 1770 and was attacked during the riots in Hillsborough that year. He also fought against the Regulators at the Battle of Alamance. See Robert Charles Kneip, "William Hooper, 1742–1790: Misunderstood Patriot" (PhD diss., Tulane University, 1980).

64. Michael McDonnell, "The Struggle Within: Colonial Politics on the Eve of Independence, in *The Oxford Handbook of the American Revolution*, ed. Edward Gray and Jane Kamensky (New York: Oxford University Press, 2015), 103-106.

65. Breen, *American Insurgents*, 162, 188-189.

66. "Proclamation of Governor Josiah Martin," March 1, 1775, in *Colonial and State Records of North Carolina*, Vol. 9, 1146-1147.

67. "Proclamation of Governor Josiah Martin," April 7, 1775, in *Colonial and State Records of North Carolina*, Vol. 9, 1211.

68. North Carolina had a large Scots community in Cross Creek, most of whom had fled Scotland following their failed efforts to support Charles Edward Stuart at the Battle of Culloden in 1745. See Wallace Brown, *The Good Americans: The Loyalists in the American Revolution* (New York: Morrow, 1969), 46-48. British general Thomas Gage sent Donald Macdonald to recruit supporters from North Carolina's Highland Scots community in 1775, and many of these men served under Macdonald during the Battle of Moore's Creek in

1776. See Sabine, *Biographical Sketches*, 59, for more about Donald MacDonald, and Lee, *Crowds and Soldiers*, 152-155, for more about the Battle of Moore's Creek. Further evidence of local support for Governor Martin can be found in an undated address delivered to him by "two hundred and twenty-seven of the Inhabitants of the county of Anson." See "Address of inhabitants of Anson County to Josiah Martin concerning loyalty to Great Britain," in *Colonial and State Records of North Carolina*, Vol. 9, 1161-1164.

69. "Resolves Adopted in Charlotte Town, Mecklenburg County, North Carolina, May 31, 1775," Avalon Project, accessed May 1, 2021, https://avalon.law.yale.edu/18th_century/charlott.asp.

70. "Proclamation of Governor Josiah Martin," June 16, 1775, in *Colonial and State Records of North Carolina*, Vol. 10, ed. William Saunders, (Raleigh: Winston, 1886), 16-19.

71. Josiah Martin returned to the Carolinas during the American Revolution in 1780 with General Charles Cornwallis, who hoped to rally local support for the British cause, though this proved unsuccessful. See Clyde Ferguson, "Carolina and Georgia Patriot and Loyalist Militia in Action, 1778–1783," in *The Southern Experience in the American Revolution*, ed. Larry Tise and Jeffrey Crow (Chapel Hill: University of North Carolina Press, 1978), 174-175, and Powell, *North Carolina*, 197-199.

72. See Howard to Iredell, May 15, 1777, 363-364, for evidence of the friendship between Howard and Iredell. See Ekirch, *"Poor Carolina,"* 37, for more about the connections between James Iredell and Samuel Johnston. Johnston was also the author of the "Johnston's Riot Act."

73. Howard to Iredell, May 15, 1777, 363-364.

74. Abigail Greenleaf Howard and Annie Howard returned to Massachusetts in 1783 after the Treaty of Paris was signed. See Chandler, "Loyalists and the Birth of Libraries," for a longer discussion of Abigail Howard's life in Massachusetts after the American Revolution.

75. See Minutes of the Provincial Congress of North Carolina, April 4, 1776–May 14, 1776, in *Colonial and State Records of North Carolina*, vol. 10, ed. William Saunders (Raleigh: Winston, 1886), 499-590.

76. See "May 4, 1776 Act of Renunciation," State of Rhode Island, accessed March 21, 2023, https://www.sos.ri.gov/divisions/Civics-And-Education.

77. British occupations were common in both the Mid-Atlantic and Southern states. Acquidneck Island, home to the communities of Newport, Middletown, and Portsmouth, was the only New England region occupied by the British army after 1776. See Donald Johnson, *Occupied America: British Military Rule and the Experience of Revolution* (Philadelphia: University of Pennsylvania Press, 2020), 5-15.

78. John Shy, *A People Numerous and Armed: Reflections on the Military Struggle for American Independence* (Ann Arbor: University of Michigan Press, 1990), 198-200.

79. William Hooper to Abner Nash, June 7, 1780, in Saunders, *Colonial and State Records of North Carolina*, 8:843-844. For more about North Carolina's experiences during the Revolution, see Maas, "North Carolina and Public Spirit."

80. "The Articles of Confederation," Avalon Project, accessed March 19, 2023, https://avalon.law.yale.edu/18th_century/artconf.asp.

81. See John Ferling, *A Leap in the Dark: The Struggle to Create the American Republic* (New York: Oxford University Press, 2003), 274-275, for more on the collective debt of the indi-

vidual states and the federal government after the American Revolution. See George William Van Cleeve, *We Have Not a Government: The Articles of Confederation and the Road to the Constitution* (Chicago: University of Chicago Press, 2019), 4-6, for more on the challenges of collecting taxes under the Articles of Confederation.

82. Sean Condon discusses similarities between the Regulator Rebellion and Shays's Rebellion in Condon, *Shays's Rebellion*, 57.

83. "The United States Constitution," Avalon Project, accessed March 21, 2023, https://avalon.law.yale.edu/18th_century/usconst.asp.

84. "Article Seven," ibid., accessed March 21, 2023, https://avalon.law.yale.edu/18th_century/art7.asp.

85. David Oterson further notes that Rhode Island and North Carolina became "independent political societies that had no constitutional relationship with the United States" once the first nine states had voted to ratify the Constitution." See Oterson, "The Admission of North Carolina and Rhode Island into the Union," *Journal of the American Revolution*, February 18, 2021, accessed March 21, 2023, https://allthingsliberty.com/2021/02/the-admission-of-north-carolina-and-rhode-island-into-the-union/.

86. This language is similar to the language used in the Articles of Confederation in 1781. "Resolves Adopted in Charlotte Town, Mecklenburg County, North Carolina, May 31, 1775," Avalon Project, accessed March 21, 2023, https://avalon.law.yale.edu/18th_century/charlott.asp.

87. Maier, *Ratification*, 406.

88. See ibid., 408-423, for a detailed description of the ratification debates in Hillsborough that took place between July 21 and August 4, 1788.

89. See Carol Berkin, *The Bill of Rights: The Fight to Secure America's Liberties* (New York: Simon and Schuster, 2015), 126-127. Pauline Maier notes that "being associated with Rhode Island, the only other nonratifying state, pleased nobody in North Carolina," but I question this assessment given Rhode Island and North Carolina's long history of economic and cultural connections. Maier, *Ratification*, 457.

90. See Thompson, "Ward-Hopkins Controversy," 363-375.

91. Crane, *Dependent People*, 126. These same divisions also drove much of the dissent over the Constitution in other states.

92. See Maier, *Ratification*, 223-225, for a detailed description of the debates between the Federalists and the "Country Party" in Rhode Island.

93. Maier, *Ratification*, 225.

94. Berkin, *Bill of Rights*, 128-129.

Bibliography

PRIMARY SOURCES IN ARCHIVES

American Antiquarian Society, Historical Periodicals Collection
  Boston Chronicle
  Massachusetts Spy
  New Hampshire Gazette
  Providence Gazette
  Williamsburg Gazette
Newport Historical Society
  Newport Mercury, 1764–1772
  Vernon Family Papers
New York Public Library, Manuscripts and Archives Division
  William Smith, "Introduction to the History of Governor Tryon's Administration from 1764 to 1768"
  William Smith, "Introduction to the History of Governor Tryon's Administration from 1769 to 1771"
  William Smith, Notes and Extracts from Papers of Governor William Tryon
Rhode Island Historical Society, Rhode Island Miscellaneous Manuscripts
  Papers Relating to the *Gaspee*, compiled by Walter Edwards Mss, 434.
State Archives of North Carolina
  Fanning-McCulloh Papers, 1752–1806
  James Iredell Papers, 1770–1773
  Military Collection War of the Regulation, 1768–1771

North-Carolina Gazette (Wilmington, NC), 1765–1766
North-Carolina Gazette (New Bern, NC), 1768–1774
North Carolina General Assembly Session Records, 1766–1771, boxes 3-5
William Tryon, 1765–1771, Colonial Governors Papers
Yale University
Beinecke Rare Book and Manuscript Library
Ezra Stiles's "Stamp Act Notebook"

Published Primary Sources

Bailyn, Bernard, ed. *Pamphlets of the American Revolution, 1750–1776*. Vols. 1-2. Cambridge, MA: Harvard University Press, 1965.

Bartlett, John Russell, ed. *Records of the Colony of Rhode Island and Providence Plantations in New England*. Vol. 6. Providence, RI: Knowles, Anthony, 1861.

———. *Records of the Colony of Rhode Island and Providence Plantations in New England*. Vol. 7. Providence, RI: A. C. Greene and Bros, 1862.

Bennet, William, ed. *Orange County Records*. Vols. 1-7. Raleigh, NC: privately published, 1987–1991.

Boyd, William K., ed. *Some Eighteenth Century Tracts Concerning North Carolina*. Raleigh, NC: Edwards and Broughton, 1927.

Bradford, Allen, ed. *Speeches of the Governors of Massachusetts, 1765–1775; the answers of the House of Representatives thereto; with their resolutions and addresses for that period. And other public papers relating to the dispute between this country and Great Britain which led to the independence of the United States*. New York: Da Capo Press, 1971.

Clark, Walter, ed. *Colonial and State Records of North Carolina*. Vols. 11-25. Raleigh: P. M. Hale, 1895–1906.

Cobbett's Parliamentary History of England from the Earliest Period to the Year 1803. Vols. 8-16. London: T. C. Hansard, 1813.

Franklin, Benjamin. *The Papers of Benjamin Franklin*. Founders Online, National Archives. Accessed March 21, 2023, https://franklinpapers.org/.

Greene, Nathanael. *Papers of Nathanael Greene*. Vol. 8. Edited by Dennis Conrad. Chapel Hill: University of North Carolina Press, 2015.

Hopkins, Stephen. *A True Representation of the Plan Formed at Albany for Uniting All the British Colonies*. In *Rhode Island Historical Tracts*. Providence, RI: S. S. Rider, 1877, 3-46.

Iredell, James. *Life and Correspondence of James Iredell: One of the Associate Justices of the Supreme Court of the United States*. Vol. 1. Edited by John Griffith. New York: Peter Smith, 1857.

Johnson, William. *The Papers of Sir William Johnson*. Vol. 3. Edited by James Sullivan. Albany: University of the State of New York, 1921.
Journal of the Commissioners for Trade and Plantations. Vol. 8. London: His Majesty's Stationery Office, April 1704 to May 1782.
Kimball, Gertrude Selwyn, ed. *The Correspondence of the Colonial Governors of Rhode Island, 1723–1775.* Vol. 2. Freeport, NY: Books for Libraries Press, 1969.
Lawson, John. *A New Voyage to Carolina; Containing the Exact Description of that Country: Together with the Present State thereof.* Edited by Hugh Talmadge Lefler. Chapel Hill: University of North Carolina Press, 1967.
Locke, John. "The Fundamental Constitutions of Carolina: March 1, 1669." Avalon Project: Documents in Law, History and Diplomacy. Accessed March 21, 2023, https://avalon.law.yale.edu/17th_century/nc05.asp.
Mercantini, Jonathan, ed. *The Stamp Act of 1765*. Peterborough, ON: Broadview Press, 2018.
Morgan, Edmund S., ed. *Prologue to Revolution: Sources and Documents on the Stamp Act Crisis, 1764–1766.* Chapel Hill: University of North Carolina Press, 1959.
Potter, Elisha Reynolds, ed. *The Early History of Narragansett: with an appendix of original documents, many of which are now for the first time published.* Providence, RI: Marshall, Brown, 1835.
Powell, William S., James K. Huhta, and Thomas J. Farnham, eds. *The Regulators in North Carolina: A Documentary History, 1759–1776.* Raleigh: North Carolina Department of Cultural Resources, Division of Archives and History, 1971.
Price, William, ed. *Not a Conquered People: Two North Carolinians View Parliamentary Taxation.* Raleigh: North Carolina Department of Cultural Resources, Division of Archives and History, 1975.
Rhode Island Historical Tracts. Providence: S. S. Rider, 1877.
Saunders, William Laurence, ed. *Colonial and State Records of North Carolina.* Vols. 4-9. Raleigh, NC: P. M. Hale, 1886.
———. *Colonial and State Records of North Carolina.* Vol. 10. Raleigh, NC: Winston, 1886.
Smith, William. *Historical Memoirs 1763 to 1778*. Vol. 1. Edited by William Sabine. New York: Colburn and Tegg, 1971.
Staples, William R., ed. *The Documentary History of the Destruction of the Gaspee.* Providence: Rhode Island Publications, 1990.
Stiles, Ezra. *The Literary Diary of Ezra Stiles.* Edited by Franklin Bowditch Dexter. New York: Charles Scribner's Sons, 1901.

Tryon, William. *The Correspondence of William Tryon and Other Selected Papers.* Vols. 1-2. Edited by William S. Powell. Raleigh: North Carolina Department of Cultural Resources, Division of Archives and History, 1980–1981.

Wood, Abraham. "The Travels of James Needham and Gabriel Arthur through Virginia, North Carolina, and Beyond, 1673–1674." Edited by R. P. Stephen Davis, Jr. *Southern Indian Studies* 39 (1990): 31-55.

SECONDARY SOURCES

Allen, Robert. "The Industrial Revolution in Miniature: The Spinning Jenny in Britain, France, and India." *Journal of Economic History* 69, no. 4 (2009): 901-927.

Amory, Hugh. "Printing and Bookselling in New England, 1638–1713." In *The Colonial Book in the Atlantic World.* Edited by Hugh Amory and David Hall. Chapel Hill: University of North Carolina Press, 2007.

Anderson, Fred. *Crucible of War: The Seven Years' War and the Fate of Empire in British North America, 1754–1766.* New York: Alfred A. Knopf, 2000.

Anderson, Mark. *Battle for the Fourteenth Colony: America's War of Liberation in Canada, 1774–1776.* Lebanon, NH: University Press of New England, 2013.

Archer, Richard. *As If an Enemy's Country: The British Occupation of Boston and the Origins of Revolution.* New York: Oxford University Press, 2012.

Austin, John. *Genealogical Dictionary of Rhode Island.* Albany, NY: J. Munsell's Sons, 1887.

Balsera, Viviana Díaz, and Rachel May, eds. *La Florida: Five Hundred Years of Hispanic Presence.* Gainesville: University of Florida Press, 2016.

Bannister, Jerry. *The Rule of the Admirals: Law, Custom, and Naval Government in Newfoundland, 1699–1832.* Toronto: University of Toronto Press, 2014.

Barrow, Thomas. *Trade and Empire: The British Customs Service in Colonial America, 1660–1775.* Cambridge, MA: Harvard University Press, 1967.

Barry, John. *Roger Williams and the Creation of the American Soul: Church, State, and the Birth of Liberty.* New York: Penguin, 2012.

Bates, Albert Carlos. "Sketch of William Pitkin." In *The Pitkin Papers: Correspondence and Documents during William Pitkin's Governorship of the Colony of Connecticut, 1766–1769.* Hartford: Connecticut Historical Society, 1921.

Beattie, J. M. *Crime and the Courts in England, 1660–1800.* Princeton, NJ: Princeton University Press, 1986.

Beatty, Joshua Fogarty. "'The Fatal Year': Slavery, Violence, and the Stamp Act of 1765." PhD diss., College of William and Mary, 2014.

———. "Thinking Globally, Acting Locally: The Struggle for Community in Revolutionary Newport." Master's thesis, College of William and Mary, 2002.

Berg, Maxine. "In Pursuit of Luxury: Global History and British Consumer Goods in the Eighteenth Century." *Past & Present* 182 (2004): 85-142.

Berkin, Carol. *The Bill of Rights: The Fight to Secure America's Liberties*. New York: Simon and Schuster, 2015.

Berry, Christopher. *The Idea of Luxury: A Conceptual and Historical Investigation*. New York: Cambridge University Press, 1994.

Bicknell, Thomas Williams. *The History of the State of Rhode Island and Providence Plantations*. New York: The American Historical Society, 1920.

Bilder, Mary Sarah. "English Settlement and Local Governance." *The Cambridge History of Law in America*. Vol. 1. Edited by Michael Grossberg and Christopher Tomlins. New York: Cambridge University Press, 2008.

———. *The Transatlantic Constitution: Colonial Legal Culture and the Empire*. Cambridge, MA: Harvard University Press, 2004.

Bond, Edward. *Damned Souls in the Tobacco Colony: Religion in Seventeenth-Century Virginia*. Macon, GA: Mercer University Press, 2000.

Breen, T. H. *American Insurgents, American Patriots: The Revolution of the People*. New York: Farrar, Straus and Giroux, 2010.

———. "'Baubles of Britain': The American and Consumer Revolutions of the Eighteenth Century." *Past & Present* 119 (1988): 73-104.

———. "An Empire of Goods: The Anglicization of Colonial America, 1690–1776." *Journal of British Studies* 25, no. 4 (1986): 467-499.

———. "Ideology and Nationalism on the Eve of the American Revolution: Revisions Once More in Need of Revising." *Journal of American History* 84, no. 1 (1997): 13-39.

———. *The Marketplace of Revolution: How Consumer Politics Shaped American Independence*. New York: Oxford University Press, 2004.

———. "Narrative of Commercial Life: Consumption, Ideology, and Community on the Eve of the American Revolution." *William and Mary Quarterly* 50, no. 3 (1993): 471-50.

Brenton, Chester. "Descendants of William Brenton, Governor of Rhode Island. Unpublished manuscript. Newport Historical Society.

Bridenbaugh, Carl. *Peter Harrison, American Architect*. Chapel Hill: University of North Carolina Press, 1949.

Brooks, Christopher. *Pettyfoggers and Vipers of the Commonwealth: The "Lower Branch" of the Legal Profession in Early Modern England*. New York: Cambridge University Press, 1986.

Brown, Wallace. *The Good Americans: The Loyalists in the American Revolution*. New York: Morrow, 1969.

Browning, Reed. *The Duke of Newcastle*. New Haven, CT: Yale University Press, 1975.

Brunsman, Denver. *The Evil Necessity: British Naval Impressment in the Eighteenth-Century Atlantic World*. Charlottesville: University of Virginia Press, 2013.

Bullion, John. *A Great and Necessary Measure: George Grenville and the Genesis of the Stamp Act, 1763–1765*. Columbia: University of Missouri Press, 1982.

Cannon, John. "Henry McCulloch and Henry McCulloh." *William and Mary Quarterly* 15, no. 1 (1958): 71-73.

Carp, Benjamin. *Defiance of the Patriots: The Boston Tea Party and the Making of America*. New Haven: Yale University Press, 2011.

———. *Rebels Rising: Cities and the American Revolution*. New York: Oxford University Press, 2007.

Caruthers, E. W. *A Sketch of the Life and Character of the Rev. David Caldwell*. Greensborough, NC: Sherwood, 1842.

Champlin, George Mason. *Annals of the Redwood Library and Athenaeum*. Newport, RI: Redwood Library, 1891.

Chandler, Abby. "'The Basis of Alienation will never be healed': The Historicity of Protest in Ezra Stiles' Stamp Act Notebook." In *Protest in the Long Eighteenth Century*. Edited by Yvonne Fuentes and Mark Malin. New York: Routledge, 2021.

———. "'But by the Law of this Colony': The *Gaspee* Affair in American History." In *The Bridge: The Gaspee Affair in Context*, a joint edition of the *Rhode Island History Journal* and the *Journal of Newport History* (2022): 1-14.

———. "'Let us unanimously lay aside foreign Superfluities': Textile Production and British Colonial Identity in the 1760s." *Early American Studies: An Interdisciplinary Journal*, 19, no. 1 (Winter 2021): 138-165.

———. "Loyalists and the Birth of Libraries in New England: The Marriage of Martin and Abigail Howard." Selected Papers of the Consortium of the Revolutionary Era, 2020. *Age of Revolutions*. Accessed March 21, 2023, https://ageofrevolutions.com/2021/01/13/loyalists-and-the-birth-of-libraries-in-new-england-the-marriage-of-martin-and-abigail-howard/.

———. "Reexamining the Remarkable Career of Martin Howard." *Newport History* 90, No. 1 (2019): 1-30.

———. "'Unawed by the Laws of their Country': Finding Local and Imperial Legitimacy in North Carolina's Regulator Rebellion," *North Carolina Historical Review*, 93, no. 2 (April 2016): 1-28.

Chaput, Erik. *The People's Martyr: Thomas Wilson Dorr and his 1842 Rebellion*. Lawrence: University Press of Kansas, 2013.

Clark-Pujara, Christy. *Dark Work: The Business of Slavery in Rhode Island*. New York: New York University Press, 2016.

Coakely, Robert. *The Role of Federal Military Forces in Domestic Disorders, 1789–1878*. Washington, DC: Center of Military History, 1988.

Coggeshall, Charles Pierce. *The Coggeshalls in America: Genealogy of the Descendants of John Coggeshall of Newport, with a brief notice of their English antecedents*. Boston, MA: C. E. Godspeed, 1930.

Compton, Stephen. "'James Pugh,' Regulator Sharpshooter: A Conundrum Unfolded." *North Carolina Historical Review* 90 (April 2013): 173–196.

Condon, Sean. *Shay's Rebellion: Authority and Distress in Post-Revolutionary America*. Baltimore, MD: Johns Hopkins University Press, 2015.

Conforti, Joseph. *Saints and Strangers: New England in British North America* Baltimore, MD: Johns Hopkins University Press, 2006.

Conley, Patrick. *Democracy in Decline: Rhode Island's Constitutional Development, 1776–1841*. Providence: Rhode Island Historical Society, 1977.

Conniff, James. *The Useful Cobbler: Edmund Burke and the Politics of Progress*. Albany: State University of New York Press, 1994.

Connor, Robert. *Revolutionary Leaders of North Carolina*. High Point, NC: Petrie, 1916.

Corbitt, David Leroy. *The Formation of the North Carolina Counties, 1663–1943*. Raleigh: North Carolina Department of Cultural Resources, Division of Archives and History, 1975.

Coughtry, Jay. *The Notorious Triangle: Rhode Island and the African Slave Trade 1700–1807*. Philadelphia, PA: Temple University Press, 1981.

Crane, Elaine Forman. *A Dependent People: Newport, Rhode Island in the Revolutionary Era*. New York: Fordham University Press, 1985.

———. *Ebb Tide in New England: Women, Seaports, and Social Change, 1630–1800*. Boston, MA: Northeastern University Press, 1985.

Creviston, Vernon. "'No King unless it be a Constitutional King': Rethinking the Place of the Quebec Act in the Coming of the American Revolution." *Historian* 73, no. 3 (2011): 463-479.

Daniels, Bruce. *Dissent and Conformity on Narragansett Bay, The Colonial Rhode Island Town*. Middletown, CT: Wesleyan University Press, 1983.

DeGennaro, Jeremiah. "North Carolina's Regulators, the Battle of Alamance, and Public Memory." *Emerging Revolutionary Era*. Accessed March 21, 2023, https://emergingrevolutionarywar.org/2021/05/16/north-carolinas-regulators-the-battle-of-alamance-and-public-memory/.

Demond, Robert. *The Loyalists in North Carolina during the Revolution*. Durham, NC: Duke University Press, 1940.

Deutsch, Sarah. "Those Elusive Guineamen: Newport Slavers, 1735–1774." *New England Quarterly* 55, no. 2 (1982): 229-253.

De Vries, Jan. *The Industrious Revolution: Consumer Behavior and the Household Economy, 1650 to the Present*. New York: Cambridge University Press, 2008.

Dickerson, Oliver. *The Navigation Acts and the American Revolution*. Philadelphia: University of Pennsylvania Press, 1951.

Dill, Alonzo Thomas. *Governor Tryon and His Palace*. Chapel Hill: University of North Carolina Press, 1955.

Drake, Francis S. *The town of Roxbury: its memorable persons and places, its history and antiquities, with numerous illustrations of its old landmarks and noted personages*. Roxbury, MA: self-published, 1878.

Du Rivage, Justin. *Revolution against Empire: Taxes, Politics, and the Origins of American Independence*. New Haven, CT: Yale University Press, 2017.

Duval, Kathleen. *Independence Lost: Lives on the Edge of the American Revolution*. New York: Random House, 2015.

Eacott, Jonathan. *Selling Empire: India in the Making of America and Britain, 1600–1830*. Chapel Hill: University of North Carolina Press, 2016.

Edelson, S. Max. *The New Map of Empire: How Britain Imagined America before Independence*. Cambridge, MA: Harvard University Press, 2017.

Edes, Henry. "Memoir of Martin Howard, Chief Justice of the Supreme Court of North Carolina." *Publications of the Colonial Society of Massachusetts*. Boston: Colonial Society of Massachusetts, 1904.

Ekirch, A. Roger. *"Poor Carolina": Politics and Society in Colonial North Carolina, 1729–1776*. Chapel Hill: University of North Carolina Press, 1981.

Ellery, Harrison. "The Vernon Family and Arms." *New England Historical and Genealogical Register* (1879): 312-319.

Ernst, Joseph. *Money and Politics in America, 1755–1775: A Study in the Currency Act of 1764 and the Political Economy of Revolution*. Chapel Hill: University of North Carolina Press, 1973.

Ezell, Margaret. "John Locke's Images of Childhood: Early Eighteenth Century Response to Some Thoughts Concerning Education." *Eighteenth-Century Studies* 17, no. 2 (1984): 139-155.

Feng, Cho-Chien. "The Revolutionary Memories of New York Loyalists Thomas Jones and William Smith, Jr." *Journal of the American Revolution*, January 31, 2019. Accessed March 21, 2023, https://allthingsliberty.com/2019/01/the-revolutionary-memories-of-new-york-loyalists-thomas-jones-and-william-smith-jr/.

Ferguson, Clyde. "Carolina and Georgia Patriot and Loyalist Militia in Action, 1778–1783." In *The Southern Experience in the American Revolution*. Edited by Larry Tise and Jeffrey Crow. Chapel Hill: University of North Carolina Press, 1978.

Ferling, John. *A Leap in the Dark: The Struggle to Create the American Republic*. New York: Oxford University Press, 2003.

Fitch, William. *Some Neglected History of North Carolina, Being an Account of the Revolution of the Regulators and of the Battle of Alamance, the First Battle of the Revolution*. New York: Neale Publishing, 1906.

Flavel, Julie. *When London Was Capital of America*. New Haven, CT: Yale University Press, 2010.

Garland, Katherine. "African Spirituality in Newport." *Spectacle of Toleration*. Accessed March 21, 2023, http://www.spectacleoftoleration.org/african-spirituality-in-newport/.

Gerlach, Don. "A note on the Quartering Act Act of 1774." *New England Quarterly* 39, no. 1 (1966): 80-88.

Golway, Terry. *Washington's General: Nathanael Greene and the Triumph of the American Revolution*. New York: Holt Paperbacks, 2006.

Goodman, Phebe. *The Garden Squares of Boston*. Hanover, NH: University Press of New England, 2003.

Gould, Philip. *Writing the Rebellion: Loyalists and the Literature of Politics in British America*. New York: Oxford University Press, 2013.

Griffins, Patrick. *The Townshend Moment: The Making of Empire and Revolution in the Eighteenth Century*. New Haven, CT: Yale University Press, 2017.

Hall, David D., John M. Murrin, and Thad W. Tate, eds. *Saints and Revolutionaries: Essays on Early American History*. New York: W. W. Norton, 1984.

Hatley, Tom. *The Dividing Paths: Cherokees and South Carolinians through the Era of Revolution*. New York: Oxford University Press, 1993.

Haulman, Kate. *The Politics of Fashion in Eighteenth-Century America*. Chapel Hill: University of North Carolina Press, 2011.

Henderson, Archibald. *The Star of Empire: Phases of the Westward Movement in the Old Southwest*. Durham, NC: Seeman Printery, 1919.

Herndon, Ruth Wallis. *Unwelcome Americans: Living on the Margin in Early America*. Philadelphia: University of Pennsylvania Press, 2001.

Higginbotham, Don. *Daniel Morgan: Revolutionary Rifleman*. Chapel Hill: University of North Carolina Press, 1979.

Higginbotham, Don, and William Price. "Was It Murder for a White Man to Kill a Slave? Chief Justice Martin Howard Condemns the Peculiar Institution in North Carolina." *William and Mary Quarterly* 54, no. 4 (1979): 593-601.

Hinderaker, Eric. *Boston's Massacre*. Cambridge, MA: Harvard University Press, 2017.

Hogeland, William. *The Whiskey Rebellion: George Washington, Alexander Hamilton, and the Frontier Rebels Who Challenged America's Newfound Sovereignty*. New York: Scribner, 2006.

Honeyman, Abraham Van. *The Honeyman Family in Scotland and America, 1504–1598*. Plainfield, NJ: Honeyman's Publishing House, 1909.

Hudack, Leona. *Early American Women Printers and Publishers, 1639–1820*. Metuchen, NJ: Scarecrow Press, 1978.

Hudson, Arthur Palmer. "Songs of the North Carolina Regulators." *William and Mary Quarterly* 4, no. 4 (1947): 470-485.

Humphrey, Carol Sue. *The American Revolution and the Press*. Evanston, IL: Northwestern University Press, 2013.

Hutchins, Zachary McLeod. *Community without Consent: New Perspectives on the Stamp Act*. Hanover, NH: Dartmouth College Press, 2016.

James, Sydney. *Colonial Rhode Island: A History*. New York: Scribner, 1975.

———. *John Clarke and His Legacies: Religion and Law in Colonial Rhode Island, 1638–1750*. University Park: Pennsylvania State University Press, 1999.

Jasanoff, Maya. *Liberty's Exiles: American Loyalists in the Revolutionary World*. New York: Alfred A. Knopf, 2011.

Johnson, Donald. *Occupied America: British Military Rule and the Experience of Revolution*. Philadelphia: University of Pennsylvania Press, 2020.

Jones, Lewis Hampton. *Captain Roger Jones of London and Virginia, Some of his antecedents and descendants*. Albany, NY: Joel Munsell's Sons, 1891.

Kamensky, Jane. *A Revolution in Color: The World of John Singleton Copley*. New York: W. W. Norton, 2016.

Kars, Marjoleine. *Breaking Loose Together: The Regulator Rebellion in Pre-Revolutionary America*. Chapel Hill: University of North Carolina Press, 2002.

Kay, Marvin Michael. "The Payment of Provincial and Local Taxes in North Carolina, 1748–1771." *William and Mary Quarterly* 26, no. 2 (1969): 218-240.

———. "Provincial Taxes in North Carolina during the Administrations of Dobbs and Tryon." *North Carolina Historical Review* 42, no. 4 (1965): 441– 443.

Kennedy, Edwin Wexler. "Quit-rents and currency in North Carolina 1663–1776." PhD diss., Johns Hopkins University Press, 1897.

Kerber, Linda. *Women of the Republic: Intellect and Ideology in Revolutionary America.* Chapel Hill, NC: Omohundro Institute of Early American History and Culture, 1997.

Kishlansky, Mark. *Parliamentary Selection: Social and Political Choice in Early Modern England.* New York: Cambridge University Press, 1986.

Klein, Milton, and Jacob Cooke, eds. *Colonial Rhode Island: A History.* New York: Scribner, 1975.

Kneip, Robert Charles. "William Hooper, 1742–1790: Misunderstood Patriot." PhD diss., Tulane University, 1980.

Laird, Michael. *A Natural History of English Gardening.* New Haven, CT: Yale University Press, 2015.

Lang, Sean. *Parliamentary Reform, 1785–1928.* New York: Routledge, 1999.

Langley, Lester. *The Americas in the Age of Revolution, 1750–1850.* New Haven, CT: Yale University Press, 1996.

Lawson, Philip. *George Grenville: A Political Life.* Oxford: Clarendon Press, 1984.

Lee, Wayne E. *Crowds and Soldiers in Revolutionary North Carolina: The Culture of Violence in Riot and War.* Gainesville: University Press of Florida, 2001.

———. "Fortify, Fight, or Flee: Tuscarora and Cherokee Defensive Warfare and Military Culture Adaptation." *Journal of Military History* 68, no. 3 (2004): 714-770.

Lepore, Jill. *The Whites of Their Eyes: The Tea Party's Revolution and the Battle over American History.* Princeton, NJ: Princeton University Press, 2011.

Lewis, Wilmarth, ed. *The 1764 Catalogue of the Redwood Library Company at Newport, Rhode Island.* Hartford: Connecticut Printers, 1965.

Littlefield, George Emery. *Early Boston Booksellers, 1642–1711.* New York: Burt Franklin, 1969.

Locke, John. *The Two Treatises of Civil Government.* Edited by Thomas Hollis. London: J. M. Dent, 1924.

Lovejoy, David. *Rhode Island Politics and the American Revolution, 1760–1776.* Providence, RI: Brown University Press, 1958.

Maass, John. "North Carolina and Public Spirit in the American Revolution, 1775–1783." *Journal of the American Revolution,* May 4, 2021. Accessed March 21, 2023, https://allthingsliberty.com/2021/05/north-carolina-and-public-spirit-in-the-american-revolution-1775-1783/.

Maier, Pauline. *From Resistance to Revolution: Colonial Radicals and the Development of American Opposition to Britain, 1765–1776.* New York: W. W. Norton, 1972.

———. *Ratification: The People Debate the Constitution, 1787–1788*. New York: Simon and Schuster, 2010.

Mather, Cotton. *Magnalia Christi Americana or the Ecclesiastical History of New England*. Hartford, CT: Silas Andrus and Son, 1853.

McConville, Brendan. *The King's Three Faces: The Rise and Fall of Royal America, 1688–1776*. Chapel Hill: University of North Carolina Press, 2006.

McDonnell, Michael. "The Struggle Within: Colonial Politics on the Eve of Independence. In *The Oxford Handbook of the American Revolution*. Edited by Edward Gray and Jane Kamensky. New York: Oxford University Press, 2015.

McGlynn, Margaret. *The Royal Prerogative and the Learning of the Inns of Court*. New York: Cambridge University Press, 2003.

Merrell, James. *The Indians' New World: Catawbas and Their Neighbors from European Contact through the Era of Removal*. Chapel Hill: University of North Carolina Press, 2009.

Merrens, Harry Roy. *Colonial North Carolina in the Eighteenth Century: A Study in Historic Geography*. Chapel Hill: University of North Carolina Press, 1964.

Messer, Peter. "A Most Insulting Violation: The Burning of the HMS Gaspee and the Delaying of the American Revolution." *New England Quarterly* 88, no. 4 (2015): 582-622.

Meyers, Debra. *Common Whores, Vertuous Women, and Loveing Wives: Free Will Christian Women in Colonial Maryland*. Bloomington: Indiana University Press, 2003.

Minty, Christopher. "Mobilization and Voluntarism: The Political Origins of Loyalism in New York, c. 1768–1778." PhD diss., University of Stirling, 2014.

Monod, Paul Kléber. *Jacobitism and the English People*. New York: Cambridge University Press, 1993.

Moore, Rosemary. "Seventeenth-Century Context and Quaker Beginnings." In *The Oxford Handbook of Quaker Studies*. Edited by Stephen Angell and Pink Dandelion. New York: University of Oxford Press, 2015, 13-28.

Morgan, Edmund. *The Gentle Puritan: A Life of Ezra Stiles, 1727–1795*. New York: W. W. Norton, 1962.

Morgan, Edmund S., and Helen M. Morgan. *The Stamp Act Crisis: Prologue to the Revolution*. Chapel Hill: University of North Carolina Press, 1995.

Morser, Eric. *The Fires of New England: A Story of Protest and Rebellion in Antebellum America*. Amherst: University of Massachusetts Press, 2018.

Mulcahy, Matthew. *Hubs of Empire: The Southeastern Low Country and British Caribbean*. Baltimore: Johns Hopkins University Press, 2014.

Murrin, John. "The Legal Transformation: The Bench and Bar of Eighteenth-Century Massachusetts." In *Colonial America: Essays in Politics and Social Development*. Edited by Stanley N. Katz and John Murrin. New York: Alfred A. Knopf, 1983.

Myers, Ruth Kennedy, and Bradford A. Becken. "Who Was John Webber?" *Newport History* 70, no. 2 (2000): 1-21.

Nash, Claude. *Some Nashes of Virginia: Two Hundred Years of an American Family, 1774–1974*. Self-published, 1975.

Nash, Gary. "The Failure of Female Factory Labor in Colonial Boston." *Labor History* 20 (1979): 165-188.

Nelson, Dana. *Commons Democracy: Reading the Politics of Participation in the Early United States*. New York: Fordham University Press, 2015.

Nelson, Paul David. *William Tryon and the Course of Empire: A Life in British Imperial Service*. Chapel Hill: University of North Carolina Press, 1990.

Newman, Paul Douglas. *Fries's Rebellion: The Enduring Struggle for the American Revolution*. Philadelphia: University of Pennsylvania Press, 2004.

Norton, Louis Arthur. "Print Media and Isaiah Thomas." *Journal of the American Revolution*, April 13, 2021. Accessed March 21, 2023, https://allthingsliberty.com/2021/04/print-media-and-isaiah-thomas/.

Oatis, Steven. *A Colonial Complex: South Carolina's Frontiers in the Era of the Yamasee War, 1680–1730*. Lincoln: University of Nebraska Press, 2008.

Oberg, Michael Leroy, and David Moore. "Voyages to Carolina: Europeans in the Indians' Old World." In *New Voyages to Carolina: Reinterpreting North Carolina History*. Edited by Larry Tise and Jeffrey Crow, 41-59. Chapel Hill: University of North Carolina Press, 2017.

Olson, Alison. "The London Mercantile Lobby and the Coming of the American Revolution." *Journal of American History* 69, no. 1 (1982): 21-41.

O'Shaughnessy, Andrew Jackson. *An Empire Divided: The American Revolution and the British Caribbean*. New York: University of Pennsylvania Press, 2000.

———. *The Men Who Lost America: British Leadership, the American Revolution, and the Fate of the Empire*. New Haven, CT: Yale University Press, 2014.

Oterson, David. "The Admission of North Carolina and Rhode Island into the Union." *Journal of the American Revolution*, February 18, 2021. Accessed March 21, 2023, https://allthingsliberty.com/2021/02/the-admission-of-north-carolina-and-rhode-island-into-the-union/.

Park, Steven. *The Burning of His Majesty's Schooner* Gaspee. Yardley, PA: Westholme, 2016.

Pavord, Anna. *The Naming of Names: The Search for Order in the World of Plants*. New York: Bloomsbury, 2005.

Petty-Fitzmaurice, Edmond George. *Life of William, Earl of Shelburne*. London: Macmillan, 1912.

Potvin, Ron M. "Washington Slept Here? Reinterpreting the Stephen Hopkins House." *History News* 66, no. 2 (2011): 17-20.

Powell, William. *North Carolina through Four Centuries*. Chapel Hill: University of North Carolina Press, 1989.

———. *The War of the Regulation and the Battle of Alamance, May 16, 1771*. Raleigh: North Carolina Department of Cultural Resources, Division of Archives and History, 1975.

Price, William. "'Men of Good Estates': Wealth among North Carolina's Royal Councilors." *North Carolina Historical Review* 49, no. 1 (1972): 72-82.

Purdue, Theda, and Christopher Oakley. *Native Carolinians: The Indians of North Carolina*. Raleigh: North Carolina Department of Natural and Cultural Resources, Division of Archives and History, 2010.

Ramsey, William. *The Yamasee War: A Study of Culture, Economy, and Conflict in the Colonial South*. Lincoln: University of Nebraska Press, 2010.

Rao, Gauthram. *National Duties: Customs Houses and the Making of the American State*. Chicago: University of Chicago Press, 2016.

Reeves, John. *A History of the Law of Shipping and Navigation*. London: Thomas Burnside, 1792.

Reid, John Phillip. *Constitutional History of the American Revolution: The Authority of Rights*. Madison: University of Wisconsin Press, 1995.

Riordan, Liam. "A Loyalist Who Loved His Country Too Much: Thomas Hutchinson, Historian of Colonial Massachusetts." *New England Quarterly* 54, no. 3 (2017): 344-84.

Sabine, Lorenzo. *Biographical Sketches of Loyalists of the American Revolution, with an Historical Essay*. Vol. 2. Boston: Little Brown, 1864.

Sainty, J. C. *Office-Holders in Modern Britain*. Vol. 3, *Officials of the Boards of Trade 1660–1870*. London: University of London and History of Parliament Trust, 1974.

Schlesinger, Arthur. *Prelude to Independence: The Newspaper War on Britain, 1764–1776*. Boston: Northeastern University Press, 1980).

Schocket, Andrew. *Fighting over the Founders: How We Remember the American Revolution*. New York: New York University Press, 2015.

Sellers, Charles. "Private Profits and British Colonial Policy: The Speculations of Henry McCulloh." *William and Mary Quarterly* 8, no. 4 (1951): 535-551.

Shammas, Carole. "How Self-Sufficient Was Early America?" *Journal of Interdisciplinary History* 13, no. 2 (1982): 247-272.

Shannon, Timothy. *Indians and Colonists at the Crossroads of Empire: The Albany Congress of 1754*. Ithaca, NY: Cornell University Press, 2000.

Sherman, Constance. "An Accounting of His Majesty's Armed Sloop *Liberty*." *American Neptune* 20 (1960): 243-249.

Sherman, Kimberly. "A Spirit of Industry: The Colonial Origins of Rice Culture in the Lower Cape Fear." *North Carolina Historical Review* 91, no. 3 (2014): 255-287.

Shumate, Ken. "The Molasses Act: A Brief History." *Journal of the American Revolution*, January 24, 2019. Accessed March 21, 2023, https://allthingsliberty.com/2019/01/the-molasses-act-a-brief-history/.

———. *1764: The First Year of the American Revolution*. Yardley, PA: Westholme, 2021.

———. "The Sugar Act: A Brief History." *Journal of the American Revolution*, September 17, 2018. Accessed March 21, 2023, https://allthingsliberty.com/2018/09/the-sugar-act-a-brief-history/.

Shy, John. *A People Numerous and Armed: Reflections on the Military Struggle for American Independence*. Ann Arbor: University of Michigan Press, 1990.

Skemp, Sheila. "Newport's Stamp Act Rioters: Another Look." *Newport History* 47, no. 2 (1989): 41-59.

Slaughter, Thomas P.. *The Whiskey Rebellion: Frontier Epilogue to the American Revolution*. New York: Oxford University Press, 1986.

Smith, Barbara Clark. *The Freedoms We Lost: Consent and Resistance in Revolutionary America*. New York: New Press, 2010.

Smith, S. D. "The Market for Manufactures in the Thirteen Continental Colonies, 1698–1776. *Economic History Review* 51, no. 4 (1998): 676-708.

Smith, Scott M. "William Tryon and the Park That Still Bears His Name." *Journal of the American Revolution*, May 17, 2021. Accessed March 21, 2023, https://allthingsliberty.com/2021/05/william-tryon-and-the-park-that-still-bears-his-name/.

Smith, William. *The history of the province of New-York: from the first discovery to the year MDCC. XXXII, to which is annexed a description of the country, with a short account of the inhabitants, their trade, religious and political state, and the constitution of the courts of justice in that colony*. London: T. Wilcox, 1757.

Snydacker, Daniel. "The Remarkable Career of Martin Howard." *Newport History* 61, no. 1 (1988): 2-17.

Spero, Patrick. *Frontier Country: The Politics of War in Early Pennsylvania*. Philadelphia: University of Pennsylvania Press, 2016.

Stanwood, Owen. *The Empire Reformed: English America in the Age of the Glorious Revolution*. Philadelphia: University of Pennsylvania Press, 2011.

St. George, Robert Blair. *Conversing by Signs: Poetics of Implication in Colonial New England Culture*. Chapel Hill: University of North Carolina Press, 1998.

Strobel, Christoph. *Native Americans of New England*. Santa Barbara, CA: Praeger, 2020.

Stumpf, Vernon. "Josiah Martin and His Search for Success: The Road to North Carolina." *North Carolina Historical Review* 53, no. 1 (1976): 55-79.

Taylor, Alan. *American Colonies: The Settling of North America*. New York: Penguin, 2002.

Thomas, Allen Mansfield. "'Circumstances not Principles' Elite Control of the Newport Stamp Act Riots." *Newport History* 67, no. 2 (1996): 1-29.

Thomas, Isaiah. *The History of Printing in America, with a Biography of Printers & an Account of Newspapers*. New York: Weathervane Books, 1970.

Thompson, Mack. "The Ward-Hopkins Controversy and the American Revolution in Rhode Island: An Interpretation." *William and Mary Quarterly* 16, no. 3 (1959): 363-375.

Troxler, Carole Watterson. *Farming Dissenters: The Regulator Movement in Piedmont North Carolina*. Raleigh: North Carolina Office of Archives and History, 2011.

———. "Land Tenure as Regulator Grievance and Revolutionary Tool." In *New Voyages to Carolina: Reinterpreting North Carolina History*. Edited by Larry Tise and Jeffrey Crow, 110-143. Chapel Hill: University of North Carolina Press, 2017.

Ulrich, Laurel Thatcher. *The Age of Homespun: Objects and Stories in the Creation of an American Myth*. New York: Alfred A. Knopf, 2001.

———. "'Daughters of Liberty': Religious Women in Revolutionary New England." In *Women of the Age of Revolution*. Edited by Ronald Hoffman and Peter Albert, 211-243. Charlottesville: University of Virginia Press, 1989.

———. "Of Pens and Needles: Sources in Early American Women's History." *Journal of American History* 77, no. 1 (1990): 200-207.

———. "Wheels, Looms, and the Gender Division of Labor in Eighteenth-Century New England," *William and Mary Quarterly* 55, no. 1 (1998): 3-38.
University of London Institute of Historical Research. *Office-Holders in Modern Britain.* Vol. 2. London: J. C. Sainty, 1973.
Updike, Wilkins. *A History of the Episcopal Church in Narragansett, Rhode Island: Including a History of Other Episcopal Churches in the State.* Boston: Merry Mount Press, 1907.
Van Cleeve, George William. *We Have Not a Government: The Articles of Confederation and the Road to the Constitution.* Chicago: University of Chicago Press, 2019.
Van Horn, Jennifer. *The Power of Objects in Eighteenth-Century British North America.* Chapel Hill: University of North Carolina Press, 2017.
Vickers, Daniel. *Farmers & Fishermen: Two Centuries of Work in Essex County, Massachusetts, 1630-1850.* Chapel Hill: University of North Carolina Press, 1994.
Ward, H. Warwick, and R. P. Stephen Davis. *Time before History: The Archaeology of North Carolina.* Chapel Hill: University of North Carolina Press, 1999.
Watson, Alan. *Money and Monetary Problems in Early North Carolina.* Raleigh: North Carolina Department of Cultural Resources, Division of Archives and History, 1980.
Whittenberg, James. "Planters, Merchants, and Lawyers: Social Change and the Origins of the North Carolina Regulation." *William and Mary Quarterly* 34, no. 2 (1997): 215-238.
Wickwire, Franklin. *British Subministers and Colonial America, 1763–1783.* Princeton, NJ: Princeton University Press, 1966.
Williams, Glenn. *Dunmore's War: The Last Conflict of America's Colonial Era.* Yardley, PA: Westholme, 2018.
Wilson, Kathleen. *The Island Race: Englishness, Empire and Gender in the Eighteenth Century.* New York: Routledge, 2003.
———. *The Sense of the People: Politics, Culture and Imperialism in England, 1715–1785.* New York: Cambridge University Press, 1998.
Wilson, Mary Tolford. "Amelia Simmons Fills a Need: American Cookery, 1796." *William and Mary Quarterly* 14, no. 1 (January 1957): 23.
Wood, Bradford. *This Remote Part of the World: Regional Formation in Lower Cape Fear, North Carolina, 1725–1775.* Columbia: University of South Carolina Press, 2004.
Wright, Albert. *History of the State of Rhode Island with Illustrations.* Philadelphia: Hong, Wade, 1878.

Wroth, Lawrence C. *The Colonial Printer*. Portland, ME: Southworth-Anthoensen Press, 1938.

Wulf, Karin. "Situating Self, Seeking Lineage: Family Histories in 17th and 18th Century British North America." In *The Uses of First Person Writings: Les Usages des ecrits du for prive*. Edited by Francois-Joseph Ruggiu, 203-216. New York: Peter Lang, 2013.

Yirush, Craig. "The Imperial Crisis." *The Oxford Handbook of The American Revolution*. Edited by Edward Gray and Jane Kamensky. New York: Oxford University Press, 2015.

Young, Alfred. "Ebenezer Mackintosh: Boston's Captain General of the Liberty Tree." In *Revolutionary Founders: Rebels, Radicals, and Reformers in the Making of the Nation*. Edited by Gary Nash Young and Ray Raphael. New York: Vintage Books, 2012.

Zabin, Serena. *The Boston Massacre: A Family History*. New York: Houghton Mifflin Harcourt, 2020.

Zaret, David. *Origins of Democratic Culture: Printing, Petitions, and the Public Sphere in Early-Modern England*. Princeton, NJ: Princeton University Press, 2000.

Zobel, Hiller B. *The Boston Massacre*. New York: W. W. Norton, 1970.

Index

abolition movement, 12
agrarian interests
  vs. mercantile interests, 8, 12, 22, 28–29, 143
  in Rhode island's early economy, 6
  and textile production, 30–38
  in Virginia and South Carolina, 9
  See also North Carolina elite
Alamance, Battle of, 80, 81, 110, 118–121, 136–137
Albemarle province, North Carolina, 14–16
Allen, John, 135–136
Almy, William, 62, 63
American Duties Act. *See* Sugar Act
American Museum, 37
American Revolution
  casting of Battle of Alamance as start of, 136–137
  economic interests and, 59
  and inter-colonial tensions, 128
  Newport Junto members as Loyalists during, 25
  North Carolina's embrace of, 111, 117, 144
Anglican Church, 1, 15–16, 78, 88–89
Antrobus, Charles, 132
Archdale, John, 15
Arthur, Gabriel, 9

Articles of Confederation, 142
Ash, Abner, 142
Ashe, John, 68, 69
"Atticus" (pen name), 120, 125–126
attorneys vs. justices of the peace, 102
Avery, John, 47

Bass, Henry, 48
Berkeley, Norborne, 112
Bernard, Francis, 48, 52, 56, 57, 58, 60–61
Bill of Rights, 143, 144
Bird, Valentine, 14
Boston, Massachusetts
  Loyal Nine in, 47–48
  publication of *A Fan for Fanning* in, 106–107
  Stamp Act crisis in, 55–56, 57–61
Boston Chronicle, 106
Boston Massacre, 107
Boston Sons of Liberty. *See* Sons of Liberty in Boston
Boston Tea Party, 135, 138
Bowler, Metcalf, 48, 49
Brantley, Joseph, 97
Bray, Henry, 96–97
Brenton, Ebenezer, 33
Brenton, Jahleel, 24, 33
British common law, 44

British naval vessels, 71, 72
British Parliament
  Carteret's influence in, 17
  and colony types, 4, 5
  and Culpepper's Rebellion, 15
  encouragement of hemp production by, 32
  and Johnston's Riot Act, 122–123
  Newport Junto's support of, 28
  and North Carolina's colony status, 16
  representation in, 44–46, 67–68
  See also specific tax acts passed by
Brown, John, 134
Brown, William, 120
Bryan, Needham, 115
Butler, William, 83, 84, 95, 120

Caldwell, David, 118, 119
Cape Fear region, 66, 68, 71–72, 113
Caribbean trade, 8, 40, 129
Carolina Charter, 67–68
Carolina Colony, founding of, 4–6
Carteret, John, 6, 16–17
Cary, Thomas, 16
Cary's Rebellion, 15–16
Catawba tribe, 10, 74
Channing, Henry, 48, 49
Charles II, 4, 5
chartered colony status, 4, 27, 28, 41, 55
Chase, Thomas, 48
Child, Thomas, 17
Cider Tax, 39–40
Clarendon province, North Carolina, 14, 15
Clarke, John, 2, 4, 11
clerks, fees for. *See* nonsalaried officials, payments for
Cleverly, Stephen, 48
Coddington, William, 2
Coercive Acts, 138–139
Collins, John, 48, 49
Colony House, 21, 25, 63
colony types, 4, 5
"Commission of Inquiry into Burning of the Gaspee," 134–135
commissions and fees. *See* nonsalaried officials, payments for
Committees of Safety, North Carolina, 140

Connecticut
  chartered colony status of, 27
  internal conflicts in, 11
  reaction to the Stamp Act in, 41
constitutional conventions, Rhode Island, 12–13
consumerism, 37–38
Conway, Henry Seymour, 65
Cooper, Anthony Ashley, 15
Copeland, James, 120
Corbin, Francis, 17–18
county organization, North Carolina, 86, 87, 89
Cox, Hermon, 120
Crafts, Thomas, 47
Crandall, Samuel, 132–133
Craven, Peter, 84
Crook, Robert, 48, 49, 63, 64, 65
Culpeper, John, 14–15
Culpepper's Rebellion, 14–15
Cumberland County, 86
currency, lack of, 76, 84, 87, 89
Currency Act of 1764, 76
customs officials, 41, 57, 61, 132–136
Cygnet (ship), 62, 64, 132

Dartmouth, Earl of (William Legge), 134–135
De Grey, William, 98–99
De Rosset, Moses John, 68, 69
Declaration of Independence, 141–142
Diligence (ship), 71–72
Dobbs, Arthur, 18, 66, 77, 94, 108
Dobbs (ship), 71
Dorr, Thomas, 12, 13
Dorr Rebellion, 12–13
Dudingston, William, 133, 134, 135
Dudley, Charles, 133
Dunmore, Lord (John Murray), 112
Durant, George, 14, 15
Duties in American Colonies Act. *See* Stamp Act

Eastchurch, Thomas, 14
eastern North Carolinian interests. *See* North Carolina elite
Edes, Benjamin, 48
effigy hanging, 57–58, 63, 67, 69
Ellery, William, 48, 49, 61, 63, 64, 65

Ellis, Richard, 19
Emmerson, James, 120
Enfield Riots, 16–18
English Riot Act, 109, 122
"An Essay on the Trade of the Northern Colonies" (Hopkins), 40
Evening Post, 104
execution of Regulators, 120, 121
extortion trial of Edmund Fanning, 96, 97–99

A Fan for Fanning (Husband), 92, 107
Fanning, Edmund
   Allen on, 136
   background of, 95
   confrontations between Regulators and, 95–96
   extortion trial of, 93, 96, 97–99, 108
   and "Regulators' Advertisement No. 11," 86
   Regulators' attack of, 103–104
   replacement of Moore by, 68
   Sandy Creek Association's requests of, 82–83
Fauquier, Francis, 67
Few, James, 120
Fields (Regulator), 102–103
First Continental Congress, 139–140
flax production, 30, 31, 32–33, 34, 36, 37
Fonville, John, 19
Fort Dobbs, 10
Fortune (ship), 133
Franklin, Benjamin, 27–28
Franklin, James and Ann, 21
Frohock, John, 101, 116
Frohock, Thomas, 101
Frohock, William, 101
frugality, 37–38
The Fundamental Constitutions of Carolina, 5, 15, 78
Fyke, Malachi, 84

Gaspee Affair, 127, 128, 133–136, 138
General Assembly of North Carolina. *See* North Carolina General Assembly
George III
   appointment of Stuart by, 39
   and the burning of the *Gaspee*, 134–135

Hopkins' petition to, 53
and Johnston's Riot Act, 122–123, 137–138
Newport Junto's petition to, for royal colony status, 27, 28
Glover, William, 16
Gorton, Samuel, 2
government organization, North Carolina, 76–77
governor appointments, 100, 112
governor- colonists relations, 137–138
governor's mansion, North Carolina, 72, 78, 106, 113, 115, 119
Gower, Lord (Granville Leveson-Gower), 112
Granville County, North Carolina, 90, 94
Granville District, North Carolina, 6, 17, 96, 97
Greene, William, 29
Greene family, 133
Greenleaf, Abigail, 65–66
Greenleaf, Stephen, 25, 58, 60–61, 65–66
Grenville, George, 39, 40
Gross, Solomon, 84

Halifax Resolves, 141
Hall, Samuel, 26, 31, 34, 50–51
Hallowell, Benjamin, 58, 59
Halton, Robert, 17
Hamilton family, 82, 84, 96
Hannah (ship), 134
Harding, Jane, 19
Harnett, Cornelius, 68
Harris, Tyree, 78, 83, 86
Harrison, Elizabeth Pelham, 24
Harrison, James, 62
Harrison, Joseph, 24, 27, 61, 63
Harrison, Peter, 24, 25, 30, 33, 66, 130
Harvey, John, 139, 140
hemp production, 30–32, 34, 52, 63
Henderson, Elizabeth, 94
Henderson, Josiah, 100, 101–103, 104
Henderson, Richard, 94, 97
Henderson, Samuel, 94
Henry, Patrick, 56
Hillsborough, Lord (Wills Hill)
   and currency policy, 76
   Hutchinson to, on trouble in Machias, 106

Martin to, on the Regulators, 124–125
and Martin's appointment as governor, 121
and New York governorship, 112
Tryon to, on pardons, 120
Tryon to, on the Regulators, 105, 114–115
and Tryon's appointment, 94
Hillsborough, North Carolina
Fanning in, 82
militia's planned march to, 117
ratifying convention in, 143
riots in, 102–106, 108
as seat of Orange County, 80
as trial location, 115–116
See also Orange County, North Carolina
Hillsborough District Superior Court, 91, 96, 97, 102–103
Hinton, James, 115
Honeyman, James, Jr., 24
Honeyman, James, Sr., 24
Hooper, William, 139, 141–142
Hopkins, Stephen
"An Essay on the Trade of the Northern Colonies," 40, 129
at the First Continental Congress, 143
Howard's feud with, 41–47
and letter in the *Providence Gazette*, 33
Moore's arguments compared to those of, 67
on the Navigation Act, 129
pamphlet writing of, 92
petition of, to George III, 53
and questioning of Hall, 51
The Rights of the Colonies Examined, 32
to Sherwood, on the Newport Junto's petition, 28
Ward's feud with, 29–30
Houston, William, 68–69
Howard, Abigail, 141
Howard, Ann Brenton Conklin, 23, 24, 30
Howard, Annie, 64, 65, 66, 141
Howard, Martin
after dissolution of royal government, 140–141
and aftermath of Battle of Alamance, 124–125

appointment of, as North Carolina chief justice, 18–19
background of, 23
communications of, with Franklin, 27–28
departure of, for England, 132
departure of, from Rhode Island, 33–34
family connections of, 30
feud of, with Hopkins, 41–47
A Letter from a Gentleman at Halifax, 32, 50, 90, 130
and libel charges against Husband, 114
marriage of, 65–66
Moore's similarities with, 68
oversight of trial after Battle of Alamance, 120, 136
pamphlet writing of, 92
and the Redwood Library, 25, 26
Regulators' petition addressed to, 100, 101–102
relationship of Regulators to, 126
and the Stamp Act riot, 61–65
Stiles on, 19–20
Howell, Redknap
bounty for, 120
on Fanning, 82, 95
letter of, to Hunter, 116
and "Regulators' Advertisement No. 11," 81, 86, 96
Hunter, James
at Alamance Creek, 118
bounty for, 120
financial downturn of, 80
Howell's letter to, 84, 116
indictment of, 115
letter of, in the *North-Carolina Gazette*, 114
on Martin, 137
reassurances to Henderson by, 103
and "Regulators' Advertisement No. 11," 86, 96
in Tryon's proclamation, 84
Hunter, William, 24, 25, 130
Husband, Herman
at Alamance Creek, 118
arrest of, 83–84, 95
background of, 81
bounty for, 120

in the General Assembly, 87, 91, 96
imprisonment and release of, 114–115
indictment of, 115
and "Leonidas" pen name, 125–126
as mentioned in Howell's letter to Hunter, 116
pamphlets by, 92, 106–107
removal of, from the General Assembly, 113–114
sale of land to Bray by, 97
Hutchinson, Thomas, 58, 59–60, 61, 106, 107
Hutchinson family, 25, 30
Hutchison, Anne, 2
Hyde, Edward, 15, 16

An Impartial Relation (Husband), 91, 92, 106–107
imports, textile. *See* textile production debate
impressment, 54, 132
Intolerable Acts. *See* Coercive Acts
Iredell, James, 140

Jackson, Isaac, 84
Jackson, Richard, 27, 59, 60
Jenkins, John, 14, 15
Johnston, Augustus, 23–24, 25, 30, 63, 64, 130
Johnston, Samuel, 108, 140, 143
Johnston's Riot Act, 108–109, 110, 111, 113, 114, 122–123
Jones, Robert, 17
Jones family, 19
The Justice and Policy of Taxing The American Colonies… (Moore), 67
justices of the peace vs. attorneys, 102

King, Samuel, 13

land issues, North Carolina, 16–18, 94–95, 96
landed families. *See* agrarian interests; North Carolina elite
Landholder's Constitution, 12–13
Lawson, John, 9–10
Leamington Farm, 24
Lennox, Charles, 65
"Leonidas" (pen name), 125–126

A Letter from a Gentleman at Halifax (Howard), 32, 42–43, 44, 50, 90, 130
Lewis, Howell, 81–82, 91, 97
Lindsay, Benjamin, 134
Lloyd, Caleb, 67
Lobb, Jacob, 71–72
Locke, John, 5, 15, 67–68, 78
lords proprietor, 5, 6, 14, 15–16
Loyal Nine, 47–48, 50, 57
luxury goods, debate on, 36–37
Lyndon, Josias, 42, 48, 49

Machias settlers, 106
Mackintosh, Ebenezer. *See* McIntosh, Ebenezer
Magnalia Christi Americanai (Mather), 6, 8
Maidstone (ship), 54, 132
Martin, Alexander, 101, 102, 116
Martin, Josiah, 110, 112, 113, 121–126, 127, 137–141
Martin, Samuel, 121, 123–124
Massachusetts
    and the Coercive Acts, 138
    imperial ambitions of, 2
    internal conflicts in, 11
    opposition of, to the Stamp Act, 53
    Stamp Act riot in, 57–61
    voting rights in, 11
Massachusetts House of Representatives, 53, 57
Massachusetts Resolves, 61
Massachusetts Spy, 125, 126
Mateer, Robert, 119, 121
Mather, Cotton, 6
McCulloh, Alexander, 18
McCulloh, Henry, 16–17, 18, 68, 94–95
McCulloh, Henry Eustace, 82, 95
McCulloh family, 18, 94–95, 97, 99
McGuire, Thomas, 98, 107
McIntosh, Ebenezer, 57, 59, 60–61
Mecklenburg Resolves, 111, 126, 127, 140, 142–143
mercantile interests
    vs. agricultural interests, 8, 12, 22, 28–29, 42, 143
    in Boston, 57

and the Newport Sons of Liberty, 48–49
in the Piedmont region, 74–75
and tensions with customs officials, 132–136
and textile production, 36
Mercer, Forester, 120
Mercer, George, 67
Merrell, Benjamin, 121
Messer, Peter, 135
Messer, Robert, 121
militia
  at Battle of Alamance, 119–120
  in Boston, 61
  in defense of New Bern, 114
  and the Dorr Rebellion, 13
  at Fort Dobbs, 10
  ordering of, to Orange County, 81, 84, 115–117
Miller, Thomas, 14
modernity and the Hopkins-Howard feud, 46–47
Moffat, Thomas
  background of, 24
  departure of, for England, 132
  as librarian for Redwood Library, 26
  as member of professional class, 130
  and the Stamp Act riot, 61–65
Moffatt, William, 84
Montagu, John, 134, 135
Moore, James, 68
Moore, Maurice
  accusations of Husband and Hunter by, 114
  and "Atticus," 126
  Howard's similarities with, 68
  The Justice and Policy of Taxing the American Colonies by, 67
  Regulators' petition addressed to, 100, 101–102
  Tryon's replacement of, 95
Morgan, John, 98–99
Moseley, Edward, 17
Moser, Adam, 96–97
Murray, John. *See* Dunmore, Lord

Narragansett tribe, 2, 6
Nash, Abner, 19

Nation, Christopher, 82, 84, 87, 88, 91, 96
Native Americans, 5, 9. *See also* Catawba tribe; Narragansett tribe
Navigation Acts, 14, 40, 129–130
Needham, James, 9
New Bern, North Carolina
  General Assembly's December 1770 meeting in, 107–108
  Husband's imprisonment in, 114
  Provincial Convention at, 139, 140
  Smith, on the Regulators' advance on, 111
  Tryon's preparation of, 115
New Jersey, internal conflicts in, 11
A New Voyage to Carolina (Lawson), 9–10
New York
  governorship of, 112, 121, 122
  Howard in, 141
  Martin's flight to, 140
  reaction to the Stamp Act in, 56
  Smith's depiction of Tryon to the people of, 77
  Stamp Act Congress in, 57, 69
New York Gazette, 104
Newport, Rhode Island
  conflicts of, with Providence, 11, 28–30
  founding of, 2
  and patent for Rhode Island, 4
  Stamp Act crisis in, 61–65, 72–73
  See also Newport Junto
Newport Harbor, 132–133
Newport Junto
  background of leaders of, 23–24
  compared to Regulators, 75
  desire of, to become royal colony, 27–28
  and the *Newport Mercury*, 26–27, 51, 52
  Otis on, 23
  Sons of Liberty's opposition to, 22
  and the Stamp Act riot, 61–64, 65
  support of the Stamp Act by, 47, 54
  support of Ward by, 30
  textile production campaign of, 30–34, 36
Newport Mercury
  essay of April 23, 1764 in, 21–22, 26–27, 75

"An Essay on the Trade of the Northern Colonies" in the, 40
Hopkins's essay published in the, 129
Howard's letter in, of August 26th, 62
and reaction to the Sugar and Stamp Acts in, 49–53
reporting on parade of August 27, 62–63
textile production essays in, 30–38
Newport Sons of Liberty. *See* Sons of Liberty in Rhode Island
nonsalaried officials, payments for, 77, 82–83, 88, 97–98, 114, 124
North Carolina
  and the Articles of Confederation, 142
  delegates to the Continental Congress from, 139–140
  economics of, 9
  formation of, 6
  and the Halifax Resolves, 141–142
  and the Mecklenburg Resolves, 111, 126, 127, 140, 142–143
  political and judicial systems of, 76–77, 84–85, 93–94
  and ratification of the U.S. Constitution, 142–143, 144
  Rhode Island's connections to, 18–20
  Rhode Island's similarities to, 1–2
  settling of, 9–11
  Stamp Act crisis in, 68–72, 73
  taxation in, for support of the Anglican Church, 78
  See also Carolina Colony
North Carolina Committees of Safety, 140
North Carolina elite, 74, 89, 93–94, 98, 123, 126. *See also* North Carolina General Assembly
North-Carolina Gazette, 69, 70, 72, 114
North Carolina General Assembly
  Cary's Rebellion and, 15–16
  composition of, 76
  effect of Regulator movement on, 126
  efforts of, to stop government corruption, 77
  election of Regulators to the, 87
  frustration of members of, with Tryon, 106
  and funding for construction of governor's mansion, 72
  Husband's removal from, 113–114
  and Johnston's Riot Act, 110, 111
  Martin's dissolution of, 140
  meeting of, in December 1770, 107–108
  and the Provincial Convention of North Carolina, 139
  Sons of Liberty in the, 137
  tactics of, 76
  Tryon's proroguing of, 69
  use of proclamations by, 75, 79
North Carolina Sons of Liberty. *See* Sons of Liberty in North Carolina
North Carolina Standing Committee of Correspondence, 138–139

Oliver, Andrew, 25, 57–58, 61, 62, 63
Oneal, John, 84
Orange County, North Carolina
  Fanning as registrar of, 82, 95, 96, 99
  letter to Tryon, from farmers of, 117–118
  request of residents of, for new county, 86
  Tryon's ordering of the militia to, 84
  See also Alamance, Battle of; Hillsborough, North Carolina
Otis, James, 23, 29, 43–46, 51
Otis, Jonathan, 48, 50
oyer and terminer courts, 109, 115–116, 120
O.Z. letters, 31–33, 36, 37, 49, 51–52

pamphlets
  and the imperial crisis, 91–92
  in London, 51
  Newport Junto's use of, 23
  vs. proclamations, 75, 79
  See also Hopkins, Stephen; Howard, Martin; Husband, Herman
pardons
  after Culpepper's Rebellion, 15
  of Dorr, 12
  petition requesting Wellborn's, 124
  and Tryon's proclamations, 84, 120–121

parliamentary representation, 44–46, 67–68
patent for Rhode Island and Providence Plantations, 4
Patience (ship), 71
patriotism, and the Hopkins-Howard feud, 46–47
patronage system, 95, 99–101
Payne, William, 84
pen names, 125–126
Pennsylvania, 27–28
People's Constitution, 12–13
Person, Thomas, 81, 87, 91, 96, 118
petitions
 after the Regulator Rebellion, 124
 on currency problems, 76
 of Regulators, 80, 81, 84–91, 96–98, 100–102, 125
 submitted by the Regulators, 118–119
 use of, 75, 79
"Phocion" (pen name), 126
Piedmont area, North Carolina, 10–11, 74–75, 93–94, 111, 137. *See also* specific locations in
Plantation Duty Act, 14
political and judicial system
 of Carolina Colony, 5–6
 of North Carolina, 6, 76–77, 84–85, 93–94
 of Rhode Island, 4
 Sons of Liberty members' involvement in, 49
Polly, seizure of, 130, 132
Pope's Day, 46, 57, 61
Porter, John, 16
Portsmouth settlement, 2, 4, 11
Preston, Thomas, 107
prisoner exchange plan, 119
Pritchet, Jeremiah, 115
Privy Council, 17
proclamations, 47, 75, 79, 140. *See also* Tryon, William
property ownership and voting rights, 12
proprietary colonies, 5, 27
Providence, Rhode Island
 conflict of, with Newport, 11, 28–30
 and the *Gaspee* Affair, 134
 meeting of August 13th in, 52–53
 settlement of, 2, 4, 6
 textile debate in, 22, 35
 See also Hopkins, Stephen
Providence Gazette, 32–33, 46
Providence Library Company, 42
Provincial Convention (Congress) of North Carolina, 139, 140
Pryor, John, 82, 87, 91, 96, 97
Pugh, James, 121

Quakers, 15–16, 118
Quartering Act, 138
Quebec Act, 138
quitrent system, 5, 6, 16–17, 94

ratification of the U.S. Constitution, 142–144
Redwood, Abraham, 25
Redwood Library, 25–26, 42, 66
Regulator Rebellion
 Allen on the, 136
 Enfield Riots compared to, 17–18
 General Assembly's attempt to quell, 108–109
 and the Hillsborough riots, 102–106
 Husband's pamphlets on, 92
 reports on, outside of North Carolina, 125–126
Regulators
 areas of concern of, 75, 76–78
 in the Battle of Alamance, 119–121
 Boston press and, 106–107
 compared to the Newport Junto, 75
 confrontations between Fanning and, 95–96
 election of, to General Assembly, 87
 final petition of, 118–119
 halting of Waddell's troops by, 117
 in the Hillsborough riots, 102–104
 large planters associated with, 81–82
 members of, 79–81
 petitions submitted by, 84–91, 97–98, 100–102
 and the Sons of Liberty, 137
 tactics of, 75
 tension between legal and extralegal centers of, 111
 trial and execution of, 110
 Tryon's proclamations against, 83, 84
 use of petitions and pamphlets, 75, 79

"Regulators' Advertisement No. 11," 80, 81, 86
religion, 2, 4, 5, 15–16, 78, 88–89
Rhode Island
  and the American Revolution, 128
  and the Articles of Confederation, 143
  and the burning of the *Gaspee*, 127
  connections of, with North Carolina, 18–20
  economy of, 6, 8
  founding of, 3–4
  internal conflicts in, 11–13
  and ratification of the U.S. Constitution, 143–144
  reaction to the Stamp Act in, 41
  renunciation of allegiance to the Crown, 141
  similarities of, with North Carolina, 1–2, 20
  Stamp Act crisis in, 61–65
  tensions between customs officials and merchants in, 132–136
  See also Newport Junto
Rhode Island General Assembly, 28, 49, 50, 52–53, 54, 64
Rhode Island Sons of Liberty. *See* Sons of Liberty in Rhode Island
The Rights of the British Colonies Asserted and Proved (Otis), 43–44
The Rights of the Colonies Examined (Hopkins), 32, 42–44, 53
Robinson, John, 24, 62, 64, 130, 132–133
Rome, George, 24, 25, 30, 130
Romney (ship), 133
Rowan County, North Carolina, 84, 101
royal colonies, 27, 28, 41, 55

Salisbury Superior Court, 101, 116
Sandy Creek Association, 82–83, 92, 95, 123
Sanford, Margaret, 25
Sanford, Mary, 25
Saxby, George, 67
Second Continental Congress, 141–142
Selwyn, George, 18
Sessions, Darius, 135
Seven Years' War, 39–40, 49, 129
Shay's Rebellion, 11
Shays's Rebellion, 142

sheriffs, fees for. *See* nonsalaried officials, payments for
Sherwood, Joseph, 28, 53, 65
slave-owning North Carolinians. *See* North Carolina elite
Smith, John, 48
Smith, William
  on the building of the governor's mansion, 78
  condemnation of the Regulators by, 118
  on Hunter, 118
  on the planter economy, 9
  portrayal of Tryon's North Carolina governorship by, 112
  on raising a militia, 116
  on Regulators in winter 1770-1771, 111
  on trial after Battle of Alamance, 120
  on Tryon's and the Stamp Act crisis, 66
  on Tryon's handling of the Regulators' concerns, 77, 83
social contracts, 75, 85, 100, 125
Sons of Liberty in Boston, 57, 61
Sons of Liberty in North Carolina, 68, 71–72, 137
Sons of Liberty in Rhode Island
  conflict of, with the Newport Junto, 22, 52
  members of, 48–50
  and the Newport riots, 64, 65
  parades organized by, 61
  and textile production, 34, 44
Sothel, Seth, 15
South Carolina, 6, 8–9, 67
South-Carolina Gazette, 51, 52, 115
Southwick, Solomon, 34
Special Court of Oyer and Terminer, 115
Spooner, John, 48, 50, 64–65
Stamp Act
  and the colonial power structures, 55
  common themes in responses to, 56
  Hopkins' objections to, 42–43
  Howard's support of, 43
  London pamphlet objecting to the, 51
  Loyal Nine's opposition to, 47–48
  Newport Junto's defense of, 130
  and the *Newport Mercury*, 52–53
  provisions of, 40–41

purpose of, 130
Rhode Island's opposition to, 54
Stamp Act Congress, 53–54, 57, 69
Stamp Act crisis
  in Boston, 57–61, 72
  in Newport, 61–65, 72–73
  news of, in southern colonies, 67
  in North Carolina, 68–72, 73
"Stamp Act Notebook" (Stiles), 48, 50
Stamp Tax distributors
  in Massachusetts, 58, 61
  in North Carolina, 68–69
  in Rhode Island, 63, 64
  in Virginia, 67
Standing Committee of Correspondence, 138–139
Steuart, Andrew, 69, 70, 72
Stewart, James, 120
Stiles, Ezra
  on the Battle of Alamance, 136
  and correspondence of Rhode Island residents, 52
  on Dudley, 133
  pro-Revolutionary stance of, 135
  and Rhode Island residents' correspondence, 53
  on Spooner, 64
  on the Stamp Act crisis, 60
  "Stamp Act Notebook" of, 48–50, 56
  Whiting's letter to, 19–20
Story, Elisha, 62, 63
Story, William, 58, 59
Stuart, John, 39–40, 58
Sugar Act
  Hopkins' objections to, 42–43, 44
  Howard's support of, 43
  implementation of, 54
  London pamphlet objecting to the, 51
  Newport Junto on, 31–32
  provisions of, 40, 129–130
  reaction to, in North Carolina, 66
Sugar Creek War of 1765, 18

taxation
  and Culpepper's Rebellion, 14–15
  quitrent system, 5, 6, 16–17, 94
  Regulators' concerns over, 77–78, 82–83, 84–86

  for support of the Anglican Church, 78
  See also specific tax acts
Temple, John, 132
textile production debate, 30–38, 48–49, 52, 63–64
Thomlinson, John, 25
Thompson, Robert, 119
Tory Junto. *See* Newport Junto
Townshend Acts, 36, 91, 100, 108, 112–113, 127
trade
  with Caribbean colonies, 8, 40, 129
  between Rhode Island and North Carolina, 19
  and the Sugar Act, 44
Trobridge, Edmund, 29–30
Trott, George, 48
Tryon, William
  and aftermath of Battle of Alamance, 120–121
  Allen on, 136
  alliance of, with the General Assembly, 123
  appeal to McGuire for advice, 107
  appointment of, 94
  closing of Cape Fear ports by, 70–71
  cultivation of connections by, 94–95
  and Currency Act of 1764, 76
  depiction of Regulator movement by, 118
  dissolution of the General Assembly by, 91, 100, 101
  and government corruption, 77
  governor's mansion of, 72, 113
  on the Hillsborough riot, 105–106
  and Howell's letter to Hunter, 81
  imprisonment of Husband by, 114
  and Johnston's Riot Act, 109
  letter to, from farmers of Orange County, 117–118
  and location of second oyer and terminer court, 115–116
  Martin as successor to, 110
  and militia expedition to Orange County, 115–117
  and New York governorship, 111, 112, 122
  and the Orthodox Clergy Act, 78
  Polk's petition to, 18

primary interests of, upon taking office, 66–67
proclamations of, against the Regulators, 83, 84, 86–87, 102
reform attempts by, 108
"Regulators' Advertisement No. 11" sent to, 86
Regulators' final petition to, 118–119
Regulators' relations with, 137
and relations with the General Assembly, 56
replacement of Moore with Fanning by, 68, 95
response of, to demonstrations, 69–70
response of, to petitions, 96
and the Stamp Act crisis, 55
and status of the Anglican Church, 88
tactics of, 75
use of proclamations, 75, 79
Tryon's Palace. *See* governor's mansion, North Carolina
Tyler, John, 13

U.S. Constitution, 142–144

Vail, Mary, 19
Vernon, Samuel, 34, 48, 49, 61–62, 63, 64–65
Vernon, William, 34, 48, 49
A Vindication of the British Colonies (Otis), 46, 51
Viper (ship), 66, 71
Virginia
  economics of, 8, 9
  governorship of, 112
  reaction to the Stamp Act in, 56, 67
Virginia Gazette, 104, 115, 120, 126
Virginia House of Burgesses, 67
Virginia Resolves, 56
voting rights, 11–13, 44–46

Waddell, Hugh, 10, 68, 117, 118
Walker, Henderson, 15
Wanton, Joseph, 50, 133–134, 135
Ward, Henry, 48, 49
Ward, Richard, 29
Ward, Samuel
  feud of, with Hopkins, 29–30, 42
  at the First Continental Congress, 143

and Howard's request for repayment for losses, 65
Moffat's and Howard's request for assistance from, 61
and Newport Harbor incident, 132, 133
opposition of, to the Stamp Act, 54
and Rhode Island politics, 49
Ward, Thomas, 49
Warwick settlement, 2, 4, 11
Webber, John, 50, 64, 65
Wellborn, Thomas, 124
Wells, Henry, 48
Wentworth, John, 66
White, Samuel, 53
Whiting, John, 19
Whiting, Mary, 19
Williams, John, 94, 103
Williams, Roger, 2, 6, 11, 29
Wilmington, North Carolina, 69, 70, 71
Wood, Abraham, 9, 74
wool production, 33, 34, 36, 37

Yamasee War, 6, 16

Z.Y. (pseudonym), 22, 23, 26–27, 28

Other Titles in the Series

1764: The First Year of the American Revolution
by Ken Shumate

Anatomy of a Massacre: The Destruction of Gnadenhutten, 1782
by Eric Sterner

The Burning of His Majesty's Schooner Gaspee*:
An Attack on Crown Rule Before the American Revolution*
by Steven Park

General Peter Muhlenberg: A Virginia Officer of the Continental Line
by Michael Cecere

Grand Forage 1778: The Battleground Around New York City
by Todd W. Braisted

The Invasion of Virginia 1781
by Michael Cecere

John Adams vs. Thomas Paine: Rival Plans for the New Republic
by Jett B. Connor

*March to Independence:
The American Revolution in the Southern Colonies, 1775–1776*
by Michael Cecere

*The Road to Concord: How Four Stolen Cannon Ignited
the Revolutionary War*
by J. L. Bell

The Sugar Act and the American Revolution
by Ken Shumate

*United for Independence:
The American Revolution in the Middle Colonies, 1775–1776*
by Michael Cecere

Washington's War, 1779
by Benjamin Lee Huggins